TELLING TALES ON TECHNOLOGY

For Eryl

Telling Tales on Technology:
Qualitative studies of technology and education

NEIL SELWYN
School of Social Sciences
Cardiff University

LONDON AND NEW YORK

First published 2002 by Ashgate Publishing

Reissued 2018 by Routledge
2 Park Square, Milton Park, Abingdon, Oxon OX14 4RN
711 Third Avenue, New York, NY 10017, USA

Routledge is an imprint of the Taylor & Francis Group, an informa business

Copyright © Neil Selwyn 2002

The Author has asserted his right under the Copyright, Designs and Patent Act, 1988, to be identified as the Author of this Work.

All rights reserved. No part of this book may be reprinted or reproduced or utilised in any form or by any electronic, mechanical, or other means, now known or hereafter invented, including photocopying and recording, or in any information storage or retrieval system, without permission in writing from the publishers.

Notice:
Product or corporate names may be trademarks or registered trademarks, and are used only for identification and explanation without intent to infringe.

Publisher's Note
The publisher has gone to great lengths to ensure the quality of this reprint but points out that some imperfections in the original copies may be apparent.

Disclaimer
The publisher has made every effort to trace copyright holders and welcomes correspondence from those they have been unable to contact.

A Library of Congress record exists under LC control number: 2002025868

ISBN 13: 978-1-138-36871-2 (hbk)
ISBN 13: 978-1-138-73401-2 (pbk)
ISBN 13: 978-1-138-36873-6 (ebk)

Contents

List of Tables and Figures vii
List of Abbreviations viii

PART I: TAKING A QUALITATIVE APPROACH TO TECHNOLOGY AND EDUCATION 1

1   Introduction 3

2   Taking a Qualitative Approach to Technology and Education 7

PART II: THE POLITICS AND ECONOMICS OF TECHNOLOGY AND EDUCATION 21

3   The Discursive Construction of 'Educational Computing' in the UK, 1979-1989 23

4   The Discursive Construction of the National Grid for Learning, 1997-2002 38

5   The Role of Big Business in UK Education Technology Policy and Practice 52

PART III: INDIVIDUAL LEARNERS AND TECHNOLOGY 71

6   Children's Engagement with ICT in Primary School 73

7   A-Level Students and ICT 89

8   Exploring Accountancy Undergraduates' Use of ICT 103

PART IV: QUALITATIVE EXPLORATIONS OF 'VIRTUAL' EDUCATION 117

9   Perspectives of Adult Learners on ICT and Learning (*With Stephen Gorard & Sara Williams*) 119

10   School Teachers' Use of an Electronic Discussion Group 134

PART V: LESSONS TO BE LEARNT? 157

11 The Dilemmas of Critically Researching Technology and Education 159

12 Conclusions 171

Bibliography 183
Index 201

List Of Tables and Figures

Table 5.1   Descriptions of Interviewees (n=12)   57

Table 6.1   Sample Characteristics Across the Five Schools   75

Figure 10.1   Numbers of Messages Posted and Active Contributors to the SENCo Forum between October 1996 and October 1998   138

List of Abbreviations

BBC	British Broadcasting Corporation
BECTa	British Educational Communications and Technology agency
BJET	British Journal of Educational Technology
BT	British Telecom
CD-ROM	Compact Disc Read Only Memory
CLAIT	Computer Literacy and Information Technology
CMC	Computer Mediated Communication
CoP	'Code of Practice' for the identification and assessment of special educational needs
DfEE	Department for Education and Employment (now DfES)
DfES	Department for Education and Skills
DTI	Department of Trade and Industry
EBD	Emotional and Behavioural Difficulties
EDSi	Education Department Superhighways initiative
EMO	Education Management Organisation
ESRC	Economic and Social Research Council
FE	Further Education
GCSE	General Certificate of Secondary Education
GNVQ	General National Vocational Qualification
HE	Higher Education
IBM	International Business Machines
ICL	International Computers Limited
ICT	Information and Communications Technology
ISDN	Integrated Services Digital Network
IT	Information Technology
ITAP	Information Technology Advisory Panel
ITEC	Information Technology and Enterprise Centre
JANET	Joint Academic Network
LEA	Local Education Authority
MA	Master of Arts postgraduate degree
MEP	Micro-electronics in Education Programme
MLD	Moderate Learning Difficulties
NCC	National Curriculum Council
NCET	National Council for Educational Technology
NGfL	National Grid for Learning
NIACE	National Institute for Adult and Continuing Education
NVQ	National Vocational Qualification
OECD	Organisation for Economic Co-operation and Development
OfSTED	Office for Standards in Education
PC	Personal Computer

List of Abbreviations

PCAST	Presidential Committee on Educational Technology
PE	Physical Education
PFI	Private Finance Initiative
RM	Research Machines
RSA	Royal Society of Arts
SCAA	Schools' Curriculum and Assessment Authority
SENCo	Special Needs Co-ordinator
TVEI	Technical and Vocational Education Initiative
UfI	University for Industry
UK	United Kingdom
USA	United States of America
YTS	Youth Training Scheme

PART I
TAKING A QUALITATIVE APPROACH TO TECHNOLOGY AND EDUCATION

PART I

Chapter One

Introduction

It is now taken for granted that the use of technology in education is a 'good thing'. This reaction stems in part from the deeply-held and often voiced belief amongst many educators that 'information and communications technology' (ICT) will transform and revolutionise teaching and learning processes. This trust amongst proponents of educational technology has solidified over the last two decades into an unquestioning orthodoxy that now pervades and colours most discussion of technology and education. To observe, for example, that personal computers have maybe not had the far-reaching and transformatary effect on schools that has been predicted over the last twenty years is likely to be met with a fair degree of hostility. Indeed, to challenge the 'technological orthodoxy' is seen by many educators as heresy – as somehow being obstructive and backward in one's thinking, to be part of the problem not part of the solution.

Of course, an uncritical faith in technology is not the sole preserve of educationalists. As Langdon Winner (1993) observes, the bulk of technological change in society has occurred in a social and intellectual vacuum – and it would seem that the rise of educational technology has been no different. Since the microcomputer's introduction into school and university classrooms towards the end of the 1970s, academic research into education and technology has often presented little more than an uncritical reflection of societal faith in technology. Whilst a positive approach towards technology is not in itself a disadvantage, it can be strongly argued that educational research has long been limited by an *excessive* technological optimism bordering on 'technophillia'. Although a succession of authors have attempted to point out these fundamental shortcomings (e.g. Beynon & Mackay 1989, Kenway 1996, Young 1984, Kerr 1996) much educational technology research is still characterised by an underlying distrust and avoidance of theory coupled with an unwillingness to consider the social, political, cultural and economic aspects of ICT in educational settings. As Kenway (1996) concludes, social science research in this area has often been too 'micro-focused', with a 'wilful blindness' to the social and cultural contexts and wider implications of technology. One particular symptom of this wilful blindness (and the driving motivation behind this book) is manifested in the way that educational technology studies distanced themselves from the rest of social science research over the 1980s and 1990s by exhibiting an almost overt distrust of *qualitative* data.

Back in 1997 I wrote a very short piece for educational technology researchers discussing some of these issues. The choice of journal for this piece was deliberate – the 'British Journal of Educational Technology' is a specialist academic journal frequented by some of the leading lights in the field. As such the decidedly technicist tenor of 'BJET' made it an ideal arena in which to air my views. Having written the piece I was equally deliberate in choosing a title: 'The Continuing Weakness of Educational Computing Research'. As a fledging writer and researcher I assumed naively that a provocative title alone would make some impact on the BJET readership. Now, with the benefit of hindsight, I would not be so presumptuous to imagine that a journal article could hope to raise anything more than a flicker amongst the six or so academics that are likely to come across it when published. Looking back I am not surprised that this thought-piece has failed resoundingly to change the world of educational technology research, or whatever similar lofty intention I had in mind when writing it.

Yet, if this article had one saving grace then it was short. At just under three pages long it briefly set out its stall and, for this alone, it *has* begun to gradually provoke a reaction from the wider world. In particular, the piece has proved a popular choice for graduate students of Educational Technology in US universities when asked by their lecturers to summarise and critique an article and then disseminate their thoughts via the world-wide web. As I have surreptitiously come across these online reactions over the last five years the arguments presented by the students have often prompted me to revisit and reconsider my original broadside against the educational technology research community.

Some of the students' responses are as stridently dismissive as the article itself - arguing that I was obviously feeling nothing more than 'mean-spirited', 'down' and 'disillusioned' at the time of writing (although feeling disillusionment with what is never made entirely clear). A few students have contended that my arguments are now redundant given the wealth of quantitative research carried out in this area over last five years (although my over-riding point was that educational technology was lacking in quality not necessary quantity of research). A few students very kindly claim to have had some of their perceptions altered in light of the article's arguments. These more supportive responses are occasionally extended to the point of taking my initial arguments further that I would have felt comfortable at the time. As this Graduate Student from the Iowa State class of 2001 argues in her response:

> 'Selwyn's point that there is too much quantitative research and not nearly enough qualitative research struck a real chord within me. I would argue that there little *research* from either paradigm. Far too many of the research studies I read leave me asking too many questions about methodology, research questions, results, interpretation *etc*. Many activities occur under the guise of quantitative research, but almost invariably I find myself asking if the researcher(s) measured what they thought they were measuring, and if they measured anything at all [....] It would be a stretch to attach any real significance to these findings, and yet a great many researchers attempt to do so'.

Yet the most provocative responses have come from students who read my piece as a wholly negative attack on educational technology research – adding nothing to the field and only 'offering criticism and never any answers'. This was never my intention. On the contrary, I had hoped idealistically to provoke myself and other researchers to address the gaping holes in academic examination of education and technology and forge a 'new wave' of education technology research. I had intended to make a case for in-depth, considered, rigorous research which was rooted in and reflected the wider 'real world(s)' of education and technology. So to read five years on that I was merely pointing out the shortcomings of others without doing anything about it was, I felt, a little unfair. There *has* been some good work in this area since the mid 1990s but obviously not with enough prominence to register with everybody in the educational research community.

This book, therefore, is a belated personal response to these criticisms. It presents a selection of my work carried out in Cardiff University and the University of Bristol which has tried to adopt a careful, qualitative approach towards education and technology. In empirically examining education and technology I have adhered to a research framework which is discussed in more detail in Chapter Two, essentially based around the strength of qualitative methodologies in providing views of education and technology at different levels - from the 'macro' level of government and industry to the 'micro' level of the individual learner. Adopting this multi-layered perspective in organising the empirical bulk of the book then leads onto three discrete sections. Chapters Three, Four and Five give a flavour of the 'macro' level of education and technology in the UK – in particular the politically and economically constructed nature of 'educational technology' in the early days of the Thatcher government as compared to the present day New Labour administration; arguably the two defining periods of educational IT policymaking in the UK. This is illustrated through two discursive analyses of the rhetoric surrounding technology and education – each providing a view of the different shaping forces behind what we have come to regard as 'educational technology'. This 'macro' level picture is complemented in Chapter Five by an in-depth interview study with some of the key political and commercial interests in the shaping and implementation of the current 'National Grid for Learning' initiative - revealing the extent and nature to which education and technology almost unavoidably falls prey to a combination of 'public' and 'private' shaping forces and motivations.

The second empirical section of the book consists of three studies which examine educational technology from the perspective(s) of individual learners. When first engaging with the literature during the mid-1990s as an undergraduate student, I was surprised by the absence of learners' voices amidst all the earnest discussions of education and technology that I came across. Yet as the ultimate 'end users' of technology in education hearing the voice(s) of learners stuck me as crucial in developing a realistic understanding of new technologies in education. An integral strand of my work over the last seven years has, therefore, focused on individuals' responses to technology in education – represented here in three chapters looking at seven and eleven year old primary school children, sixteen and seventeen year-old sixth form students and, finally, undergraduate students at university. When reading these accounts in succession I am struck by the remarkable similarities in the responses of these learners, particularly the way that the bounded nature of the educational context has a profound effect on the way that ICT is approached and rationalised.

The final empirical section of the book presents two contrasting pictures of what many technologists would currently consider as the 'future' of education and technology – 'e-learning' and 'virtual' scholarly collaboration. Beyond the rhetoric of 'virtual' education chapters nine and ten attempt to empirically unpack the realities for teachers and learners, highlighting the often mundane nature of these over-hyped and under-critiqued areas of education. Finally, given the preceding empirical barrage the book concludes with a consideration of what lessons can be learnt. Chapter eleven reflects on the dilemmas of taking a critical, qualitative approach to researching technology and education, whilst chapter twelve maps out the strengths, weaknesses and future necessities for work in this area.

In carrying out this work over the past seven years I have been assisted greatly by a variety of funding sources: my work examining A-level and vocational students was funded by the Economic and Social Research Council; the work on adult learners' use of ICT was funded by the Spencer Foundation in the USA; the project examining undergraduate students was funded by the Association of Certified Chartered Accountants; my work looking at primary school children was funded by a Cardiff University Young Researcher grant; and my time looking at the public and private foundations of educational technology policy making was supported by the Cardiff University 'Learning Capital Project'. I am particularly grateful to all the participants in these research projects – the learners, teachers and representatives from government and industry – who have patiently explained to me their experiences of, and perspectives on, educational and technology. I have also been aided immensely throughout the past seven years by the numerous academic colleagues who I have worked with on the research projects presented within this book – especially Stephen Gorard, John Fitz, Sara Williams, Neil Marriott, Pru Marriott and Kate Bullon. I would also like to thank Gareth Rees, Emma Renold, Trevor Welland and Keri Facer for their discussion and advice along the way. However, as is always the case, the responsibility for any inaccuracies or blatant mistakes is mine.

Neil Selwyn
Cardiff 2002

Chapter Two

Taking a Qualitative Approach to Technology and Education

Introduction

A belief in the power of information and communications technologies such as the computer has fast become orthodoxy as 'developed' societies such as the UK are seen to lurch from the industrial to the post-industrial (Bell 1973, Touraine 1969, Reich 1991). Indeed, the growing development of the computer has been heralded by many commentators as one of the defining features of the last two decades of the twentieth century and of profound significance for the first years of the twenty-first (Negroponte 1995, Gates 1997, Dyson 1998). Currently, this 'techno-romance' continues in the guise of widespread enthusiasm for the convergence of multimedia and telecommunications technologies into 'information and communication technologies' and associated applications such as 'e-commerce', 'e-tailing' and even 'e-government' – thus further cementing the computer at the heart of 'modern' British society.

This technological faith has proved especially deep-rooted with regards to technology and education. Over thirty-five years ago, Patrick Suppes (1966) reasoned that the flexibility and interactive nature of computer technology would have an almost immediate and permanent effect on the educational process. Two decades later this claim was echoed by Seymour Papert (1980) who, from a Piagetian perspective, argued that forging new relationships between computers and humans would result in 'a future where the computer will be a significant part of every child's life' (Papert 1980, p.18) and later that schools, as a result, would be obsolete (Papert 1995). Other authors have enthusiastically echoed these claims over the years, typified by Stonier and Conlin's (1985, p.10) assumption that:

> [The] entire educational system will begin to revolve increasingly around the computer. Combined with teachers and parents, books and classrooms, the system over the next few decades will change. At the core of it will be the computer.

Such hyperbole has not just been the preserve of a few over-zealous educators. Indeed, this enthusiasm has been stridently reflected in educational policymaking over the last twenty years. The current new Labour government in the UK, as we shall see in following chapters, has invested considerable faith, and more importantly finances, into information and communications technology as part of their quest for the 'modernisation' of schools and the raising of educational 'standards'. Via 'National Grids for Learning', 'Universities for Industry', 'e-universities', 'ICT learning centres' and 'Virtual Teacher Centres', the current educational climate has been infused with a sense of technological evangelism, reminiscent of the utopianism prevalent at the beginning of the 1980s and the Thatcher administration. Moreover, unceasing expenditure by parents anxious to augment their children's education has given rise to a multi-billion pound industry in computer-based home learning. Education and learning have been at the heart of Britain's conceptualisation *and* consumption of new technologies over the last two decades.

Although the exact nature of the technology may have altered, ICT in its various forms has proved unique in educational terms in that, unlike any other innovation, its benefits to schools and colleges, learners and teachers have remained largely unchallenged, quickly becoming an established educational orthodoxy (Robins and Webster 1989). Against such consensual optimism the prospect of critically questioning education and technology would appear to be an unproductive and churlish option.

Yet given this increasing ideological and financial importance it is more vital than ever to ask awkward questions of education and technology. It is important to highlight the advantages *and* disadvantages of educational technology, its strengths and weaknesses and, above all, the often messy and never straight-forward nature of its implementation and insertion into the social settings of the school, college and university. In short, academic engagement with technology and education needs to adopt an objective air – one that has, more often than not, been sadly lacking. Indeed, as a field of academic enquiry over the past thirty years, educational computing has until recently remained the preserve of small groups of well-intentioned, enthusiastic yet under-funded and isolated 'hobbyists' – individuals whose driving motivation was often an intrinsic interest in technology, often from a purely personal perspective. However, the rapid policy expansion of educational technology now means that such a 'closed' capture of the field can no longer afford to continue. The 'hobbyist era' of education technology appears increasingly anachronistic as ICT enters the mainstream of educational policy and practice. Nevertheless the current salience of technology in educational policy and practice terms has, as yet, been slow to permeate the field of educational technology *research* – which continues to remain rooted in rigid technicist paradigms and a narrow perspective of what 'educational technology' entails. The remainder of this chapter seeks to redress this imbalance by discussing in more detail the present limitations of educational technology research and then outlining a conceptual agenda for the preceding empirical chapters in the book.

Present Weaknesses of Research into Education and Technology

Over the past three decades there have been many individuals examples of groundbreaking and exemplary work focusing on the role of 'new' technologies in education. However, through-out the bulk of the literature there are also a number of recurring limiting features. Primarily, some researchers have tended towards an optimism which, in its extreme form, has approached a utopian outlook on technology. Whilst an optimistic view of technology is not in itself a bad thing, such a reticence to consider negative or less successful aspects of educational technology has long been seen as fundamentally restricting the field (Maddux 1989, Kearsley 1998). For example, such has been the enthusiasm and expenditure vested in educational computing over the last twenty years that any suggestion of doubt is often dismissed as being 'anti-progress' or 'Luddite' (e.g. Somekh 1999, Bennett 1999). Indeed, the whirl of public discourses surrounding educational use of new technologies has tended to offer only two entrenched positions – to be either *for* or *against* the use of ICT in education, with little room for discussion in-between (de Vaney 1998).

In many ways, this optimistic rationalism can be seen as a failure to take into account the 'wider picture' of educational technology beyond the 'efficiency' of the technology in question. Furthermore there has been a conspicuous tendency to mistrust, or even avoid, theoretical approaches when formulating the direction of research – despite many attempts to introduce theoretical perspectives to an education technology audience (e.g. Bryson and de Castell 1994, Seals 1997, Wilson 1997, Carr *et al.* 1998). All these characteristics have been translated into a body of research which, although substantial in size, remains narrowly focused and executed. Thus, much educational technology research continues to take the form of small/medium-scale surveys and case-studies, experimental descriptions and classroom-focused analysis; succinctly characterised by Barry Wellman (2001, p.2031) as 'pundit suppositions, traveller's tales and laboratory studies'. How, then, can this situation be redressed and educational technology research begin to reflect the increasing importance of information and communications technology both in education and society at large?

Recognising the Need to Embrace Diverse Methods of Research

Perhaps the most obvious area for change is the way that education technology research goes about asking questions. Here, the opportunities to methodologically improve would appear to be two-fold. Despite a predominance of small and medium-scale survey approaches to research there has historically been less of an emphasis on the large-scale quantitative analyses that have so advanced other areas of educational inquiry. It can be strongly argued that education technology research is lacking the large-scale data-sets to illustrate how ICT is 'working out' in practice – across school districts, regions and even countries – and not just in smaller samples of localised institutions which cannot necessarily be held indicative of any wider context of technological implementation. To date, such an approach has tended to be limited to 'official' statistical reports, such as the US Presidential Committee on Educational Technology report (PCAST 1997) and OECD (1998) global indicators, which provide useful national and international pictures of education technology use; albeit at a general level. Yet, as technology is rapidly introduced into educational settings there is a pressing need to replicate and expand on work such as the large-scale IEA comparative survey of ICT use in twenty-one countries carried out nearly a decade ago (Pelgrum and Plomp 1991, 1993) as well as larger scale work carried out in UK and US schools over the last decade (e.g. Watson *et al*. 1993, Underwood 1997, Underwood *et al*. 1999, Anderson and Ronnkvist 1999). By providing *large scale* pictures of education technology use it should be possible to highlight patterns and conditions of success and failure, good and bad practice and the strategies which lead to the effective implementation of technology.

Yet from the perspective of this book, there is an equally pressing need for more qualitative approaches to educational technology research to also be adopted. Unlike the vast majority of other areas of social science research, education technology as a field of inquiry has remained peculiarly impervious to qualitative methodology and analysis. Although an overt reliance on qualitative methods can be as restrictive as a purely quantitative approach, the addition of a qualitative dimension to education technology research allows a focus on what *does* happen (as opposed to what has apparently happened or what *could* happen) when technology is used in educational settings. Indeed, using the example of research concerning students' attitudes towards computer based learning, Weinholtz *et al*. (1995, p.388) were anxious to show:

> ... just how ambiguous and misleading results from quantitative studies can be if not supplemented by qualitative data ... Use of supplemental qualitative methods by quantitative researchers can serve as a prudent hedge against obtaining inconsequential or erroneous results.

In this way, qualitative findings can be used to 'illuminate' quantitative data (Parlett & Hamilton 1972), reducing the need for speculation or subjective interpretation on the part of the quantitative researcher. Such use of 'triangulation', in terms of a combined methods approach in social science research, has been well established (Williamson *et al*. 1977, Denzin 1978). As Connidis (1983, p.334) points out, 'the usual assumption underlying this view is that any single method has its own inherent weaknesses; combining approaches helps fill the gaps left by each one'. However, perhaps founded in traditional misconceptions of such methods as lacking 'rigour', educational technology researchers have tended to shy away from a qualitative approach to data gathering and analysis.

The Need to Ask 'Wider' Questions of Educational Technology

Allied to this need to broaden methodological horizons towards the qualitative is the fundamental need to start asking wider questions of education technology. If we are to attempt a more objective, detached analysis of ICT in education then it would seem appropriate to move beyond the linear 'cause and effect' model of technological and social determinism and explore alternative perspectives on society and technology. There is clearly a pressing need to step beyond the limitations of previous analyses if we are to gain a deeper understanding of educational technology. Above all, researchers need to be aware of the social, cultural, political and economic aspects of educational technology; the 'soft' as well as the 'hard' concerns. By considering alternative theoretical perspectives we can begin to form a multi-dimensional view of what is a very complex area of educational policy and practice. Given the increasing salience of ICT, researchers cannot afford to spare educational technology the analyses that technology has been subjected to in other areas of the social sciences.

At this point it is worth reconsidering Qvortrup's (1984, p.7) argument that ICT 'cannot be properly understood if we persist in treating technology and society as two independent entities'. This perspective strongly suggests that we move beyond the view that educational technology is separate from society in either its cause or effect. Thus researchers need to make a conscious effort to move away from positions of either technological or social determinism towards a perspective that avoids drawing a technology/society distinction, and focus on the social, cultural, political and economic contexts where technologies are developed, and the ones where they are used (Bromley 1997).

The Social Aspects of Education and Technology

From this perspective there is a need for educational researchers to pay more attention to opening up the 'black box' of technology (Grint and Woolgar 1997). Educational innovation can be understood as a 'garden of forking paths' (Williams and Edge 1995) where every stage in the development of a technology is reliant on social and technological factors, resulting in a direction, or 'trajectory', of development shaping both the content of the artefact and potential technological outcomes. Educational technology, then, is borne of a series of technical and social influences from its conception to implementation.

From this social shaping perspective, the idea that technology is inherently neutral is obviously a nonsense. Yet educational technology continues to be justified by many of its advocates in terms of social justice and equality of opportunity – as a great social leveller for learners and teachers alike. But the popular political portrayals of, for example, African classrooms and remote Vietnamese villages enjoying on-line access to state-of-the-art Western education (e.g. Clinton 1998, Barber 1999) show little sign of being realised. Indeed, on a global level, social inequalities in terms of access to ICT appear to be widening rather than diminishing. For example, whereas one in four Australians were 'online' at the end of the twentieth century, in Africa the ratio was nearer as 1 in 4000 (Vidal 1999). In the same vein, research repeatedly tells us that disparities in ICT between 'rich' and 'poor' schools or male and female students persist even in technologically-rich countries such as the USA, Australia and UK (Hickling-Hudson 1992, Shashanni 1993, Durndell and Thomson 1997). This is not to say that the social aspects of education technology should be seen merely in terms of 'information rich' and 'information poor'. After all, as Webster (1995, p.97) reasons:

To distinguish between the 'information rich' and 'information poor' both avoids precise delineation of who these are and fails to consider the range of different positions ... In short the model lacks sufficient sociological sophistication.

Instead, researchers need to develop more precise understandings of the patterns and implications of different levels of access to, and exclusion from, educational ICT. This is allied to the wider social effects that differential levels of use of technology may entail; for example, in terms of changing patterns of communication, interaction and social relationships between learners, teachers and institutions as well as the 'social construction' of educational technology.

The Cultural Aspects of Educational Technology

Any analysis of educational technology needs to also consider the cultural contexts in which technology is being used. Although a fiercely contested concept, conventional definitions state that cultures are systems of ordinary, taken-for-granted meanings, values and symbols, with both implicit and explicit content that are, deliberately and indeliberately, shared amongst members of a social group (i.e. Erickson 1987). Thus, it has been strongly argued that cultures and sub-cultures have an important influence on educational processes in a way that is common across individual institutions, districts and even countries (Siskin 1991).

At a global level, there are already indications that countries' approaches towards educational technology have been strongly mediated by 'national' cultures; from the 'village market' national cultures of the USA and UK reflected in their 'laissez-faire' market-driven policies, to the Singaporean 'family' national culture reflected in the centralised, government-directed visions of policies such as IT2000 and Singapore One (Garfield and Watson 1998). Thus cultural variations in individualism and collectivism, norms of power distribution and short-term/long-term orientation can both affect and be affected by the implementation of educational ICT. For example, the ambitious goals of recent education technology policies in countries such as Japan, Malaysia and Singapore can be traced (at least in part) to a strong cultural faith in technology (Latzer 1995). Similarly, issues of national culture are also prevalent in Singapore's on-going attempts at controlling, and in some cases censoring, individuals' access to the Internet (Birch 1998), where other Western countries have tended to shy away from any notion of overtly controlling the Internet. The extent to which national cultures affect the eventual 'shape' and effectiveness of education technology policies remains to be seen, but nevertheless suggests that caution should be taken when trying to directly compare the experiences of one country with another.

Similarly, at a more 'micro level' one must also be aware of the importance of educational institutions as cultures on the implementation and eventual effectiveness of education technology. As Ball and Bowe (1992) contend, even the implementation of a relatively 'rigid' educational policy is shaped by the influence of educational sub-cultures. Indeed, there is little reason to assume that education technology is any different, with technology constantly fighting a battle against pre-existing educational cultures, occasionally succeeding but generally failing to be effectively adopted (Goodson and Mangan 1995).

The Political and Economic Aspects of Educational Technology

Finally, there has been a general reluctance within the literature to recognise that educational technology is also shaped by political and economic concerns. Thus researchers have tended to ignore the dynamics of advanced industrial society in shaping the development and implementation of technology. As Webster & Robins (1986, p.65) reason, 'technology ought to be perceived as a product of capitalist development, as constitutive of capitalist social relations, and as a means of perpetrating those relations'. However, in adopting this perspective we should not just view technologies as simple direct translations of economic and political imperatives into tangible artefacts and practices but take a more sophisticated, less reductionist focus on the role of various groups and interests involved in the processes of technological innovation.

For example, much has been written about the economic and military shaping of computers. It is an often repeated argument that the genesis of computerised technology intrinsically embodies capitalist over public interest criteria, reflecting the commercial and military research and development that has initiated most of society's technology (Noble 1991). Thus, information technologies such as the computer are developed and shaped primarily with corporate capitalism in mind. Although ICT may serve 'nicely the world business system's requirements' (Schiller 1981, p.16) this 'construction' of ICT is not necessarily based upon the fundamental requirements of educational systems.

Adopting a political economy view of educational technology has gained renewed importance with the rise of global telecommunications networks presently embodied in emerging information networks. With digital information seen as fast becoming the dominant form of capital (Castells 1996) the political-economy perspective looks set to continue in its relevance to the macro shaping of educational technology. Similarly, at the classroom level, some commentators have begun to extend the work of Braverman in identifying the long-term tendency of educational technology to de-professionalise, or de-skill, the work of the teacher (e.g. Apple 1987, Apple and Jungk 1990, Bryson and de Castell 1998). Concerns have also been raised over surveillance aspects of the Internet as a 'Super Panopticon' (Poster 1995) and means of extending centralised control over educational processes rather than the notions of liberation popularly associated with telecommunications technology.

Forging the Way Ahead in Education Technology Research

All these points are not made to dismiss or devalue the vast body of education technology literature that has accumulated over the part thirty years. Such work has, after all, laid the invaluable foundations upon which the field now finds itself today. However, as ICT and education move into a new era of heightened importance so must education technology research. If ICT is to become an integral part of day-to-day educational processes there is an urgent need to find out *how* education technology is currently working out in practice. To this end, researchers must recognise and explore the web of mediating factors that technology comes into contact with once it is placed in educational settings. The social, cultural, economic and political dimensions of educational technology must be addressed if research is to go any way to effectively analysing the success or failure of the many national initiatives currently being implemented to bring technology to education.

There are already some encouraging pointers among the body of recent literature to guide such a progression. The Australian work of Chris Bigum and Bill Green (1993, 1997, 1998) and Parlo Singh (1993, 1997), alongside the work of Hank Bromley (1992, 1995) and Angelos Angalianos (2001) provide invaluable insights into the day-to-day negotiations between technology and other educational actors. The Canadian work of Goodson and Mangan (1995) and Bryson and de Castell (1998) offer similar insights into the socio-cultural aspects of computers and classrooms. Moreover, excellent discussions of the political and economic aspects of educational technology can be found in the writing of Michael Apple (1987, 1990, 1997) and Robins and Webster (1989, 1999). Yet the challenge now facing educational researchers is to empirically build upon these foundations and make such work an integral, rather than marginal, part of education technology research. While a need for the traditional paradigms of experimental and small-scale survey work remains, at the very least such work needs to be re-enforced and contextualised with the type of research questions and approaches that this chapter has considered.

The Use of Qualitative Approaches in this Book

It is from this research agenda that the following empirical chapters of this book are presented – all offering summaries of various qualitative studies of technology and education. In many cases the qualitative nature of the inquiry is secondary to the questions being asked. When carrying out research I have tried to be careful to avoid what Rorty (2000) describes as 'methodolatry' and must profess to have had no slavish desire or ideological leaning towards any particular research strategy or paradigm – just a desire to use techniques that result in deeper, richer and more accurate understandings of technology and education. Indeed many of the qualitative data presented in this book were used as part of larger studies to complement and build upon quantitative findings. Yet, taken on their own, these 'qualitative' data have also proven useful in developing an understanding the economic and political construction of 'educational technology' as well as the social and cultural understandings of individual learners and educators faced with engaging with this technology 'on the ground'.

In particular my research has tended to return to three distinct approaches to collecting and analysing data: focus group interviews with learners; individual interviews (both face-to-face and technology-based) with 'significant others' and discourse analysis of government and commercial rhetoric. These methods shall now be considered briefly as a preface to the following eight empirical chapters.

Focus Group Interviews with Learners

Given one of my primary concerns with capturing the *learner's* experience of technology and education my choice of method of research has often hinged around encompassing as great a cross-section of learners as possible whilst also offering as deep an understanding of learners' engagement with ICT as possible. Thus, throughout many of my studies, individual student interviews were felt to be too restrictive in terms of generalisability to the overall population, given the often limited time and resources available. An alternative methodology, long established in market research and rapidly gaining acceptance in both social science and educational research has been the focus group interview (Morgan and Spanish 1984, Morgan 1988, Flores and Alouso 1995, Wilson 1997). As Kitzinger (1994 p.159) describes:

> Focus group interviews are group discussions which are organised to explore a specific set of issues. The group is focused in the sense that it involves some kind of collective activity – such as viewing a film, examining a single education message or simply debating a particular set of questions. Crucially, focus groups are distinguished from the broader category of group interviews by the explicit use of the group interaction as research data.

In this way, focus groups have allowed me access to relatively large numbers of respondents but, unlike conventional group interviewing, also offered the chance to observe participants engaging in interaction that is concentrated on attitudes and experiences of direct interest to the researcher; thus providing data directed by the researcher but collected via interaction within groups of informants (Morgan & Spanish 1984). Focus groups have, therefore, proved invaluable for identifying the *why* as well as the *what* of education and technology (Kitzinger 1994).

Nevertheless, as with all research methods, focus groups have acknowledged limitations. Two of the primary restrictions to focus group interviewing are conventionally assumed to be their unnatural setting and the researcher's relative lack of control over the discussion (Morgan and Spanish 1984). Although the 'unnaturalness' of any interview situation is almost impossible to avoid, I have always found the 'messiness' and sometimes irrelevant nature of focus group data to be a distinct advantage. As Kitzinger (1994, p.159) continues:

> The data are messy and sometimes incoherent. However, these are precisely the sorts of problems that, I believe, make focus groups a useful method for exploring people's understandings and experiences. The technique enables the researcher to examine people's different perspectives as they operate within a social network and to explore how accounts are constructed, expressed, censured, opposed and changed through social interaction.

Indeed, throughout the course of many of my focus group interviews with learners, often very revealing data were collected from initially irrelevant interactions between participants, highlighting factors which would not have been necessarily raised in individual, informant interviews. All the focus group interviews presented in this book were intended to be phenomenological in nature (Morgan and Spanish 1984), in as much as they were designed to provide data concerning learners' common sense conceptions and everyday explanations of their use of technology in school, college and university settings. In this way, the focus for the groups was often a set of questions developed from responses to open-ended sections of survey instruments. Participants were always volunteers (although the realities of such 'volunteering' are explored in chapter eleven) and following Fern's (1982) lead, the focus groups generally consisted of between four and eight participants and took between 40-60 minutes. Furthermore, following Knodel's (1993) guidelines, the role of the moderator was primarily to improvise comments and questions within the original interview framework.

Individual Interviews with Adults

Although the principal focus of many of my studies has often been on learners in institutional settings, my work on 'distributed' adult learners necessitated the use of individual interviews. This need for individual semi-structured interviews was also imperative for my work with politicians and business-people when examining the public/private nature of educational technology presented in chapter five. The rationales, strengths and weaknesses of individual interviews have been widely discussed and require little elaboration here. Suffice to say, my experiences of interviewing some of the 'great and the good' in business and political settings has never been dull and always provides a different experience every time. This was perhaps exemplified when I found myself interviewing (or rather being 'talked at' by) a senior 'captain of industry' and prime ministerial advisor in a green leather-panelled suite overlooking St. James' Palace, when the day before I had been interviewing a group of seven year-olds in a Wendy House.

That said, my use of 'online' email interviews with virtual learners in chapter ten does merit further discussion. In theory the practical advantages of electronic interviewing are two-fold. Firstly, as Foster (1995) points out, interviewing by electronic mail is not constrained by geographical location or time-zone; the need for proximity between the interviewer and interviewee is no longer an issue. A second advantage is that fact that electronic interviewing data require no additional transcription – with a minimum of alteration the text from e-mail interviews can easily be tailored for any word processing package or computer-based qualitative analysis package. As well as obviously saving the researcher time and money this also eliminates any biases introduced through incorrect transcription. With e-mail interviewing the data that is eventually analysed exactly as the interviewee dictated. Nevertheless, having undertaken e-mail interviews one must be careful not to ignore the 'human' factors enhanced and impaired by its use. The use of e-mail interviewing also brings up a host of interpersonal factors that must be considered when assessing the applicability of the medium.

On a positive note, e-mail interviewing reduces the problem of interviewer 'effect'; whether in the form of visual and non-verbal cues or effect of interviewer status. It also can reduce the problem of dominant and shy participants, particularly in a focus group situation. As Roberts *et al.* (1997) discuss, the negative effects of shyness are often overcome when communicating via electronic mail. In this way, electronic interviewing goes a long way to alleviating some of the inter-personal problems commonly associated with conventional interviewing techniques. Nevertheless, the fact remains that e-mail interaction is, in many ways, not comparable to verbal interaction. 'On-line' discussion requires different skills to 'off-line' discussion, both on the part of the interviewer and subject, and can take different forms. As Bannon (1986) notes, the content and style of e-mail messages lie somewhere between a telephone call and a memo. Indeed, the language of all computer-mediated-communication tends toward a simplified register due to the space and time constraints of the medium, in effect making e-mail messages a hybrid of oral and written language (Murray 1995). Although it should still be seen as a less accurate reflection of a respondent's thoughts than verbal data, the 'mute evidence' of written data can offer the (sometimes necessary) convenience of both spatial and temporal distance between subject and researcher (Hodder 1994).

Discourse Analysis

The final qualitative method utilised in this book can be loosely described as 'discourse analysis' in as much as it involves the synthesis and systematic content analysis of the rhetoric surrounding educational technology. The rhetorical construction of political initiatives and commercial products can provide a valuable insight into the nature of the 'macro' level construction of educational technology. In particular, as Bromley (1997) argues, the way that technologies are described shape what we do and do not see in them, and how they are ultimately used and treated in society. It is therefore important to ask what such 'stories' omit (and therefore imply as insignificant) and question the assumptions presented to us as 'fact'. Bryson and de Castell (1994) extend this line of argument when they contend that the burgeoning discourse of educational technology defines and delimits how technology is used in the classroom. In this way we can begin to understand how technologies come to occupy the position they do in society (and therefore schools). Furthermore, as Sussman (1997, p.30) intimates, examination of such rhetoric can help reveal the structures of power and real shaping concerns behind the ostensibly bland, corporate face of the educational technology:

> Language, written and spoken (or signed), does not simply convey *objective* statements of fact or even expressions of intent. Language also transmits various semantic codes that have underlying narratives, stories and ways of seeing the world ... Clearly, language is used to establish or reinforce various representations of power, and those aspects of language are of interest to understanding politics ... Beyond the control of resources, capitalists must be able to create legitimacy for themselves in their role of resource developers, and this requires the capture of public discourse. When the captains

of industry are not capable of responding to people's real needs, it becomes necessary for them to change the popular perception and language of "need".

In this way, as well as 'unpacking' the relationship between private interests and public concerns, examination of the prevailing rhetoric and discourse has allowed me to explore the wider synergy which exists between education, technology and society after twenty years of ICT in schools. This reflects the Foucauldian notion of discourse as the historical and cultural production of systems of knowledge and beliefs which is shaped, and shapes, our behaviour (Foucault 1981), thus extending the individual text into the wider discursive field in terms of its effects rather than its internal organisation (Barker 1998). Examination of discourse production in education thereby affords an understanding of 'the multifaceted public process through which meanings are progressively and dynamically achieved' (Davies 1989, p.45).

Nevertheless, although analysis of discourse has been used in other areas of education, especially gender issues (i.e. Davies 1989, Walkerdine 1990, Weiner 1994) and media perceptions of educational issues (e.g. Pettigrew and Maclure 1997), it has been less widely applied to educational technology. Chapters three and four therefore explore the political and commercial discourses of 'educational computing' and the National Grid for Learning by presenting, and then examining, a variety of marketing and promotional material produced by industry and the government. From these texts we can therefore gain a sense of how educational technology is beginning to be shaped at a macro level by its key actors.

Analysis of Qualitative Data

Before moving onto the eight studies it is worth also briefly considering how all these data were analysed. Here, I must start by confessing to using decidedly non-technological approaches, despite the focus of my research. The use of computer-based techniques for the analysis of qualitative data has been much lauded yet, in practice, I have found them to offer little to the researcher working with only a small-to-medium number of interview transcripts (say between 30-80) and a willingness to read and re-read the data. Although the NUD*IST and latterly In-Vivo qualitative analysis packages were initially considered for the analysis of the data in many of the studies detailed in this book, on every occasion it was eventually decided to use manual, 'paper and pencil' content analysis for practical reasons and in light of the ongoing debate concerning the validity and restrictive nature of using computer-based qualitative analysis (see Holbrook and Butcher 1996, Catterall and Maclaren 1997). Therefore, the constant comparison technique was used to analyse all data generated from the studies presented in this book (Glaser and Strauss 1967). This initially involved reading all the interview transcripts to gain an overall sense of the data. All the interview data were then read again and 'open-coded' to produce an initial code list until, in the opinion of the researcher, analysis had reached theoretical saturation. Although some *in vivo* codes were adapted (i.e. directly using the language of the participant) the majority were researcher-led and analytic (Strauss 1987). From this basis the data were then selectively coded in terms of categories identified with the initial code list directly related to the aims of the particular study.

Conclusion

The fruits of this approach can now be seen over the next eight empirical chapters. Although by no means a comprehensive analysis of education and technology I hope that the chapters, when taken as a whole, provide a wide-ranging and provocative picture of education and technology from a variety of perspectives – in the spirit of the research questions and framework outlined in this chapter. Thus the next three chapters attempt to address the 'wider' economic and political construction of education and technology in the UK over the last twenty years. This perspective starts with a historical examination of the rise of 'information technology' and education during the 1980s and the Thatcher administration.

PART II
THE POLITICS AND ECONOMICS OF TECHNOLOGY AND EDUCATION

PART II

Chapter Three

The Discursive Construction of 'Educational Computing' in the UK, 1979-1989

Introduction

This chapter heads the empirical section of the book by examining the discursive foundations of what we now unproblematically refer to as 'educational technology' and 'educational computing', thereby laying bare the shaping forces and driving motivations behind education and technology in UK policymaking. As we discussed in chapters one and two, the idea that ICTs such as the computer have inherent educational qualities is firmly ingrained in the hearts and minds of public and politicians alike. The ability of the computer to act, for example, as a tireless 'individual tutor' or to provide access to an unlimited wealth of resources and information are familiar scenarios and continually used as justification for expenditure on information technology both in the classroom and at home. Furthermore, the scope of the computer's educational potential is seen by many to be limited only by technical considerations. As the processing speeds and memory capacities of computerised technologies have steadily increased so too have the educational claims made on their behalf.

Such is the force and frequency with which these 'stories' have been told, that the association of the 'computer' with 'education' and 'learning' is now seen by many as unquestionable common sense. Yet a number of educationalists are beginning to challenge this rhetoric, reasoning that the inherently educational nature of computing belies the reality in many classrooms and homes (e.g. Loveless 1996, Cuban 2001). It is argued, for example, that the increasing numbers of computers being bought for primary and secondary schools obscures the relatively limited use of these machines in day-to-day classroom activity. A similar picture emerges when children's domestic use of technology is examined, with 'educational' activities proving the exception rather the rule for many children (Furlong et al. 1999). Furthermore, despite the best efforts of researchers, there is little sustained and reliable evidence that computer use does lead to the widespread gains in learning and increases in educational standards that are persistently claimed. In short, there has been remarkably little substantial evidence over the last twenty years to support the notion of the 'educational' computer despite the widely held beliefs and multi-billion pound investment by governments, schools and parents.

Re-examining the 'Educational' Computer

This fundamental discrepancy at the heart of 'educational' computing remains over-looked by many politicians, practitioners and academics. Indeed, as we have already seen in chapter two, questioning the educational value of computing is treated as heresy among some sectors of the educational community. Yet, whilst the bi-polarised debate over whether computers are a 'good thing' for education and learning shows little sign of being resolved, there is a pressing need to explore how and why the computer came to occupy its current cultural position as 'educational' tool. Following this line of thought, one must start from the premise that the nature and qualities of the computer are *not* intrinsic and merely shaped by technological progress. As Marvin (1986, p.8) contends, 'media are not fixed natural objects; they have no natural edges. They are constructed complexes of habits, beliefs, and procedures embedded in elaborate cultural codes of communication'. As Marvin intimates, technologies have no inherent qualities. Instead they are socially constructed, shaped and configured by a variety of actors; including designers, manufacturers, distributors, the media, government and 'end-users' (Woolgar 1991, Grint and Woolgar 1997, Bromley 1997). The educational potential of the computer should therefore be seen as a site of power, reflecting a complex preceding combination of political and cultural forces. As de Vaney (1998, p.580) concludes:

> Diffuse sources of power often cohere around the dissemination of new technologies, thereby establishing conventions for use that become regulatory by their very practice and articulation.

From this conceptual basis, the present chapter explores how the computer came to be so strongly 'configured' as educational during its integration into mainstream British society and culture. In doing so it examines the various actors and routes of transmitting information that were involved in the construction of the computer as an inherently educational machine and, as a result, discusses the underlying motivations behind this process. In asking these questions the chapter focuses specifically on the period 1979-1989 as the genesis of mainstream educational computing in the UK. The end of the 1970s has been identified by sociologists of technology as a significant milestone in the history of computer technologies which were still in the process of formation and had yet to be stabilised or naturalised into the daily lives of the general public (Reed 2000). Indeed, in 1979, the computer was by no means successfully integrated into mainstream British culture. Therefore the choice of 1979 as a starting point for our present analysis has deliberate technological, social *and* political connotations. Marking as it does the election of Margaret Thatcher's Conservative government, the early development of UK-produced computers as well as a rising media interest in new technologies, 1979 can be seen as a distinctive 'turning point' in the UK's relationship with the computer and, it follows, the discursive formation of educational computing. Conversely, by the end of the 1980s 'information technology' was an enshrined part of government policymaking, legislated education practice *and* an established part of public consumption of technology. The period between 1979 and 1989 therefore marked the establishment of the computer as an information technology *par excellence* in British society and the entrenchment of the popular perception of the computer as inherently 'educational'.

Government Policy

In examining the period 1979-1989 we must consider three prominent areas of production which combined to (re)shape the computer into the image of 'educational machine'. Perhaps the most influential of these was the tenure throughout the 1980s of the Conservative government under Margaret Thatcher, arguably the first political administration to give the computer sustained attention. As McNeil (1991) reminds, the ideological dimensions of Conservative party IT policymaking throughout this time are all too easily obscured by the commonly held view that information technology was merely a personal hobby-horse for a few prominent members of the government rather than the focus of concerted Conservative activity. However, one cannot overlook the role that the Conservative administration played in the shaping of new technologies in the UK throughout the 1980s, especially with regard to education. Indeed, the emergence of educational computing policy during Thatcher's time in office should be seen as a principal catalyst of the wider 'educational' computer discourse.

Inheriting little from the departing Labour government, the Conservatives came to power in 1979 with a vague notion that 'something should be done' about new technology. As Kenneth Baker (1993, p.57) later reflected on the predicament of the newly elected government:

> [At this time] the Government had little understanding of the significance of the microchip revolution which was about to transform society. There was another industrial revolution actually in the process of happening, and it was essential that we were not left trailing behind America and Japan.

Nevertheless, the Conservatives were certainly aware of moves being made in other countries regarding new technology. Most notably, the French president Giscard d'Estaing had commissioned the hugely influential 'L'Informatisation de la Société' report in 1978 and subsequently established the Direction Générale des Telecommunications as well as increasing government subsidies to the French telecommunications industry. Similar moves were being made in Sweden, Denmark, Canada, the US and Japan, creating a world-wide impetus for action. Such political activity contrasted sharply with Britain's floundering industrial fortunes with regard to IT at the time. From being a world-leader in the development of computers in the late-1940s, British industry had been seen to consistently 'fail' in the commercial exploitation of new technology throughout the 1960s and 70s – perceived by many as symptomatic of the wider 'British problem' in industry (Hendry 1989). Thus, by 1979 world-wide firms mainly of American origin were dominating the computer marketplace – personified by the omnipresent 'Big Blue' of IBM. As Kenneth Baker's earlier quotation intimates, boosting economic competitiveness and re-establishing Britain's position as a high-tech leader were major concerns for the incoming Conservative government.

Although by no means the most prominent area of policymaking during the first years of the Thatcher administration, the new government quickly made moves to meet the emergence of computerised technologies head on. Kenneth Baker, a high-profile backbencher with no job in the government and substantial business interests in IT, was appointed to the Department for Trade and Industry (DTI) with the title of Minister of State for Industry and Information Technology in January 1981. Supporting moves were also made, such as the establishment of the Information Technology Advisory Panel (ITAP) as an independent business-orientated body to steer the Conservative's reforms. This political reorganisation therefore enabled the government to produce a policy agenda to support the beleaguered British IT industry and it was here that education was identified by the Conservatives as playing a vital role in achieving this aim. Indeed, in lobbying for the job of Minister for IT, Baker had produced an outline of a 'National Strategy for Information Technology', where one of the main plans was for 'the Government [to] identify a number of applications for advanced systems within its own activities and procure them from the British information technology industry'. In particular, Baker's strategy included the seeds of an educational computing programme:

> Schools should be provided with small and low-cost microcomputers and software systems. To give a boost to our own hardware industry they should be asked to design and supply these quickly ('National Strategy for IT' 1980, – cited in Baker 1993, p.476).

As well as revitalising the British IT industry the other strand of the emerging Conservative policy agenda was focussed on 're-educating' the British population about the potential of information technology. Here the young (or 'the keyboard generation' as they were often referred to in government rhetoric) were seen as a primary target; as Kenneth Baker again reflects:

> In all of this [the government] was acting partially as a missionary for the new technologies. It was essential that Britain should focus on them as they were to be as important in changing society as had been the early inventions of the Industrial Revolution in the eighteenth century [...] People had to understand the job opportunities that the new technologies would bring. If we didn't adapt and use them then we would have to settle for economic decline and permanently high levels of unemployment. I particularly wanted to appeal to the young, because they knew more about the new technology than their parents (Baker 1993, p.64).

Thus, even early into the first term of office, both 'the young' and their educational institutions were being targeted by the government as key sites for launching the 'IT revolution' and soon this discursive focus was reinforced by a series of high profile centrally-funded initiatives. Most notable of these was the 'Micros for Schools' scheme launched in 1981 by the DTI, offering to fund 50 per cent of the cost of a microcomputer to every computerless school in the country – with the school financing the remainder. The Micros in Schools scheme was distinguished by restricting schools' choice of machine to one of two British-made machines and quickly made an impact on the UK educational system. Whereas in 1980 there were only around 700 microcomputers in UK schools (Hubbard 1981), by 1982 over 4000 secondary schools had ordered microcomputers. For schools, at least, microcomputing had fast become a matter for attention. This message was further reinforced by the concurrent £12million 'Microelectronics in Education Programme' (MEP) with its dual brief to promote the use of microcomputers in schools and to develop the teaching of IT. In practice the MEP entailed the dissemination of information, curriculum and software development and teacher training. The need, if not the reason, for schools, teachers and students to 'get on board' with the IT revolution was being made explicit through both government discourse and policy.

In initiating these schemes alongside parallel higher education and work-based training initiatives over the first half of the 1980s the Conservatives were committing unprecedented amounts of central government money and support towards IT and education. A further example of this model of central 'bankrolling' of educational computing was the introduction of the Technical and Vocational Education Initiative (TVEI); a vocational educational programme launched in 1982 but largely usurped by the introduction of the National Curriculum in 1988. As a broad curricular programme primarily designed to consolidate and progress vocational education, TVEI informed curricula by promoting the use of new technologies, equal opportunities and a range of vocational courses for all, as well as the funding of local initiatives. The over-arching theme of the initiative was to bring together education with the world of work; an aim achieved with varying degrees of success. TVEI did, in fairness, act as a catalyst for much educational policy-making which followed it; certainly paving the way for the National Curriculum and the wider acceptance of 'mainstream' vocational courses. Crucially, it was also responsible for bolstering levels of schools' IT resourcing with much of the TVEI money gained by institutions actually being used to purchase computer hardware and software.

Significantly policy commitments such as TVEI, Micros in Schools and the MEP were beginning to send clear signals to schools, parents and students about the educational importance of IT. Yet, any tangible *educational* rationales for these schemes remained tenuous and were ultimately couched in terms of deferred economic gratification:

> The use of computers outside school is not confined to calculation. There is no reason why schools should be any less innovative. We must not forget that when we move on out of this recession we shall need trained young people ready to cope with the latest technology has to offer (Boyson 1981).

> Having seen young children become fascinated with the interplay of keyboard and screen and also seen them acquiring operating skills so quickly, I was persuaded that computers could assist learning, particularly in basic numeracy and literacy. Children

had to learn keyboard skills at school, since whatever they were to do in life they were going to come into contact with the microchip. We have to train the young people of today for the jobs of tomorrow (Baker 1993, p.61).

This emerging government focus on IT, the young and education was sustained throughout the 1980s with the formation of the National Council for Educational Technology and the DTI's continued funding of school IT equipment purchases through the £3.5 million Software in Schools and £1.5 million Modems in Schools programmes. Then, in 1987 the government's educational IT agenda subtly but dramatically became more focussed with the publication of *'New Technology for Better Schools'* (DES 1987). The central stated aim of this policy document was 'to harness the potential of IT for enhancing the quality of teaching and learning across the curriculum'. As Boyd-Barrett (1990) contended at the time, government discourses on computer use thereby shifted from the general notion of preparing children for the information society to the specific notion of IT helping children learn. In other words, after seven years of encouraging computer use for future economic benefit, the government was now boldly promoting computer use largely for its perceived educational benefits. Thus the story of the computer as a powerful tool for teaching and learning and 'improving education' was now an explicit part of government discourse. As Kenneth Baker (now Secretary of State for Education) argued at the time of the announcement:

> Information technology has already shown its potential to improve the education of school pupils of all ages and in most subjects. I seek now to spread its benefits more widely through the provision to schools of more micros and more advisory teachers (cited in Penfold 1987, p.5).

In practice, the 'New Technology for Better Schools' document outlined a five-year plan based on Education Support Grant money bid for by LEAs, promising £8.5 million for more hardware and £10.5 million for the training of a corps of advisory teachers. Again the policy of restricting schools' choice of hardware to British-made machines continued, with schools having to gain permission to purchase machines not manufactured by Acorn or Research Machines. In doing so, *'New Technology for Better Schools'* was more or less a continuation of the original economically-driven agenda pursued via the Micros in Schools and MEP initiatives yet now couched in explicitly educational rather than economic terms. As Boyd-Barrett (1990, p.175) observed soon after:

> It is also important because it suggests a process of greater clarification at central level of the educational rationale for the promotion of educational computing. The economic arguments for the inclusion of computing in the curriculum, after all, were not invincible ... In *New Technology for Better Schools* the government was clearly taking the line that computers in education were important because they could improve both the delivery and above all the quality of education. This was not an unassailable argument, but at least it was an educational argument, one with a better chance of convincing teachers.

Then, at the end of the 1980s, the political construction of IT for educational purposes culminated with the government's moves to dictate 'the general principles which must be reflected in the curriculum of all pupils' (NCC 1989, 2.1) via the National Curriculum. Indeed, the introduction of the National Curriculum in 1988 reaffirmed the government's commitment to making IT an integral part of education by placing 'basic IT skills at the heart of the curriculum' (Dearing 1993, p. 28) as one of the so-called 'cross curricular themes' to be taught across conventional academic subjects. In this way, the National Curriculum continued the now dominant government discourse about the use of IT to 'enhance and enrich' pupils' learning and 'extending the scope of pupils' learning potential'. Thus, almost ten years on from the Micros in Schools scheme which has been loosely justified in terms of benefiting industry and the economy, the government ended the decade by explicitly enshrining the educational capabilities of IT into legislation which every school in England and Wales had to follow. Politically, at least, the notion of the 'educational' computer had been affirmed in UK schools.

IT Firms

Nevertheless, government policy and rhetoric alone do not account for the societal shaping of the computer in the UK throughout this time. A concurrent integral element to the shaping of the computer throughout this time was the growth of the IT industry and rise of the home computer market. During the 1970s computer manufacturing was still a nascent industry, in spite of the presence of large firms such as IBM and ICL who were well established in business and research markets. As Haddon (1988) has observed, at this time the computer had no discernible image amongst the general public and no perceived tangible use beyond office equipment. Nevertheless, throughout the latter half of the 1970s a new breed of small and localised IT manufacturer catering for individual computer users had begun to emerge on both sides of the Atlantic.

These early machines produced by companies such as Sinclair and Apple were solely aimed at the 'hobbyist' market; electronics enthusiasts enthralled by learning about microcomputing and willing to self-assemble rudimentary computers from kits. Thus any initial pretensions about the utility of these machines on the part of IT firms were limited to educating enthusiasts about the construction and operation of computers. For example, when discussing the early microcomputer kit developed by the Sinclair company in the UK, Adamson and Kennedy (1986, p.76) reflected:

> It is clear that this early micro was never intended to be much more than an educational aid. Certainly [the accompanying] book about the machine emphasised its value as a tool for learning about the way microprocessors work, and never claimed that it offered a computing power that was of any practical use .

Yet as the 1970s drew to a close, US firms such as Apple and Commodore began to toy with the idea of producing microcomputers for the wider public as well as hard-core hobbyist consumers, although these wider intentions were based on little tangible demand beyond a possible home business market. In theory, therefore, the computer represented a blank canvas for those companies who believed there to be a wider latent audience. As Haddon (1988, p.25) continues:

> In principle the computer was a universal machine – you could do many things on it. While each type of micro could share the same underlying principles of operation, they could be designed and marketed in very diverse ways. The debate [during the 1970s and 80s] was about the best way to develop and market a computer for the domestic context.

So, just as the Conservative government was looking to establish the role of the computer in the UK, firms such as Commodore, Atari, Sinclair and Apple were also faced with the problem of convincing the general public on both sides of the Atlantic to buy into the new computer technology. From this perspective, as Reed (2000, p.172) observes, the mass-marketing of the computer was wrought with difficulties as its development remained overtly supply-side in focus. Consequently, much of the early justification for early personal computers was decidedly post-hoc in nature (Bardini 1995). At best the thrust taken by many companies was completely self-referential and relied solely on the allure of the future benefits of information technology in society. Thus, during the early 1980s:

> One of the major triumphs of the early years of the home-computer industry is that its promotional campaigns managed to avoid questions as to why the common man [sic] should be remotely interested in the technology. The implication was that only a neo-Luddite would need to question the need to become acquainted with the world of the micro. The computer as a symbol of progress was as undeniable as the relationship between a Rolls-Royce and wealth (Adamson & Kennedy 1986, p.98).

Despite the tenuous nature of their marketing strategies, early microcomputers such as the Sinclair ZX81 and Commodore Vic 20 began to sell spectacularly well considering their very limited capabilities and software base as well as lack of real purpose. By the end of 1981 200,000 households had home computers whilst by the end of 1983 this figure had risen to two million. In particular, many of these sales were proving to be to young teenagers and adolescents. Indeed, although Sinclair's advertising copy spoke of a desire to 'produce a computer for everyman', the everyman was quickly seen specifically in terms of older children and teenagers – in particular males. In turn, the (male) adolescent market developed as the principal main target group of UK computer firms during the early 1980s. Thus, central to subsequent marketing was the idea of introducing future generations to the microcomputer. As Adamson and Kennedy (1986, p.97) argued, 'the idea was to lay the ghost of Big Brother and give birth to a New Image of computing, one that you'd feel safe letting loose on the kids'.

From their initial successes firms quickly strove to develop more sophisticated computers capable of running relatively complex software – thus giving the machines more in the way of content. Now, it was possible to point to actual applications of these machines above and beyond their role as a vague passport to the future. Thus computers and computer software began to be more 'ambiguously promoted' throughout the 1980s towards a variety of markets (Reed 2000). In particular three marketable applications emerged; the computer as a home office machine, the computer as a leisure/games machine and the computer as an educational machine. The basis for all these claims was often arbitrary. For example, the Commodore PET computer was marketed specifically at educational markets in the UK whereas in Germany it was marketed as an industrial machine (Haddon 1988). Nevertheless, marketing computers in the UK as educational tools soon proved a popular option for IT firms, reflected in the associated emergence of numerous 'software houses' being set up to develop and produce 'educational' programs.

Although the use of home computers as 'video games' machines had quickly taken off in popularity, most companies were loathe to lose the 'serious' air that had previously surrounded IT and saw an educational identity as the best way to position the home computer with a degree of respectability (Haddon 1988). Thus firms began to market aggressively their computers as educational tools – thus giving a legitimate *justification* for purchase whereas games remained the actual *reason* for purchase for many consumers (children if not their parents). Indeed, throughout the 1980s the 'Mum and Dad factor' was seen by many IT firms as a vital element of computer recruitment (Reed 2000) and the 'educational' tag was an ideal means of stimulating it:

> Eventually many of those companies emphasised the micro as an educational machine. On the one hand this had a wide-ranging meaning: education for all the family. The new term 'edutainment' soon started to appear in the vocabulary of marketers. This captured the idea that home education was also fun and part of leisure activities. The other meaning of education was geared specifically to children. This strategy appealed to parents to think of their children's future, based on the premise that somehow computer skills were the route to future jobs and prosperity. A few years later, the introduction of micros into the education systems of many Western countries was used by manufacturers to support their marketing claims (Haddon 1988, p.26).

Thus education was quickly constructed as a viable 'niche' for both British and US firms competing in the fast growing home computer market and, building on the earlier discourse of preparing future generations for the computer age, firms' marketing of the 'educational' computer continued, with bolder and bolder (yet often unsubstantiated) claims being made on behalf of what were still relatively simple machines:

> Learn everything from languages to chess and touch-typing, all at your own pace, from a teacher than never gets tired or impatient. Learning has never been more effective or more fun. Learn to invent your own games, create your own music and art, make your own experiments and discoveries. Or develop deeper understanding of nuclear energy issues as you simulate the fascinating workings of a power plant (Atari – promotional literature for Atari 400 – 1983).

> Ample room to accommodate your child's learning development. The BBC Master Compact's educational software takes children from their first grasp of words and numbers to A-level and beyond ... With a BBC Master Compact at home, your child's ability with computers will progress by leaps and bounds. Before too long you may find

that you have a Businessman of the Year in the family. At which stage, our micro could well be handling your young tycoon's financial forecasting and planning ... You owe it to yourself to buy them something they won't grow out of easily (Acorn Advertisement for BBC Master Compact – 1987).

Commercially the discourse of the computer as a powerful and flexible teaching and learning machine was firmly established by industry marketing and discourse throughout the 1980s; both reflecting and building upon the image of the 'educational computer' constructed in government discourse. However far-fetched and unsubstantiated these claims may have been at the time, the strategy became an integral and enduring part of the home computing market in the UK.

Broadcast and Print Media

Yet, whilst the political activities of government and the marketing activities of IT firms must be seen as integral forces in the shaping of the computer during the 1980s, the role of the print and broadcast media should also be acknowledged as playing a significant role in the shaping of this new technology in the UK. As Berdayes and Berdayes (1998, p.109) argue:

> The media are full of stories about how emerging communication technologies will change our lives and unify the planet. Yet, what tends to go unnoticed is that these stories shape the development of technologies by conveying assumptions about how these instruments will be used and the interests that shape their development. Such narratives tell us where we have been, who we are and what we might expect. Thus, they have a role in articulating or reproducing social reality.

Throughout much of the post-war period any portrayal of 'computers' in the media tended to be simplistic and limited to reporting the latest application of the 'awesome thinking machines' (Martin 1993). During the 1950s and 1960s there were many public displays of computers as 'electronic brains' playing chess games and predicting election results (Lubar 1994) but, on the whole, media perceptions of computers throughout this time were generally vague and often highly fanciful. However, by the end of the 1970s the media were quick in picking up on the information technology revolution. Perhaps the most celebrated example of this was when Time magazine famously announced the computer as their prestigious 1982 'Man of the Year', pointing to the 'irresistible invasion of computers into American homes' as evidence for their decision. Yet in the UK it was the BBC (British Broadcasting Corporation) that most forcibly led the early media introduction of IT to the British public.

Indeed, BBC television can be seen as a highly influential actor in the initial shaping of the computer as a societally desirable machine and, more importantly, cementing the link between education and IT in the public's mind. From 1978 onwards the corporation broadcast a succession of highly influential programmes heralding the arrival of IT with titles such as 'When the Chips are Down', 'The Mighty Micro', 'Goodbye Guttenberg' and 'the Silicon Factor'. As Adams (1982, p.21) argued at the time, 'the aim of all these programmes is to demystify microtechnology and to present a layman's picture of what computers actually are and do'.

Aside from these documentary programmes, the key element of the BBC's output was the production of a series of educational programmes outlining the principles, practice and application of microcomputers – backed up by BBC produced software and based around a BBC endorsed computer. Thus, in early 1982 the BBC launched the Computer Literacy Project involving a television series about computing which was loosely based around an Acorn microcomputer, a corresponding book and a 30 hour correspondence course on BASIC programming by the National Extension College. This project was quickly heralded a success with initial viewing figures of 400,000, sales of 60,000 books and 12000 microcomputers as well as 1000 students signing up for the correspondence course.

The Computer Literacy Project had a profound impact on the public perception and use of IT. In particular, the choice of Acorn Computers' new 'Proton' machine – subsequently rebranded as the BBC computer and launched in January 1982 – effectively acted as a state endorsement of the BBC micro and ensured that that machine enjoyed a long life as the official computer of choice for both parents and schools. Subsequently, when Margaret Thatcher announced the Micros in Schools scheme, the BBC Micro was one of the two machines of choice and took the lion's share of the fledging education market (Adamson and Kennedy 1986). Yet, more importantly, the BBC series along with UK schools' extensive purchase of BBC Microcomputers further promoted the educational aspect of computing in the eyes of the viewing public:

> The widespread concern with computer literacy helped to push the burden of Britain's position in the IT world simultaneously on to the backs of educationalists and individual citizens. It became the duty of those within the educational system to make sure that new generations of citizens would be capable of making Britain technologically competitive and stopping the process of economic decline (McNeil 1991, p.132).

The BBC's education department continued to support computers and education via the weekly computer programme Micro Live and the 1986 schools-based Doomsday Project, and were equally enthusiastically supported by other sections of the media. In particular, the printed media also were keen throughout the 1980s to promote this brave new world of computer-based learning, often indulging in speculation and futurology with headlines such as 'Children Will Learn from Computers at Home in the 1980s' (*Daily Telegraph* September 28 1979, p.8) and a 'Brighter Future for the Computer Kids' (*New Scientist* August 18 1983, p.462). At both home and schools, computers were therefore portrayed as powerful and desirable educational tools by journalists, reflecting the prevailing political and commercial discourses of the time:

> The explosion of the television games market and the exposure given children, even at primary school level, to the uses and fun of the microchip has brought increasing pressure to bear on parents to 'get with it' 'Computers – Every Home Should Have One' (*Times* February 28 1981, p.21).

The computer will be as important as books and paper in the classroom of the 1990s – and far more important that overhead projectors and videos' 'High Marks for Classroom Micro' (*Sunday Times* 31 October 1982, p.8).

Throughout the 1980s children were reported in magazines and newspapers to be freely 'learning through play' (*What Micro?* April 1, 1984, p.103) via 'the electronic Disneyland of computer programming' (*Times* March 29, 1983) with the computer being presented to readers as a benevolent and powerful tutor lending 'power to the pupils' (*Guardian* January 14, 1988, p.15). Moreover, newspapers also featured stories on children's natural ability to use and learn from computers in schools; highlighting information technology as an area 'Where Pupils Outshine Their Teachers' (*Times* September 6, 1983, p.19) and predicting a new generation of 'Computer Kids: the 21st Century Elite' (*Science Digest* November 1, 1982, p.84). Even popular magazines such as Good Housekeeping were extolling the virtues of children learning through playing computer games ('Computer Games Defended' *Good Housekeeping* January 1, 1984, p.93). Popular recurring stories also featured school children who had learned to use computers to the extent that they were earning substantial amounts of money from their newly gained skills; 'Software Kids – Online for Fortune' (*Sunday Times*, September 5, 1982, p.45). Papers' interest in educational computing even extended to collaborating with computer companies in promotions and competitions. The Sunday Times in association with Commodore held a 'Young Computer Brain of the Year' competition from 1982 and a year later launched their 'Classroom Computer Competition' with support from Atari. Thus, complementing and reflecting the prevailing efforts of the government and IT industry, the story of the educational computer became a key element (and easy journalistic device) for the reporting of the 'information revolution' during the 1980s regardless of the reality in UK schools and homes.

Discussion

There can be little doubt that the 1980s were a key shaping period in the development of information technology in the UK and saw the establishment of the computer as a mainstream application in settings other than the traditional confines of the research laboratory and office. In particular, as we have seen, the discursive construction of the 'educational computer' throughout this time was fervently pursued by the government, IT industry and media for a variety of reasons. As a site of power educational computing was clearly configured by a host of actors intent on pursuing primarily non-educational goals behind apparently educational aims. Thus the notion of the computer as a powerful home tutor or tool to modernise schools gradually became an accepted part of the 'information revolution' discourse during the 1980s regardless of government or industry's prime motivations. Yet two decades hence, it is all too easy for us to overlook the inherent economic, commercial and political influences underpinning the discursive construction of the computer as educational machine and the therefore arbitrary foundations of this discourse as it still endures. Thus if we are to make more sense of *present* day use of information and communications technology in education, it is vital that the historically constructed nature of the 'educational computer' is laid bare.

On the one hand, the Thatcher government's rationales for pursuing their educational computing agenda can be seen as a straight-forward combination of industrial, economic and political motivations, which were very much rooted in the wider problems of the day. Indeed, the desire to make UK industry competitive and upskill future generations of workers is a perennial driving force behind the majority of education policymaking – yet was exemplified in the government's construction of educational computing policy over the 1980s. From this perspective, Conservative IT policymaking can be firmly positioned within the context of Britain's economic decline over the 1970s and early 1980s and the subsequent concern with the so-called 'British Disease'. In the midst of rising levels of unemployment and perceived British failure to adapt to industrial change information technology was furiously seized upon by politicians as a high-profile antidote to the economic difficulties of the times (Robins and Webster 1989). Education was therefore seen as a key site in combining this goal with the government's other concern of establishing a national 'frame of mind' at ease with, and supportive of, the IT revolution. This cultural approach was firmly based around the ideologising of 'information technology' and the British IT industry – and then making these notions concrete via a programme of education and training reform for preparing upcoming generations of computer users. As McNeil (1991) concluded, this 'peculiarly British' approach made education the obvious choice to 'carry the burden for Britain's place in the international IT race' (p.133).

However, this is not to argue that the government's focussing on IT use in UK schools was bereft of any educational intention. Indeed, allied to the view of the 'British Disease' in industry were concurrent concerns about the state of UK education – initiated by Callaghan's 1976 Ruskin speech and the subsequent so-called 'Great Debate' about education. Thus the emergence of the educational IT policy agenda over the 1980s must also be seen as being entwined with wider Conservative intentions to rationalise, standardise and generally 'tighten up' the supposedly failing UK education system. As McNeil (1991, p.127) argues, both in terms of ideology and the political personalities involved, IT policies and wider education reforms were inexorably connected:

> [The Great Debate's] main outcome was to lay the responsibility for Britain's economic decline at the feet of the educational system and to provide ammunition for those who wished to halt the democratisation of, and progressive movements, within education [...] It is impossible to separate out the specific integration of IT within British education in the 1980s from this more general restructuring of education. In this respect, Kenneth Baker's move from the position of minister of IT to that of Minister of Education was indicative.

Yet, if government rationales for pursuing the educational computing discourse throughout the 1980s could be argued to include an often uneasy combination of economic, industrial and educational motivations, the role of the home computing industry in also presenting the computer as an inherently educational tool was more singularly focused on the over-riding intention to sell more hardware and software to the domestic market. As Adamson and Kennedy (1986) observe:

> Although in the end most home microcomputers were exclusively applied to running arcade games, they were nevertheless regarded as inherently educational. Predictably, this misapprehension was milked for all it was worth by the manufacturers. Any parents without a micro in their home were made to feel that they were impeding their children's future employment prospects.

Certainly, the decision of some firms to commercially exploit perceptions of the educational potential of their computers were expedited by the concurrent Conservative policies which has the effect of transposing education into firm's 'bounded vision' much quicker than otherwise would have happened (Fransman 1990). Yet, bearing the mind the concurrent emergence of the 'edutainment' market in other countries, the discursive construction of the educational computer by IT firms was primarily motivated by commercial interests, regardless of UK government encouragement. For example, even before the Micros in Schools initiative the commercial benefits of marketing the computer as an educational tool for both schools and the home was seen as a prompt by UK firms such as Sinclair to concentrate on developing the trigonometric functions in their early machines (Adamson and Kennedy 1986).

Thus, behind an amalgam of commercial, political and economic interests, it is clear that the discursive construction of 'educational computing' by government and industry throughout the 1980s was certainly justified by tenuous educational claims yet were founded on non-educational intentions. At the time the spuriousness of the educational assertions surrounding computing was noted with suspicion by some academic commentators, reasoning that such stories were wholly unsustainable in the light of most people's experience of actually using computers and would soon subside (McNeil 1991). Nevertheless, as we shall see in the next chapter, such stories are continuing to be told in the early twenty-first century with even more vigour and even higher levels of investment. Politically, educational IT policymaking has proved to be a curiously bi-partisan affair whilst from a commercial perspective IT firms have continued to find the promotion of their products as educational to be increasingly profitable. Indeed throughout the 1990s and into the first decade of the twenty-first century the relentless reification of 'information and communications technology' by the Major and Blair governments, multinational IT firms and the media has embellished and legitimised the 1980s construction of the 'educational computer' to the point of becoming an unchallangeable orthodoxy. Thus, far from fading away, the notion of the educational computer has been firmly appropriated as myth within UK society. From this perspective, the continuing presentation of such stories over the last twenty years has led to the situation where now the computer is seen by educators, parents, politicians and businessmen as 'naturally' educational; an embodiment of Barthes' (1973, p.143) conceptualisation of 'myth':

Myth does not deny things, on the contrary, its function is to talk about them; simply it purifies them, it makes them innocent, it gives them a natural and eternal justification, it gives them a clarity which is not that of an explanation but that of a statement of fact.

Crucially, it can be argued that the full effects of the mythologising of educational computing are only now beginning to be felt as it has been sustained over the last two decades. As we shall now examine in chapter four, the continuing construction of the educational computer as 'statement of fact' by Conservative and Labour governments, the IT industry and media is now resulting in serious ramifications for the educational community. As the memory of the £12million Microelectronics in Education Programme fades into the glare of the current £1.8 billion National Grid for Learning initiative, the political pressure for these 'new' policies to be seen to succeed has been considerably heightened – all culminating in an unrealistic imperative for educators to make the myth of educational technology real.

Chapter Four

The Discursive Construction of the National Grid for Learning, 1997-2002

Introduction

Having examined the discursive construction of 'educational information technology' throughout the 1980s, it is equally revealing to take a similar approach to the macro-level construction of 'educational technology' in the present day. This chapter, therefore, offers a comparison of the 'mythologising' of education computing throughout the 1980s with the rhetoric surrounding New Labour's current flagship educational technology policy – the National Grid for Learning. After much consultation the launch of the National Grid for Learning (NGfL) in 1997 finally clarified the Labour government's commitment to integrating information and communications technology into UK schools, colleges and libraries. With the legacy of Conservative policies such as MEP fading into memory and building upon the earlier 'Superhighways for Education' (EDSi) pilot initiative (DfEE 1995) the National Grid for Learning crystallised the Stevenson Committee's (1997, par. 7.1-7.3) recommendation that:

> A strategy for information and communications technology in education must include access for teachers and students to the Internet. It will allow them to access information and to communicate in a way that has never been possible .... It should be a high priority for any government to make usage of the Internet affordable and predictable for schools.

Although isolated examples of educational Internet use preceded the National Grid for Learning, with many forming the basis of the Conservative EDSi programme in the first half of the 1990s, the initiative can be seen as the first genuine political attempt to provide a co-ordinated, nation-wide drive towards widespread, Internet-based ICT use. From this starting point, the consultation document *'Connecting the Learning Society'* (DfEE 1997a) and the subsequent *'Open for Learning, Open for Business'* (DfEE 1998a) detailed an investment of £700 million aiming to connect every one of Britain's 30,000 schools to the Internet by 2002, as well as dedicating a further £230 million of Lottery money to training teachers to use the new technology. Plans were also unveiled to create various on-line resources for schools to use, the most notable of which was a 'Virtual Teacher Centre' with access to educational software and curriculum materials as well as providing a forum for teacher discussion and information dissemination. Additional elements of the Grid were regularly announced after the October 1997 launch, including an ambitious £50 million investment to digitise and provide on-line access to every major historical artefact in the country's museums as well as the free provision of laptop computers to nearly 10000 teachers and headteachers. To help initiate these proposals 1998 was proclaimed 'UK NetYear' with a steering committee of public and private interests charged with achieving the Grid's aims.

Now in 2002 the NGfL's initial goals are nearing fruition with every school connected to the Internet and most teachers having received at least a modicum of training. Although some goals have been amended (or even dropped in the case of the initial target to provide pupils with email addresses) the emphasis is now shifting to the development of the online 'digital curriculum' and the growing role of the private sector in maintaining the initial momentum (Buckingham & McFarlene 2001, Cole 2002). Yet, now five years after its launch, in many ways the ideological significance of the National Grid for Learning initiative continues to over-shadow its actual impact on UK education. Although the NGfL was thrust upon the education sector in a blaze of publicity and hype the 'physical' construction of the Grid is proving to be a slow process with the considerable problem of improving Internet use and ICT infrastructure in schools certainly not 'solved' by the government's initial 2002 targets. Thus over the past five years a major step in the 'construction' of the NGfL has been its formation within government and official discourse. This discursive construction is important inasmuch as it makes an 'ethereal' initiative a tangible concern, shaping expectations among both the education and business communities and consequently influencing the future effectiveness of the initiative.

Examining the discursive construction of the NGfL, therefore, constitutes an important precursor to examining the eventual impact of the initiative once 'on-line'. The remainder of this chapter examines how the National Grid for Learning is being discursively constructed by government and official actors at a macro level through policy and advisory documents, official statements and other rhetoric. In this way the chapter aims to highlight how the NGfL is being shaped within a restrictive technocratic and determinist discourse, thus conforming to traditional narratives of society and technology. Moreover, the chapter then aims to show how such construction negates crucial social and economic elements of the initiative and threatens, ultimately, to restrict the eventual educational effectiveness of the Grid.

Societal Rationales for the National Grid for Learning

A National Grid for an Informational Age

The Government has taken considerable care to position the Learning Grid within the wider discourses of the 'information age' and 'computer revolution'. Thus, as these two quotes from the then Secretary of State David Blunkett and Schools

Minister Catherine Ashton illustrate, the Grid is portrayed as advancing every school into the 21st century and 'bringing the information age alive':

> We're opening up the opportunities of the information age to teachers and individual learners. In short, we're moving the education service into the twenty-first century and creating a "connected society" (Blunkett 1997).

> The Government's £1.8 billion investment in ICT is paying dividends and we are equipping our future generations for the challenges of the new century. We must ensure that all schools are connected soon and we want to help any of those who are not yet there. (Ashton in DfES 2001a).

Of course, as Castells (1996) reasons, an 'information society' has been prevalent since medieval Europe's cultural structuring around scholasticism. However, the present 'information age' discourse, as embodied within the NGfL rhetoric, refers specifically to a notion of *informational* society; in other words:

> A specific form of social organisation in which information generation, processing and transmission become the fundamental sources of productivity and power, because of new technological conditions emerging in this historical period (Castells 1996, p.21).

However, as Webster (1995) contends, although the imminent arrival of such an 'information(al) age' and ensuing 'information(al) society' have been long heralded they have, as yet, been largely unsubstantiated. Nevertheless, in many areas of society the expectation (and one could argue fear) of an 'information age' is all that is needed to coerce public, government and industry into investing heavily in the requisite information infrastructures required to survive and progress in these uncertain times. Thus by positioning the NGfL within the meta-narrative of the 'information age' the government are clearly signalling its wider societal significance. Such rhetoric is powerful and pervasive for, as Slack (1984) argued nearly two decades ago, the ideology of an 'information society' instils a common-sense consensus among parents, students and teachers to adapt by whatever means possible. Such compelling discourse is also reinforced by the parallel threat of the on-going 'ICT revolution'. As Microsoft's Education Group Manager reasoned:

> Microsoft has placed top priority on one area above all others; the use of ICT in learning. We believe that the single most important use of ICT is to improve learning at all levels ... Few people appreciate that we are in the midst of an ICT revolution – a revolution which will have as great an impact on society as the Industrial revolution of the late 1900s (Microsoft 1998).

It could be suggested that the reason, as Microsoft admit, few people are recognising the salience of the 'ICT revolution' is that few people are substantially experiencing it, least of all in schools and colleges. One could argue that, as the key actor in the 'ICT revolution', Microsoft has a vested interest in promoting ICT as 'improving learning at all levels' in order to achieve their real 'top priority' of selling ICT. In the case of the National Grid for Learning at least, such ulterior motives remain well hidden behind vague predictions and prophecies about the UK's transition into an informational age.

A Basic Right of Citizenship for the 21st Century

Such is the pervasiveness of this 'information society' discourse that the National Grid for Learning is also being presented as an unalienable right for students to become citizens of the 21st century. As Tony Blair and Michael Wills argue, such provision gives students a chance of being 'effective in tomorrow's world':

> Technological change has revolutionised the way we work and is now set to transform education. Children cannot be effective in tomorrow's world if they are trained in yesterday's skills (DfEE 1997a).

> The Government is committed to ensuring that pupils and teachers in school have access to ICT. In today's competitive world, proficiency in ICT is crucial to the ability of pupils to compete with the best in the world, and the use of ICT in subject teaching will go a long way towards achieving this (Wills in DfEE 2001a).

The sense of moral obligation surrounding the NGfL was also succinctly reflected in the official slogan of the 1998 UK NetYear initiative: *'Connecting Our Children to a Better Future'*. Such rhetoric can be seen as a continuation of wider societal belief in the centrality of telecommunications technology to future living. Amidst claims of impending 'virtual communities' and 'cyber-democracy' access to the Internet has continually been voiced within popular discourse as a basic right of citizenship for the 21st century (Jones 1997). According to proponents of the information superhighway to be 'unwired' is to be nothing short of disenfranchised and isolated from society itself. It is therefore only correct that schools afford students this basic right as preparation for living in the information age.

Yet, all these arguments are so far lacking in any substance beyond vague, but foreboding, images of an information age. In doing so such discourse falls in line with another well-worn tradition of a-critical societal response to technological change. Hence the National Grid for Learning is simply an inevitable reaction to technological developments in other areas of society. It therefore makes intuitive sense that education should try and 'keep up' with the presumed 'ICT revolution' and 'information society'. Yet discourse of this kind is conspicuously silent about the ends of the NGfL. Beyond the extensive amounts of time and money to be invested such rhetoric tells us little about what roles the Grid will play, both in society and in the classroom. As Langdon Winner (1986, p.53) argued, such evasiveness is a well-worn characteristic of information society discourse:

> The almost total silence about the ends of the 'computer revolution' is filled by a conviction that information processing is something valuable in its own right. Faced with an information explosion that strains the capacities of traditional institutions, society will renovate its structure to accommodate computerised, automated systems in every area of concern. The efficient management of information is revealed as the *telos* of modern society, its greatest mission.

Indeed, much of the discursive construction of the National Grid for Learning, especially from industry, has taken this form – preferring to rely on familiar information society justifications with little consideration of the ends of the initiative. Where the ends of the NGfL have been espoused they have taken one of two themes; the Grid's centrality to reskilling future workforces and its benefit to teaching and learning.

'Employability' and Economic Efficiency

Following on from the broader 'information society' justification has been the close aligning of the National Grid for Learning with the future economic effectiveness of the country. In this way the Grid is being portrayed as an easy means of 'priming' Britain's workforce for the demands of the global economy. As Kim Howells, then Minister for Life-Long Learning, forcibly argued:

> Today's school children are tomorrow's workforce and we need to bridge the divide between education and work. The skills for accessing information and sharing knowledge and best practice are needed in education and work – they are life-long skills (UK NetYear 1998a).

Thus the skills that students will gain from using the National Grid for Learning are presented as being essential to skilling 'tomorrow's workforce'. As the chair of the Stevenson committee reasoned, these are basic skills that employers require:

> It's perfectly clear it's a bad idea for a child to leave school without feeling adept at sending e-mails. If you look at your own business, you want people who have that basic skill, just as you want people who can read and write (in Hicks 1998).

It also follows that these are skills that students themselves require in order to appear attractive as employees. As Kim Howells again stressed, the NGfL will provide students with 'employability' throughout their working lives:

> We live in a world where technology is rapidly changing. To keep ahead, people must continue to learn and update the skills they need throughout their working lives and obtain the tools to grasp the opportunities in a modern, flexible labour market ... Employability starts with high quality education and ICT has a role to play at the earliest stages of education ... The National Grid will eventually be available to all schools, offering teachers up-to-do date material to enhance their skills and providing students with high quality educational resources and the opportunity to acquire the necessary skills for employability (DfEE 1998b).

Indeed, the predicted demands of the impending technological workplace have traditionally been a primary driving force behind government and industrial attempts to introduce computers into classrooms. There should, therefore, be little surprise that a similar discourse is now surrounding the NGfL. Yet beyond the vague predictions of the increasing need for 'knowledge workers' such discourse remains as tentative and speculative as the previously discussed information society rhetoric.

It has been strongly argued that the conventional wisdom that schools should educate 'all' students in preparation for highly skilled employment in a 'high-tech' economy ignores the actual widespread lack of 'high-skill' jobs (Apple 1997). From this perspective it is useful to distinguish between high-tech *industries* and high-tech *occupations*. As Apple (1997) points out, the majority of jobs in high-tech industries do not require a substantial knowledge of technology with only the relatively few individuals in high-tech occupations needing technological skills. Furthermore, a trend in technological deskilling looks set to continue as ICTs become more sophisticated and the need for knowledge to use them declines. Thus, as Neill (1995) contends, buttressing educational reform by pointing to the presumed high-skill information economy ignores the fact that most students will require little more than a 'MacDonald's level' of familiarity with technology, primarily consisting of lower order data-entry and limited problem solving skills. Unfortunately, as Winner (1994) concludes, for many students the 'high tech' economy may promise little more than low skilled employment and a state of increasing bewilderment.

Educational Rationales for the National Grid for Learning

'Modernising' the Classroom?

Aside from economic concerns a third central tenet of the discursive construction of the National Grid for Learning has been its role in improving education. On one level this has entailed the compelling picture of the Grid 'modernising the classroom', complementing the earlier rhetoric of bringing education into the 21st century:

> Enabl[ing] schools to get wired up to the National Grid for Learning represents the biggest ever investment in schools ICT in a single year and goes some way towards fulfilling our promise of modernising the classroom (DfEE 1998c).

This has also been extended to the notion of the Learning Grid leading to an improvement in educational standards. On the one hand this has been expressed in broad terms of increasing students' attainment and 'progress':

> The digital resources ... will encourage pupils to stretch themselves with new ways of learning, giving pupils access to the latest information, great works of art and video clips of key thinkers and writers. The technology also allows teachers to monitor progress more precisely and push pupils on to more challenging topics as soon as they are ready (David Blunkett in DfEE 2001b).

The Grid has enormous potential for improving attainment, for supporting our main goal of driving up standards in schools and for delivering material which is of immediate, practical and working use to schools (David Blunkett in DfEE 1998c).

Elsewhere it has been linked with the government's other concurrent concern with raising numeracy and literacy:

> Raising standards is our top priority. The National Grid for Learning will play a crucial role in helping us meet our new targets for literacy and numeracy. It will not be a substitute for the tried and tested methods which form the foundation of our school standards campaign, but will complement them (Blunkett 1997).

> The taskforce believes that the Grid offers potential to enhance the teaching and learning of numeracy in schools and to contribute to the continual updating of teachers' skills ... We consider it important that the government's major investment in ICT be used to reinforce the objectives of the National Numeracy Strategy (DfEE 1998d).

The view of the computer as a pedagogical saviour is certainly not a new development and can again be linked with the concept of the computer as an economic saviour (Apple 1997). Promises of computers leading to improved standards in the classroom can be seen as being closely linked to wider macro economic concerns, with the language of efficiency, production, standards, skills and discipline pushing aside other 'softer' educational concerns. Indeed, the insertion of computers into classrooms under the pretext of improving education has long been a central tenet of the 'information age' thesis. That the National Grid for Learning has been promoted along similar lines should therefore come as no surprise. As Winner (1994, p.192) argues:

> There has been a great outcry during the past decade that there is an emergency in our schools, worrisome indicators of falling achievement test scores and a decline in basic verbal and mathematical skills. A common response has been to attack the malady with a blitz of electronic information, spreading computers throughout the schools, in the hope that this would provide a remedy.

The Teacher's Friend?

The discursive construction of the National Grid for Learning has not concentrated on students alone, with the role of the Grid in assisting teachers also actively promoted in government rhetoric. As well as helping teachers access resources and disseminate good practice via Virtual Teacher Centres, the Grid has also been touted as reducing teachers' administrative workload, ultimately freeing them up to spend time with students:

> [The NGfL] represents the thin end of the wedge – the future. Increasingly teachers will come to use the Internet as a source of advice, guidance and labour-saving. They will also use it as a forum in which they can identify, debate, refine and share best practice. It will become the first place to turn for professional guidance (Barber 1998).

> The big investment we are making in the National Grid for Learning will provide the opportunity for schools to develop smart systems for dealing with information such as attendance records or test results. This should mean lean administration, again freeing resources to invest in the classroom. The Grid will also enable teachers to access up-to-date resource materials (Morris 1998).
>
> ICT must be seen as a function of all teaching, part of a joined up curriculum which serves ... to help teach a child (Puttnam 1999).

Such rhetoric may be compelling yet, as Bigum (1997) contests, despite the commonly voiced expectation of educational computing making teachers' work more efficient and less time-consuming ICT has been more commonly found to make little difference to teachers' productivity. Instead, such claims are often made to divert attention away from arguments over the deprofessionalisation and deskilling of the teaching profession that computers are seen as initiating.

Commercial Involvement with the National Grid for Learning

As the previous quotations all demonstrate, the vast majority of the discursive construction of the NGfL tends to ignore the actual means of constructing the Grid. Yet, to overlook the economic construction of the Grid is to misappropriate the significant influence that commercial concerns will continue to have on the initiative. As far as the government is concerned, the involvement of business interests in the NGfL is to be welcomed as an integral and ameliorative feature of the initiative:

> Public/private partnerships are at the heart of our proposals for the Grid – this is a new approach compared with the approaches of other countries. I'm delighted that so many of the world's leading hardware and software manufacturers are playing such a constructive role in helping to make this great project a reality. It's impossible to put a value on the enormous experience that companies like Microsoft, BT, RM, ICL, Xemplar and the cable operators are bringing to this initiative (Blunkett 1997).
>
> Never have so many influential players in the educational market come together offering consensus advice and competitive products (Dominic Savage – British Educational Suppliers Association Chief Executive, cited in Kenny 1998).

Connecting every school to the Internet has therefore been made an attractive prospect for the UK telecommunications industry. Despite the obvious financial rewards, firms have instead been keen to stress the less lucrative benefits of their involvement. Thus the IT industry prefers to speak of 'helping' schools, 'strengthening' the country and making a 'genuine commitment' to students. As David Wimpress, the Executive Chairman of the UK NetYear board claimed:

> We believe the effective use of information and communication technology could transform the UK education system. By working together, the Government, the

education sector, business and the community can help to develop the new skills and new approach to take the UK forward. We are determined that our industry will make every effort to help school governors, teachers, pupils and parents fully utilise the significant potential of ICT to enhance educational attainment (UK NetYear 1998b).

The Managing Director of Excite International followed a similar line, arguing that:

We're doing something concrete to help all schools obtain and use modern technology for teaching, communication and learning. [The NGfL] is a great opportunity for Excite to kick-start the Internet revolution in school .... I'm thrilled that Excite is able to be a part of the biggest public-private partnership in any education system anywhere in the world. We're making a genuine commitment to the UK's new generation at a grass roots level (UK NetYear 1998b).

Despite such proclamations many commentators remain sceptical about the IT industry's motives behind getting involved in educational IT initiatives such as the NGfL. Firstly, as Neill (1995) argues, telecommunications corporations are eager to exploit the school market, offering to connect schools to the Internet in exchange for controlling the wires that will hook the schools to the Internet and thus to corporate coffers. Furthermore, involvement with educational IT affords companies concentrated access to a huge base of potential consumers. As Reguly (1997, p.27) notes, 'BT and the cable companies do not want to connect schools out of pure altruism. They realise that children, if exposed to their products and services, are likely to become loyal future customers'. Yet, as far as the IT industry is concerned, their involvement with the Grid is innocent and self-effacing:

Everyone taking part has a social conscience. The grid will be a vital part of the future of this country. Enlightened self-interest is the best way to describe our motives. We will not make any money out of UK NetYear. If our work is not done, the National Grid for Learning will be a year or 18 months slower (David Wimpress – ICL Education / Head of UK NetYear, cited in Kenny 1998).

The idea of the telecommunications industry participating in the NGfL initiative purely for altruistic reasons is a gross misrepresentation of what is a complex relationship between state and private sectors. As Kenway *et al.* (1994, p.324) argue:

The line between philanthropy and marketing is often blurred, particularly given the increasing recognition in the business community of the market value of being seen as a good corporate citizen with a social conscience ... Overall the main imperative, then, is to commercialise the classroom to establish schools as legitimate sites for profits and savings, and to produce future citizens who are dedicated and uncritical consumers and dedicated and docile workers.

Perhaps more revealing, and certainly lending credence to Kenway's argument, is the press statement released by Japanese IT firm Fujitsu when they pledged commitment to the NGfL early in 1998:

The [Grid] will of course also expand the market opportunities for all PC suppliers and we hope to get a fair share of this additional business. Our new range of PCs for education have been very competitively priced and we look forward to a whole new generation of young adults who have learned to love our products (Peter Stuart, European Business Development Manager at Fujitsu in UK NetYear 1998c).

Whether or not companies are participating in the National Grid for Learning purely to teach students to 'love their products', the role of the private sector is clearly a crucial element in the construction of the initiative. Yet the role remains conspicuously simplified or overlooked in much of the rhetoric surrounding the initiative. The Grid, it seems, is being interpreted as an a-political development and for the social good of the country. As has been argued elsewhere, whatever its commercial underpinnings the NGfL is being carefully presented as a Grid for learning, not for earning (Selwyn 1998, Kavanagh 1998).

Having outlined and examined the central elements of the discursive construction of the National Grid for Learning it is now possible to adopt a detached analysis of the overarching themes pervading this discursive construction and thus highlight areas of concern for future research into the NGfL.

Discussion

It is particularly striking from all these texts that the National Grid for Learning has been predominantly constructed within a restrictively determinist discourse firmly positioned within the wider 'information revolution' narrative. The overtly technologically determinist slant of the NGfL rhetoric is unsurprising when one considers its close association with notions of societal progress and educational amelioration. As Slack (1984) reminds us, this has long been a common feature of information society discourse and, so it follows, the NGfL is perceived as an inevitable response to technological advance in other areas of society, thus having a transformative effect on both students and schools. The economic competitiveness of our future workforce will be increased, standards will be raised in classrooms and teachers' workloads lessened.

Yet adherence to such a technologically determinist vision of the National Grid for Learning is a dangerous position to adopt. Such a limited 'cause and effect' view obscures crucial elements of the initiative. In particular the deterministic framing of the Grid hides the actors who stand to benefit most from its construction. As Lyon (1988, p.18) argues, this is a recurring shortcoming of 'information society' ideology with popular rhetoric designed so that it 'obscures vested interests that are involved in IT and that in fact do so much to shape its overall direction ... yield[ing] no clues as to who wields power'. Furthermore, this discourse ignores (intentionally or otherwise) the agency of the schools, teachers and students who in effect the Grid is ultimately dependent on to succeed. In short the prevailing shaping and framing of the NGfL within a technocratic discourse ignores the social origins and context of the initiative. As Lemke (1995, p.58) asserts, 'the political advantage of this technocratic strategy to those who practice it is that it presents policy as if it were directly dictated by matters of fact and deflects consideration of *values* choices and the social, moral and political responsibility for such choices'.

It is clear that this prevailing interpretation of the NGfL only serves to obscure the inherent social and cultural nature of the initiative. From this perspective educationalists should strive to move beyond the view that the National Grid for Learning as a technology is distinct from society in either its cause or effect. Instead, as Bromley (1997, p.63) argues, there should be a move towards:

> A perspective that avoids drawing a technology/society distinction, and focuses on the social contexts where technologies are developed, and the ones where they are used. [This therefore] recognises that technologies are developed out of institutional needs and their impact is always mediated through the institutional arrangements and the social forces of which they are an integral part.

In this way, recognising the complex unity of society and educational technology and resisting the sanitised and deterministic rhetoric of the NGfL, will allow for a far more revealing, and ultimately effective, analysis of the initiative and avoid replication of the previous myopia which has so blighted and restricted educational computing in the past. Thus an alternative 'technostructuralist' framework of analysis (Tehranain 1990) should be adopted when critically examining the Grid, from its 'construction' at the macro level of government and industry to its implementation at the micro level of the school. In doing so the three following considerations present themselves.

The Economic Role of the Grid

As we have seen the present discursive framing of the National Grid for Learning ignores, or actively distorts the role of commercial interests in the initiative. As Kenway (1995) argues, when examining the role of the 'information superhighway' in education one must also adopt a *global analytic* and take into account the relationship between capitalism and national information infrastructures in terms of global economic markets. Adopting such a political economist perspective therefore allows us to position the Grid's relation to education within the broader realities and dynamics of advanced industrial society (Kitchen 1998). In this way Schiller (1995) highlights the necessity for nation states to construct electronic information highways *within* countries in order to be able to compete and be part of the emerging *global* system which, as Kenway (1996) argues, will create 'a digital world order based on information flows' (p.228). Thus, as Schiller is at pains to point out, it is global economic priorities that are primarily driving the development of Internet infrastructures throughout the world.

Although officially intended to operate in the 'public interest', the practical definition and construction of the information superhighway has been quickly appropriated by the corporate telecommunications sector. It would seem, therefore, to be no accident that educational initiatives such as the National Grid for Learning are also heavily reliant on amalgams of corporate and state finance. As Schiller (1993) argues corporate capitalists have perennially persuaded governments to subsidise new technology infrastructures until commercial interests are prepared to take over with the market well-established and the risk factors overcome. Thus, as we have already seen, in the UK the NGfL initiative has been specifically designed to be financed by government and the telecommunications industry.

The dual role of government and industry in establishing and maintaining information networks is an accepted, and indeed crucial, aspect of the 'information society' thesis. Yet, as we have seen throughout this chapter, the actual role of these actors tends to be over-simplified. Whereas post-industrialists such as Daniel Bell insist on the relative independence of the political and economic spheres 'it is quite clear that polity and economy are interdependent, and that the relationship between the two is far from simple' (Lyon 1988, p.13). The danger remains that continued government support for the NGfL ultimately depends on business' ability to make it profitable, rather than any 'soft' concerns such as education. Thus, as Sussman (1997, p.281) contends, the centrality of business interests to the 'information revolution' are usually understated:

> The hucksters of the "information age" do not remind us very often that the business of business is more business – and more profit – and that deregulation [of the information superhighway] means more concentration, monopolisation, and vertical integration in the industry.

So what chance do educational concerns stand in a technological world driven primarily by global economic concerns and profit margins? The rapid commercial development of information networks leaves many commentators in no doubt over the nature of future manifestations of the Internet. The future of national information networks, like that of the Internet, is almost entirely in private hands with the 'free and anarchic' space that characterised the earlier days of the Internet quickly being re-territorialised into a commercial extension of entertainment industries (Wise 1997). As Manuel Castells (1996, p.366) continues:

> For all the ideology of the potential of new communication technologies in education, health, and cultural enhancement, the prevailing strategy aims at developing a giant electronic entertainment system, considered the safest investment from a business perspective ... Thus, while governments and futurologists speak of wiring classrooms, doing surgery at a distance, and teleconsulting the *Encyclopaedia Britannica*, most of the actual construction of the new system focuses on "video-on-demand", tele-gambling, and virtual reality theme parks.

In this way the Internet appears to be merging towards a pay-per-use model, belying the commercial interests of those who have most stake in it; a model diametrically opposed to the Internet as we know it at present (Besser 1995). From this perspective it is hard to see how placing information and communication in the global marketplace is contiguous with general welfare concerns such as education.

Ultimately, making information available only at a price, rather than as a public service, seems to betray the opposite of a communal welfare ethic (Lyon 1988).

The Grid as a Technical Fix

Adopting a social and cultural analysis of the NGfL it is also quickly apparent that the initiative should not be seen, as it currently is being presented, as a 'technical fix' for education. Societal trust in the technological fix has been well established (Weinburg 1966) ranging from medicine to the environment to education, and has increased immeasurably since the advent of computerised technology. Indeed, as Postman (1992) argues, the over-riding 'message' of the computer is that the most serious problems that confront society require technical solutions through fast access to information otherwise unavailable. As we have seen, this certainly would appear to be the thrust of the National Grid for Learning, yet, as Postman (1992, p.119) continues, such blind faith is misdirected:

> Our most serious problems are not technical, nor do they arise from inadequate information ... Where education is impotent it does not happen because of inadequate information. Mathematical equations, instantaneous communication, and vast quantities of information have nothing whatever to do with any of these problems. And the computer is useless in addressing them.

Although educational ICT has been founded upon three decades of research focusing on its impact on teaching and learning, any sustained evidence supporting the view of the NGfL as 'technical fix' is lacking. Indeed as the chief executive of the government quango charged with the implementation of the Grid recently conceded, the evidence base linking ICT with improvements in teaching and learning is at best 'fragile'; with an overall 'lack of clear research evidence about how computers can improve results' (Johnston 1999, p.10). Thus educationalists must be careful not to fall in line with popular constructions of the Grid as a pedagogic or economic saviour and maintain a more objective, reasoned analysis of the initiative's effects. As Neill (1995, p.184) concludes, 'the savage inequalities of the past will extend into the wired savagery of the future. There is neither empirical nor theoretical reason to believe this scenario will change for the better'.

A New or 'Pseudo-New' Form of Education?

Although public use of the Internet is increasing rapidly the 'information superhighway' remains largely a hypothetical construct. The technology that will support emerging national information infrastructures is yet to be definitively established and until then we are having to second guess technological trends (Selwyn 1995). Nevertheless, as Sawhney (1996) reasons, the Internet certainly suggests that future developments in information networks will be directed along the lines of interactivity and time-space and cost-space convergence. Given this, to what extent is the National Grid for Learning model an innovative framework for educational use of the emerging technology? Although the full nature of the NGfL remains to be seen there is a sense that the discursive shaping of the initiative is adhering to the societal tendency to merely view the future as a more glamorous version of the present (Marvin 1986). Indeed, as Sawheny (1996) again argues, the 'information superhighway' model itself falls into this trap, merely amplifying the existing parameters of the quantity and speed of information transfer and overlooking the new 'liberty of action' the medium potentially offers. As regards the direction of the NGfL initiative it is therefore worth considering Jane Kenway and colleagues' (1994) distinction between *new* and merely *pseudo-new* forms of education. As Kenway *et al.* (1994, p.330) argue:

> There are new opportunities in new times: opportunities to ask new questions, to work in new ways, with different people and different ideas. New times encourage us to look at old ground differently and break new ground with a view to ensuring: (1) that education is not reduced to vocationalism, information exchange or entertainment; (2) that it is not totally absorbed into the "vortex of the commodity"; and (3) that it makes real and holistic connections with the young people of today and with their concerns about their current lives and their futures. New times also encourage new forms of educational expertise, new, not *pseudo-new*, ways of thinking about policy, curriculum and pedagogy, and new educational values ... How can education deal with the full complexity of the post-modern age rather than with its economic needs? How can it help to produce people who are not simply clever workers and committed consumers, but cultured, compassionate, creative, critical and courageous human beings?

To what extent can the National Grid for Learning be seen as a new educational form? Can the focus of the Grid be seen as transcending vocationalism and information exchange? Does it really represent a new way of approaching curriculum and pedagogy? To what extent is it encouraging new educational forms and values? Of course the answers to these questions, as with the actual Grid itself, remain to be seen. Nevertheless, we can at least gain a sense from the discursive shaping of the initiative of the form and role that the Government sees the NGfL taking. On the reading of the rhetoric discussed within this chapter it would appear that the best that can be expected is a pseudo-new distillation of the educational forms and values that have characterised the modernist/industrial model of education. Although couched under the auspices of preparing education for the 'information age' (whatever that may be) the discursive construction of the initiative remains firmly focused on issues of adequately skilling the workforce and ensuring economic prosperity, increasing students' attainment and raising standards in numeracy and literacy, increased linear access to educationally relevant (and vetted) information and improved linear communication. In other words, the likelihood of the Grid fulfilling Kenway's criteria of a 'New Educational Form' appear slim.

Chapter Five

The Role of Big Business in UK Education Technology Policy and Practice

Introduction

As has been intimated throughout the last two chapters, if education technology is of great political concern then it is also of great commercial concern. Indeed, as we saw in chapter four, business and educational technology are now inexorably linked, via the role of the IT industry in providing the technological artefacts that physically constitute 'educational technology' as well as the perceived needs of business and industry to employ future workforces educated with IT skills and 'computer literacy'. The role of the private sector has traditionally been overlooked in academic discussion of educational technology, yet constitutes one of the most significant examples of private involvement in education over the last twenty years. This chapter, therefore, examines the role of the private sector in education technology at the policy level − exploring the role that private interests play in shaping educational technology through the 'voices' of public and private actors currently involved in the National Grid for Learning and New Labour's wider education drive.

One of the most significant features of the UK Labour government's recent emphasis on 'education, education, education' has been the increased role of private interests in both policy formulation and implementation. For many commentators, this move towards 'public/private' policymaking can be located within the widespread reaction against the neo-Liberal approach of the 1980s free-marketisation that so characterised Conservative education policy during the Thatcher and Major administrations. The emerging approach, fashionably recast as a 'Third Way' in public policy formation (Giddens 1998), is viewed as attempting to pursue a less sanguine approach to market economics. In this way, the government's zeal in encouraging and fostering public/private partnerships in the development and implementation of policy is seen by many as one of the tangible manifestations of a 'Third Way' approach; especially with regards to education.

The '*Excellence in Schools*' policy document (DfEE 1997b) can be viewed as best encapsulating the newly elected Labour government's approach towards education policymaking. Foremost in the document, and a claim which Labour hung its electoral hat on at the time, was the ambition to raise standards of achievement in schools as measured by student performance in national assessment programmes. In order to accomplish this the government and its advisers assembled a pragmatic ensemble of policy initiatives. In what might be seen as 'Old Labour' – the party wedded to state action and intervention, the then newly appointed Education Secretary was given further powers to take over 'failing' schools and local education authorities. Yet, neo-liberal policy dimensions persisted in the government's retention of age-weighted per capita determination of school budgets and through its continued support for schools competing for students.

Amidst the flurry of education policy-making that has proceeded the 1997 election, 'New Labour' is perhaps best represented in the targeting of resources at schools serving socially and economically disadvantaged communities. While this runs against the grain of previous Conservative policies that were by and large profoundly unconcerned about issues relating to social justice and amelioration, schools and local education authorities are nevertheless required to bid competitively for the extra resources they require; reflecting some continuity with previous Conservative administrations. Crucially, 'New Labour' is also represented in the party's enthusiastic embrace of various kinds of public-private partnerships where these could best assist in achieving this overall policy thrust of driving up standards. It is this pragmatic approach towards policy creation rather than any underpinning principled perspective that could be argued to be the guiding character of Labour's 'Third Way'.

It could also be argued, therefore, that this 'Third Way' pragmatism fundamentally underpins New Labour's relationship with the private sector in terms of policy formation and implementation. Of course, a framework for private enterprises to take a stake in the development of public services is not without precedence in the UK, first being introduced under the Conservative government of 1992 and their introduction of Private Finance Initiatives (PFIs). Nevertheless, under the current Labour government the role of public private partnerships has blossomed in most areas of public policymaking – especially in education. Since 1997, twenty-five 'Education Action Zones' have been created as area-based initiatives thereby bringing public and private institutions and resources together and aimed at supporting schools in communities under pressure. Private Finance Initiatives have been launched to aid the rebuilding of schools in Scotland and the creation of the University for Industry. Aside from these high profile programmes various other forms of private enterprise partnerships have also featured heavily in the New Labour education policy agenda (Palast 2000, Monbiot 2002).

Yet, to accept the changing nature of private interest involvement in education policy as purely driven by a nebulous notion of the 'Third Way' is to ignore the profound implications this may have for future public policymaking. Indeed, the rapid introduction of such policies raises some fundamental questions over the nature and impact of private involvement in public education policymaking. For example, how 'new' are these policies and to what extent (and to what ends) are private interests getting involved in education policy? This chapter attempts to address these questions through an examination of one of the first tangible initiatives in this 'new wave' of public/private educational policy-making in the UK; the 'National Grid for Learning'.

The National Grid for Learning as Public/Private Policy

As discussed in the previous chapter the formation of the National Grid for Learning initiative has been treated by many commentators as a pivotal signpost for the direction of future education legislation, in particular with regard to the integral role that the private sector is seen as playing in the development and eventual provision of the NGfL. As the then Minister for ICT in Schools argued:

> We depend on an open and supportive partnership with the ICT industry if we are going to provide the high quality resources education needs and at a price schools and colleges can afford, Only if we all work together, will we ensure that the technological society we want to develop is inclusive and brings added opportunities for all (Wills 1999, p.3).

Nevertheless, as Linder (1999) observes, the notion of 'public-private partnership' has multiple meanings and, as we have already intimated, such public-private involvement in recent education policy has taken different forms. Thus in conceptualising the National Grid for Learning in these terms the UK government would appear to be looking to move beyond entering into a 'purchaser-provider' relationship with the IT industry and create a viable and sustainable commercial marketplace for educational ICT with the state acting as regulator and evaluator. This was seen as only being achievable with the integral involvement of private-sector interests during the formation as well as implementation of the policy. In this way the NGfL initiative could, therefore, be seen as potentially representing an archetypal modern/post-modern hybrid form of Kenway et al.'s (1994) 'markets/ education/ technology' triad. Although initially sponsored by the state the National Grid for Learning is also largely reliant on commercial interests, public and private expertise and is overtly informed by both educational and market values. As an emerging policy initiative of this type the NGfL would, therefore, appear to encapsulate the growing influence of market and technological forces in UK education over the last ten years, potentially constituting a 'new educational form' (Kenway et al. 1994).

Questioning Public/Private Policy Making in Education

Of course, public education has long been the focus of interest for profit oriented enterprises. The 'privatisation' of public education has taken a number of forms on either side of the Atlantic. Michael Apple, for example, drew attention to the extent to which education had been turned into a 'business' by capitalist enterprise pursuing profits via the creation and sale of curriculum and testing materials (Apple 1979). From the mid 1970s British and American sociologists have demonstrated the pressures to align the organisational and pedagogical practices of schools with the needs and interests of industry and commerce (Bowles and Gintis 1976, Dale 1989, Esland 1991, Shilling 1989). Then, and now, other analysts also noted how business has impacted on education through the formulation of employment objectives; in particular the production of appropriately skilled school-leavers and balancing the widely perceived 'needs mismatch' between schools and employers (Saunders 1992). As a result there has been a growing acceptance of 'employability skills' into educational discourse over the last twenty years, with business and industry viewed by some commentators as insidiously replacing traditional educational stakeholders such as teaching unions in the policy-making process (Taylor 1998). And in yet another turn, commentators have more recently reported the extent to which for-profit organisations have been brought in by nation states, under the banner of 'standards-driven reform', to render public education first and foremost a profit making business. Education Management Organisations (EMOs) have been created precisely for this purpose in the US and the UK and in their wake they have made visible the extent of the on-going privatisation of public education (Education Week 1999, Palast 2000).

Not surprisingly, the growing influence of business and industry in determining the educational agenda has been treated with caution within the educational community, even with regards to apparently altruistic gestures by private interests towards state education. In particular, critics have questioned industry's interest with 'social responsibility' and the 'public good' above and beyond their driving motivation of profit (Bennett 1995). As Tasker and Packham (1993, p.134) conclude:

> The two worlds of business and [education] remain profoundly different. The purpose of industry is to generate profit for private gain, usually in competition with other companies. The profit so generated may or may not benefit society; the concept of public good is not central to industry's concerns.

The increased role of business in education may well have been treated with suspicion by the educational community but much remains to be done to tease out that relationship, especially with regard to policy formation and implementation. As Wilks and Wright (1987) contend, the relationship between government and industry has been much discussed but little investigated. Certainly, the consensus among policy analysts has moved away from the overly simplistic notion that business and industry act merely as an interest group lobbying from outside the policy-making process (i.e. Truman 1981). From the 1970s onwards neo-Corporatists such as Lindbolm have instead asserted that business and industry enjoy a far more extensive role in policy formation. This view sees the business class as wielding enormous influence over public policy through the state's structural dependence on corporate investment; with businessmen in market-orientated societies, therefore, enjoying a 'privileged position' within the policy-making process. As Lindbolm (1977, p.175) concluded, '[businesses] constitute a second set of major leaders in government and politics'.

However, to date, few studies have moved beyond these different conceptions of the relationship(s) between business and education and empirically begun to examine what effect these 'new forms' of public/private policy-making may be having on the formation and implementation of public policy. Indeed, there is a pressing need to examine whether or not such policy-making does represent a distinct break with the past and can be considered 'new'. Moreover, to what extent is the state deferring control over public policy-making and implementation to private interests as some authors would argue?

The remainder of this chapter therefore takes a more detailed look at private interest involvement in education policy-making and implementation using the National Grid for Learning as a contemporary form. Thus it intends to explore the extent to which businesses are getting involved in this 'new' policy forms and the nature that the resulting government/industry links are taking. Above all the chapter is concerned with how the public/private foundation of the NGfL is 'working out' in practice. As Martin (1995, p.898) contends:

> The central problem here is to explain how firms develop their preferences for social policy initiatives and especially to understand the mechanisms by which new social policy paradigms win corporate converts. What are the conditions under which some companies sign on to far-reaching government solutions when others reject them?.

Methods of Inquiry

In examining the role of the private sector in the National Grid for Learning this chapter is based on a series of in-depth interviews with 'key actors' in the formation and initial implementation of the initiative. Interviewees included officials from the co-ordinating government department (the Department for Education and Employment – DfEE), the quasi-government agency responsible for developing and delivering aspects of the initiative (the British Educational Communications and Technology Agency – BECTa), policy advisors to the Prime Minister and DfEE as well as key executives in hardware, software and telecommunications firms and their representative bodies (see Table 5.1 for a full list of interviewees and their affiliations). Representatives from all the major national and multi-national industrial firms prominently involved in the NGfL were interviewed, apart from one firm who declined to be interviewed. All the interviews lasted between one and two hours and were carried out between October 1998 and August 1999; producing over twelve hours of interview data. All interviews were tape recorded and transcribed *verbatim*. Where appropriate the names of all the major companies have been omitted as have the individual identities of all interviewees.

Table 5.1. Descriptions of Interviewees (n=12)

Position/Role	Organisation
Director of Education Division	Multinational Software Corporation
Technical Advisor	Multinational Software Corporation
Director of Education Division	Multinational Computer Hardware Corporation
Director of Corporate and Policy Relations	UK Computer Hardware Corporation
Director of Education & Marketing	Multinational Telecommunications Corporation
Chief Executive	UK IT Industry Representative Body
Assistant Director	UK IT Industry Representative Body
Senior Civil Servant	Department for Education & Employment
Civil Servant	Department for Education & Employment
Director of Schools Division	British Educational Communications & Technology Agency [non-departmental government body]
Senior Prime Ministerial Policy Advisor	-
Prime Ministerial/DfEE Policy Advisor	-

The interviews were designed to elicit these actors' perceptions of the emergence of the NGfL initiative and the role of public and private sectors in its formation and implementation. Wherever possible these individual accounts of the policy-making process were cross-checked and verified in later interviews until a cogent picture emerged. Of course, no policy formation is a wholly straightforward or 'mapable' process and, as such, this chapter presents an unavoidably simplified account. Nevertheless, the narrative provides a strong sense of the role(s) and motivations of private and public actors during the formation and ongoing implementation of the policy. In this way, the data are presented in three distinct themes; (i) the public/private origins of the National Grid for Learning; (ii) the IT industry and its participation in the formation of the NGfL; and (iii) the sustainability of private sector involvement in the NGfL.

The Public/Private Origins of the National Grid for Learning

Throughout most of the interviews the origins of the NGfL were firmly located by the interviewees within a background of inconsistent use of educational ICT in schools over the last twenty years. Despite a series of initiatives stretching from the 1981 Microelectronics in Education Programme (MEP) programme to the Conservative's Superhighways initiative in the mid 1990s, education ICT throughout this time was seen as distinctly lacking in a co-ordinated, sustained policy agenda, often resulting in an indifference amongst schools towards ICT. On the other hand successive British governments had supported the purchase of British IT equipment by educational organisations in order to sustain a fledgling domestic computer manufacturing and software industry. For these reasons, the educational ICT market until the mid-1990s relied only on one or two domestic suppliers. As one of the computing company interviewees observed, up until the election of 1997, the education ICT marketplace was, therefore, bereft of any 'real' competition:

> ... at the time of all this RM [Research Machines] had an immensely big market share in education. And the Government's dilemma is that it had created a monopoly. ... Acorn and RM were big chunky players; Apple was always trying to get in, and ICL was never there.. Suddenly RM is a monopoly and the Government, I think, were looking for people to fill the vacuum [...] They were so desperate to get people who were education compliant to come in as a credible second source [Executive, Multi-National IT Corporation].

From this perspective, in initiating the sea-change of the NGfL the Labour party appeared to be making a break with the Conservative's 'infant industry' approach to educational IT throughout the 1980s, when policies of the time had the over-riding concern of protecting and giving an active impetus to the nascent UK IT industry as a whole rather than any specific concerns with education. That said, towards the end of John Major's Conservative administration there were emerging signs that small moves were being made towards a change, with the Department for Education at least recognising the need to open the educational marketplace:

> In the very early days the Government's money was specified only to be used on three types of computers if we go back to the very beginning. Since then there has not been that sort of prescription, and indeed we have very much supported the DfEE's increasing belief that there should be good competition in this marketplace. It would be very easy for one or two of the major international players to walk in, offer something apparently incredibly wonderful and lock this market up and kill it if the Government so wished [Chief Executive, UK IT Industry Representative Body].

However, any such belief within the DfEE was tempered by their restricted role in education IT policy at the time, lacking, as they themselves admitted, 'the huge underpinning resource programme' needed to effect such change. Therefore, in approaching educational ICT as a potential manifesto commitment, New Labour were recognising a need to break with the previous Conservative ethos and introduce an element of state direction in 'kick-starting' educational ICT:

> It's one of those things that create the climate and I think what we had was a government that was prepared to join it all up because it saw, ideologically, it saw a role for the state, sure. And, as I say, the previous administration saw a lot of these things but ideologically didn't see that as the role of the state. In fact it would have said "if the state intervenes this is how you get a Skoda or Trabant" [Executive Director, BECTa].

Thus, most interviewees were keen to play down the genesis of the NGfL coming directly from the private sector as the following extended accounts suggest:

> OK well the National Grid for Learning itself is really just a jihad slogan for a number of different strategies that the Government have really and just trying to see how they can tie them all together with one vision statement, and the Vision Statement for that was National Grid for Learning [...] So in fact the National Grid for Learning is really just a Vision Statement where lots of other smaller strategies were actually trying to lead to [Executive, Multi-National Software Corporation].

> There was a number of things that fed into it [...] As a policy it probably came from around the time of the Stevenson report to the Labour Party in opposition. At that time there was the Education Departments Superhighway Initiative, yes, There were a number of things looking at Internet use, broad band use, a whole range of things. There were Net Years there were Net Days going on in the States, there was a whole range of things ... Clinton getting photo opportunities with a shovel in his hand. The idea that in addition to infrastructure connectivity you need to start putting stuff on it ... I can remember a conference that I was involved in running in '95 when I was at the SCAA (the Schools' Curriculum and Assessment Authority) called 'Education Information Highways' ... something like that. There was a number of things around '95 time that were all saying "it's more than just connecting, it's more than just a infrastructure, its all about content". But I don't believe any of the stories that say 'we initiated this, we were the first, we had the big idea'. I don't go with any of that. Chris Yapp was certainly one of the ones that everyone was talking about. I mean he spoke in conference that I organised. Steve Heppell spoke in the conference a whole range of people, Bruce Bond who was then with BT. Right. So it was sort of in the air around then but I find it very hard to locate it [Executive Director, BECTa].

As these excerpts demonstrate, there was a strong feeling among those in the educational ICT community that the concept of a 'National Grid for Learning' had not originated from any one specific industrial or governmental source. Rather it was seen as an amalgamation on the part of New Labour of existing conditions in the marketplace coupled with a characteristic 'rebranding' into the NGfL.

This point withstanding, some interviewees also took a wider perspective of New Labour attempting to revitalise a flagging domestic marketplace; arguing that the government were recognising wider global trends in the marketplace. As this Prime Ministerial policy advisor argued, the underlying motivation to create a 'National Grid for Learning' was also firmly located within a world-wide expansion of education ICT markets:

> There's two levels to see it at. One is a global level which is why these guys are interested. Education as a market ... spending on it is rising faster than GDP in every industrialised country in the world and its one of the only markets that is doing that. So it doesn't take much for a global company to think, "well actually we should be dedicating some resources to this". But coming down to the level of what is happening in the UK. Before government spent this money what you had was a very small market that was being fought over by quite a few small players who relied on it for their bread and butter and a few players where it was just a dot on the map of what they did ... but they did it because it gave them a warm feeling and it looked good for parents. What's

happened now is that this global trend and the government money going in suddenly makes the marketplace look a lot more attractive. The challenge now for policy is to ask "how can we get the big players in?". The answer to that is to make sure that they get a sufficient return on their investment ... but at the same time making sure that the little guys who are actually developing that piece of software that will actually change things are reaping their reward from it [PM Policy Advisor].

As this last quotation intimates, the increased involvement of the private sector in educational ICT is by no means a UK phenomena. Indeed, since the telecommunications explosion of the 1980s governments round the world are having to face up to what Irwin (1987) refers to the 'dilemmas of regulating markets in eruption'. Even from a pragmatic point of view an initiative involving the nation-wide connection of the country's schools to the Internet could not be physically achieved without *some* private sector involvement. The land-lines and fibre optic networks were owned by British Telecom and an ensemble of cable telecom enterprises, all stock-market quoted enterprises. As Parker-Smith (1993) concludes, the creation of any national information infrastructure would not be 'built upon a bare field' as commercial fibre-optic networks already exist. At one level, therefore, the IT industry had to be involved with the NGfL. This point withstanding, how then were private interests involved in the formation of the initiative?

The IT Industry and its Participation in the Formation of the NGfL

Beyond a commitment to establishing a 'learning grid' being included in New Labour administration's manifesto, the initiative needed 'fleshing out' after the election of 1997. At the time this process was seen by many commentators as a collaborative process between government and the IT industry. Indeed, Bill Gates' series of high-profile meetings with Tony Blair during the latter half of 1997 were timed to coincide with the launch of the first NGfL consultation document, resulting in some disquiet within the education community over the 'hi-jacking' of the initiative by private interests. The Blair-Gates project is interesting at number of different levels and crucially important because of the timing of the meetings. It can be seen as an interesting initial manipulation of the educational ICT community, primarily because it sent a clear message to Microsoft's (would-be) competitors that the NGfL was indeed a serious venture. Politically, the rhetoric of working in partnership with private enterprises was put into practice, and moreover, gave the right signals about the Blair administration's determination to 'think big' and 'think modern'. These meetings put the stamp of legitimacy on government rhetoric about modernising government and preparing citizens and the young generation for the 'information age' as discussed in chapter four. They also further consolidated the location of the NGfL in the larger discursive 'partnership' between government and industry.

So, with the role of the IT industry in the NGfL at least partially implicit in its origins, how then were private interests further represented in the formation of the initiative? Certainly, handling the role of the private sector in a very 'public' policy was always going to be a potentially problematic area for the government. In the United States politicians and technologists had long been at loggerheads as to whether the role of central government is to build information infrastructures themselves or merely create an economic climate that will encourage private business to take action (Rothschild 1993). Therefore, although firmly recognising the integral role that industry had to play if the NGfL was to succeed, the government had to be careful in establishing a relatively open consultative relationship with the private sector, thus ensuring that all interests felt included in the process. In this way mechanisms were quickly put in place by central government agencies – BECTa and the DfEE – in order to facilitate industry/government liaison. Two respondents saw it this way:

> BECTa is working hard to foster relationships between the various players. So BETCa has certainly identified who it considers to be the key players. And the Chief Executive at BECTa actually puts quite a lot of effort in ensuring that the Chief Executives of those companies sit round tables and talk to one another. He strongly believes in partnership. He's also got this refreshing naiveté because he's never worked in a commercial environment and he doesn't think that its at all odd to get XXXX from RM and XXXX from Exemplar to sit down together and talk about doing joint promotion. And you think, well golly, that's never going to happen is it? And then on the other hand you think, but isn't it good that the conversation is going on [Executive, UK IT Firm].

> What we've got is a number of different structures – its a fairly fluid situation but we have internally in the department a liaison group that brings together all the different interests in the department and also brings together some of the key educational agencies – the Qualifications and Curriculum Agency, Teacher Training Agency, BECTa and so on ... OfSTED. Within that general umbrella there are other groups. For example we have an NGfL Industry Liaison group which doesn't involve the particular industrial players but the representative proxy groups. In other words it will involve the British Educational Suppliers Association rather than individual companies. Its partly so you don't have to hire the Albert Hall so you can have a meeting. And they meet from time to time and its a place where we can talk things through ... So we do it that way. An awful lot of it is done by simply talking to all the different players and having an open door policy. An awful lot of people come through this room. In fact all the key players have been through here two or three times. So we try and maintain a structure but also we've got to keep on the move [DfEE Senior Civil Servant].

However, the nature and purpose of such meetings was not straightforward. As Heinz *et al.* (1993) observe, contacts between government and private firms may be very casual or highly formalised, private or fully public and initiated by either party. Moreover the nature of such contact can either be one of *information* or one of *influence*. Thus, although there was tentative consultation between DfEE and industry in both a public and private *informative* capacity this contact critically gave DfEE the chance to subtly guide the actions of industry:

> At a more kind of direct 'us and Department having a relationship' level we have regular meetings with people like XXXX and his team. And we attend those meetings as we like

to provide some useful information and feedback from our position as a major supplier to the market. But we also like to feel that we are getting the detail of the story that will only come from talking to the people who are making those policies or writing those documents rather than the reported stuff that comes out ... several times later ... So, in as much as is possible, between a commercial supplier and the civil servants involved in decision making we can be kind of working as a team on this project which is "the National Grid for Learning" rather than us trying to either (a) score points off the government or (b) get them to do things in our favour. Now, that's pretty hard because there are no good models for how a company like us and an organisation like the DfEE can work as a team but it does seem to be in line with the way certainly the government is thinking and its what we want to do as well. We don't like being surprised by things. We'd much rather that the input that we can give and the value that we've got in terms of the knowledge and the experience and so on goes in at the point when the decisions are being made rather than going in at the point when the decisions have already been made and we've got to try and fix them [Executive, UK IT Firm].

Thus there was a strong realisation within the IT firms of their need to 'consult' with the government in order to fully gain from the initiative. As this industrial interviewee continued:

I think that its a game ... well "game" – that's an interesting way of putting it. Our judgement is that decisions that are being made by our customers are now not just being influenced by the direct relationship that we and our competitors have with them. They're being influenced by a whole set of other things. By BECTa, by the government saying that its going to spend a billion pounds on ICT ... Well, would we be selling our customers managed services if the government wasn't pushing down that track? Its not clear. Maybe, maybe not. But certainly, it'll move faster because of these other influences happening. And we have taken the view that given the position that we've got in the marketplace ... [we have to start] participating in that broader set of policy discussions [Executive, UK IT Firm].

But, as the IT firms readily admitted, this new need to participate in the policy process came easier to some firms than others. As Martin (1995) argues, it is important to understand firms' internal policy expertise and their capacity for policy evaluation. Moreover, one must also consider how firms are connected to external networks; in other words how they understand and 'play' the political game. Clearly from the start of the NGfL large multinational IT firms such as Microsoft and ICL were more easily involved in the policy process by dint of their already established links with government:

I think ICL were better [at lobbying] for three reasons. So ... their size and position as a technology company – despite the fact that they are mainly owned by a Japanese company – they are perceived as the UK's big technology company. So, every committee or working party that the DTI put together tends to have an ICL representative on it. So that's one reason. Second reason, they're bigger and they've been doing it for longer. So they've just got more experience and they've got more people who've done this kind of thing. And you keep coming across people at ICL who clearly it is their life and their job to do this.... So they'd kind of jumped over from just doing the DTI to doing the DfEE as well. So they were, if you like, big and professional and good at it [Executive, UK IT Firm].

Although there is now a high degree of political sophistication and convergence in *large*-firm lobbying strategy (Coen 1998) as this concluding quote demonstrates, the more 'politically naïve' UK educational IT firms were clearly lacking in experience in this 'game':

> We took the view then that we had to stop being a relatively insular, inward looking company that dealt with its customers and made them happy and to start behaving more like a big company and dealing with the wider influence base that was impacting on the marketplace that we played in. And we started trying to have meetings with ministers and trying to spend more time with Civil Servants. We'd never really done that before. Not because we didn't want it but because we didn't view it as something that we needed to do. Our success was predicated on going to an individual school and convincing the decision making team in that school to buy a product. Our success wasn't predicated on big national schemes and encouraging the government to spend more money. It was actually right down at grass roots. Clearly that was changing [Executive, UK IT Firm].

The Sustainability of Private Sector Involvement in the NGfL

Yet beyond this initial interest in the NGfL on the part of the IT companies and the reciprocal 'wooing' of industry by the Department for Education how sustainable is industrial involvement with the NGfL once it moves beyond the stages of policy formation into becoming a fully fledged policy-in-practice? In asking this question the study was first interested in exploring what maintained the attention of business to the National Grid for Learning. Clearly their involvement was never going to be entirely altruistic. Furthermore, why did government see business participation as vital to the policy's long-term success?

From the government's point of view the sustained role of the private sector was mapped out in the *'Open for Learning, Open for Business'* consultation document. Primarily, industry was seen as contributing and thereby benefiting commercially in three areas (DfEE 1998a). First was the supply of *content*, in the form of learning materials software, on-line content and broadcast media. Second, the policy required *telecommunications* to link all schools to the Internet. This included broadband, fast speed links via ISDN connections and the like. While each school had been promised one connection free of charge larger schools would require more and in addition schools would also be required to pay annual connection fees. Third the government intended to put out to tender contracts for the supply of *locally managed services*, under which organisations or consortia would bid for the supply of infrastructure and supporting service (servers, routers, browsers, software packages) to groups of educational institutions in defined geographical areas. While government documentation presented this package as a challenge to industry 'to lever change' in these areas (DfEE 1998a, p.15), the rapid development of the Grid in practice required the expertise and resources of the existing IT and telecommunications industry.

While profits could be taken, the invitation to industry came with numerous conditions, which hinged on the sensitivities about the vulnerability of children. This enabled the state to dictate the terms of the formatting of software for example. This is probably most evident in the rules which limit the amount and visibility of 'banner' advertising in NGfL content and in the safeguard that are built in to warn users that they have made or about to make links to material outside the Grid. More generally it can be argued that the state has been able to use the rhetoric of schools and children's vulnerability as an argument against enterprises seeking to dominate the market and force out other competitors.

Despite such restrictions, the NGfL certainly resulted in a vast expansion of participants in the educational ICT marketplace. As one of the interviewed Prime Ministerial advisors observed: 'All the big boys and the little boys are jockeying for position now'. While there was considerable scepticism about the extent to which the £1billion budget for the NGfL actually represented 'new' or additional funds, it has certainly been sufficient in volume to bring the policy to the attention of for-profit organisations. Yet given the centralised control of this money the automatic interest from the private sector cannot be taken as read. Indeed, businesses tend to display the most pronounced resistance to policies which weaken their control over markets (Vogel 1978). At first glance it would appear that the National Grid for Learning does exactly this. However, with most firms failing to penetrate the educational computing market over the last twenty years, the National Grid for Learning was seen by companies as at least allowing them a chance to gain a foothold in the education computing marketplace and increase profits. As these interviewees explained:

> The National Grid didn't half make my job easier selling the business plan [to the company] To say look there's Tony Blair saying that the market's good and now's the time to enter not next year or the year after because we have to in at the start of this curve....... I'm here because partly because of the National Grid, but the impetus happened without people even knowing was the National Grid was [Executive, Multi-National IT Corporation].

> Yes, I mean, I think it's an organising idea that in the first instance industry will get involved because it gives them the means of talking to their customers, being people selling equipment to schools. So it's a simple thing to say, "Do you want to connect to the National Grid for Learning?". Yes. Shortcut, bang! It all goes away and you call the National Grid for Learning standards fund and then it all gets similarly sorted. So you think all right, yes. It's a brand and it's an idea and it's those sorts of things which means that a school goes "right – I'm all ready to part with my cash" [Executive Director, BECTa].

Yet despite potentially opening up new markets, all the IT firms interviewed were vociferous in the difficulties associated with the schools market. Indeed, as one executive bluntly argued, *'Education is the worst [sector] to sell to, and it is by two orders of magnitude'*. Despite the NGfL framework there was a remaining sense of fundamental incompatibility between firms and schools when it came down to the basic level of buying and selling, with the industrial interviewees arguing that schools still simply did not 'understand' firms, therefore leading to a 'pollution' of the market:

> Well I suppose that somebody who is responsible for making a reasonable commercial return out of the market I constantly watch for like the pollution that is in the market [...] hitherto it's been difficult to compete in a market where it seems an area for freebies. Its very difficult to compete in a market that's polluted. There is still a perception in the market that large companies should give things away for free [Executive, Multi-National Telecommunications Corporation]

> Schools always want something for nothing. [emphasis added]. And the worst thing that they do, for themselves, is they use the word 'support'. Now that word, as soon as I hear the word, "we were thinking about buying 5 computers and we wondered if you would support us?". That support is the most imprecise, puts-schools-into-bad-reputation word, because it can mean anything from, "will you give us them for free?", "will you show an interest and come to our open days?", or "will you have a direct personal relationship with me for the rest of my life?" and "will you have a Samaritan's lines for all my IT needs?". Of course we can do all that, and in every other walk of life we charge for it [and] everybody else pays for it. That is the most expensive part. Now here's the school problem; manpower, and labour-intensive resources is probably the least understood by schools because they're so manpower rich [...] that's what the IT companies have a real problem with [Executive, Multi-National IT Corporation]

Thus firms' primary motivation of profitability appeared to sit uneasily with involvement in the education marketplace:

> The actual adage in the entire IT industry is that education is "high maintenance/low margin" business [Executive, Multi-National IT Corporation].

There was therefore a sense within the firms that the NGfL was not going to radically alter this situation. Furthermore, even this increased value of the NGfL-enhanced market was not necessarily seen as attractive. Although many of the large IT companies have seen both their profits and share prices dramatically increase as a direct result of the National Grid for Learning (Bannister 1998, Kavanagh 1998, Bunting 1999) the profits that firms are now expecting to chase as a result of the NGfL were not seen as being overwhelming:

> I think everyone in the industry agrees with the Vision, so the National Grid for Learning is a Vision Statement [but] we're all working independently to get there. But the education market is not a market where you've actually got a very lot of revenue. We give up to 90 per cent discount on our software there and so you have to sell an awful lot of software to actually get in any return to even pay for my team and so you actually have competing groups, who really can't afford to compete in any way [Executive, Multi-National Software Corporation].

I think that various people at various times have misjudged the attractiveness of this market. [referring here to a locally managed service contract for £50million] when it came down to the wire there weren't really that many organisations who are prepared to go out on a limb and incur costs. Routinely a company like ICL would expect to be gaining contracts in the region of £500 million not £50 million. These things are not necessarily that attractive and I'm not sure that the government realises that their £1billion investment in education is not necessarily something that is going to make all industry sit up and take notice [Executive, UK IT Firm].

Government should not be expecting commerce to bankroll education. If it wants commerce to bankroll education it should put up corporation tax. And I think that its learning some hard lessons from that with education action zones. Its been pretty difficult to get even the Shells and the BPs of this world to actually put up real cash. They give you management consultancy or this and that but when it comes to delivering real cash its hard. And if schools are going to have to be based on companies delivering real cash there's a big problem [Executive, UK IT Firm].

These firms were keen to stress that their sustained participation in the NGfL was not only based around issues of short term profit. For some benefits would accrue in the long term. One software manufacturer reflected:

For us [educational ICT] was becoming a very important area, not because we were involved in education, but obviously we need to consider providing a regular stream of employable people to our big customers who are using our technology [Executive, Multi-National Software Corporation].

Involvement in schools' ICT was therefore also seen not only in terms of creating a stream of future customers but also employees of the future who were familiar with the architecture of the software and hardware being produced; a deferred product familiarity and 'brand awareness'. For another interviewee who had been involved in selling services to schools, the NGfL also involved building human capital:

Now the government aren't doing it in my view for the fun of it, they're spending at a least a billion on it, probably more and I think we have to look at what this government is aiming to do to move us from a service industry [...] commercial companies' catalysts knowledge is probably the next one we can. It's very difficult to export knowledge in, so we need a workforce that can, that has the abilities to work in a knowledge environment and the National Grid for Learning will for sure, ensure that every child that leaves British education is at least is aware of how to gain knowledge [Executive, Multi-National Telecommunications Corporation].

So, even where short term profits might not be forthcoming there was an industry view that participation in the NGfL was worthwhile because it could see how the policy would contribute to the building of a future consumer base, a forward demand for products and work force familiar with and able to use industry products.

Discussion

The on-going expansive accommodation of IT firms into the policy formation and implementation process offers a revealing glimpse of New Labour's overall strategy towards public policy making. It is clear from these interview data that the involvement of the private sector in the National Grid for Learning is evolving as the initiative moves from its formation into policy-in-practice. Moreover, although firms can not be characterised as mere interest groups in the policy-making process, the perception of a private-sector dominated initiative would appear to be equally as groundless. Indeed, the proactive and guiding role of the government in shaping the role of industry in the NGfL should be seen as significant. The UK government appear to have distanced themselves from the model of ICT policy-making adopted in Europe, America and Japan which firmly positions the role of the state as one of facilitator and the private sector as the generator of change (Downey 1999). Instead, the UK government appear to be a driving force in generating the 'change' of the NGfL and attempting to guide the actions of industry, at least throughout the early stages of the initiative.

Yet, to argue that the technological enormities of the NGfL alone made private involvement in the initiative inevitable is misleading. As Davies (1994) has demonstrated, since the development of the telegraph the ways in which the monopoly structures of technological infrastructures have been organised has been closely determined by the *political* decisions of governments. From one perspective, therefore, the early involvement of the IT industry in the NGfL can be seen as an attempt by the government to gain an initial hold over a potentially integral yet chaotic element of education they would otherwise have little control over. Indeed, as Irwin (1987) continues, if one accepts that the 'public interest' lies in the preservation of information integrity then the seeds of regulation are inevitably sown. Moreover, public/private ventures can also act as an effective means for governments to eventually maintain an element of distance from educational policies. As Shipps (1997) points out, the Clinton administration was keen to involve corporate interests in the National Goals 2000 plan (including the educational ICT elements) in order to deflect accusations of excess government intervention into schools and provide a wider legitimacy to the programme. In the same way, it was clearly felt by the interviewees in the study that the high profile involvement of firms such as Microsoft had given New Labour the political and technological credibility (as well as a degree of detachment) that was required at the start of the NGfL.

Nevertheless, despite this governmental need for private sector involvement in the NGfL, it can be conversely argued that the IT industry required the involvement of government in order to finally open up the schools' ICT marketplace. As Jacobs (1988) points out, firms will inevitably resist and not participate in government interventions that threaten to have adverse effects on their profitability. The industry-based interviews did not see the NGfL in this light. Thus, whilst for the participant firms we interviewed the NGfL does not represent the most lucrative IT market for large, multi-national corporations, it certainly affords opportunities previously unavailable. Furthermore, as we noted earlier, firms were also keen to acknowledge that other benefits would be indirect and long term. Schools were non-conventional customers and the educational market was unlike the market in the commercial sector. Thus the NGfL certainly offered firms a hitherto unavailable route into the schools market.

Yet in making the National Grid for Learning attractive to the IT industry the UK government has been thus far successful in retaining central control over the nascent NGfL marketplace. For example, Ministers and their officials have been most effective in persuading the larger corporations to leave something on the table for the smaller, niche orientated and less robust commercial enterprises. Thus the implementation of the NGfL has avoided the worst excesses of a capitalist war against all by all. Here it can be suggested that the nature of the 'end-users', the majority of whom are likely to be children of school age, has given the state a powerful lever in its dealings with big business, a lever which may not be available in other policy arenas. In the education arena the government has fashioned strong regulatory powers which so far have enabled it to harness the expertise and resources of the IT sector and shape both schools ICT market and determine the pace and direction of industry relations with schools.

Indeed, the specific nature of educational ICT and the prior educational experience of many of the private interests concerned, means that the NGfL may provide a slightly different model of business practice in education policy. For example, a frequent assertion has been that industry has consistently misunderstood education markets. As Noble (1997, p.1321) has argued:

> From the start to the present Big Business has never really known what it was doing in this area. Again and again, major firms have exploited political opportunities to break into the education market and have flailed wildly trying to make the killing they had convinced themselves was there for the taking.

Certainly, the firms that were interviewed did not appear to be convinced that enormous profits were waiting to be made from the schools market. Indeed, this led many to argue for alternative underlying motivations for involvement in education policy. In doing so it was striking how the wider role of education as 'social instrument' provided much of the private sector's stated intention for involvement in the NGfL. The role of the NGfL as a 'route into' cohorts of future employees or future consumers was seen as a valued 'social' rationale for firms' involvement. Whilst the ambiguity of any stated 'social responsibility' motivation by firms is to be expected (Bennett 1995), crucially, as Apple (1992, p.108) argues, it is 'the *official sponsored* opening up of school content to commercial sponsorship and organisation that is the sea change here' coupled with the selling of students to private concerns as a 'captive audience'. Thus, the signs are that a more deferred human capital orientation may now be driving firms' interests in education. How this agenda complements or conflicts with the government's intentions for educational ICT lies at the heart of the long-term effectiveness of the National Grid for Learning initiative.

It was argued at the beginning of this chapter that, in theory, Labour's approach to policy making could be seen as essentially pragmatic, that it would employ whatever strategies it was believed would work regardless of their ideological underpinning in it overall pursuit of raising standards. What this study of the National Grid for Learning reveals is that, in practice, there seems to be a preferred balance between state action and public private partnerships and that looks distinctly 'Old Labourist'. For while the government actively sought the participation of the private sector in taking forward the modernisation of curriculum and pedagogy it also controlled both the direction and the detail of the NGfL's development.

This study also suggests that public-private co-operation found some enterprise wanting in their capacity to work effectively in the policy arena and that some hardware and software companies had to buy in key individuals in order to secure a position in the policy networks that developed around the NGfL. On the other hand Labour's embracing of private enterprises in policy creation certainly presented an image of a government that was not business-averse, unlike some earlier manifestations of the party in office. That adaptations were made on both sides, however, *can* also be interpreted as a 'Third Way' forward in policy making.

However, it is clear that at present the government has used the involvement of the private sector to 'kick-start' an ambitious policy process. How these initial public/private foundations go on to affect the longer-term effectiveness of the NGfL should, therefore, form the focus of on-going scrutiny. At best, it is likely that the government can maintain their present level of involvement over the next five to ten years at most. Indeed, one of the pivotal aims of the NGfL is to create a 'technological' culture of ICT within education which stimulates and provokes schools to autonomously proceed with the procurement of ICT once central funding is eventually phased out (DfEE 1997a, 1998b). Although this 'model of decreasing dependency' is based upon an obvious financial constraints it is also a pragmatic response to the nature of technology provision and the education ICT marketplace. In the words of one of the industrial interviewees, the government clearly 'recognise that they can go so far and no further'. As Levi-Faur (1999) observes, any prolonged political administration of technological competition involves complex bargaining and good technical knowledge of the sectors involved beyond the reach of most governments. So in the medium term, the government clearly intend to leave the NGfL to a revitalised education ICT marketplace, which at the moment they are quite closely directing. Thus the longevity of the NGfL rests on both the IT firms and individual schools themselves. How committed these two sets of actors remain to the centrally imposed goals of the NGfL remains to be seen.

PART III
INDIVIDUAL LEARNERS AND TECHNOLOGY

Chapter Six

Children's Engagement with ICT in Primary School

Introduction

The last three chapters have focused on 'unpacking' education and technology at a macro-level of government, quasi-government actors and the private sector. At was argued in Chapter Two, such a perspective is vital to forming a coherent understanding of education and technology. Yet this macro picture can only be of use if complemented with an in-depth understanding of how education and technology is *actually* being used by learners in the 'real-world' of schools, colleges, universities and the wider community. Thus we need to also consider not how educational technology *could* be used given the ideal technological and education conditions, but the realities of educational technology use (and non-use) in the messy, complicated and often inconsistent educational settings that educational technologists are sometimes loath to acknowledge.

This chapter, therefore, starts this section's examination of individual learners and their engagement with ICT at a relatively young level – entering the world of seven and eleven year old primary school children. This need to make sense of the voices of young learners is rooted in the fact that, despite the current political impetus, the use of computerised technology in UK primary schools has historically been, at best, inconsistent. Against the renewed government interest in educational technology that we have discussed over the last three chapters, official statistics continue to portray a variable picture of ICT use in the primary school sector. Although official statistics reveal that the ratio of pupils to computers in primary education has steadily risen from 107 pupils per computer in 1985 to around 12:1 in 2001 (DfEE 1997c, DfES 2001b), these figures disguise the often ageing state of schools' hardware provision. The same statistics show that over 33 per cent of hardware and accessories in schools is over five years old with many primary schools still relying on computer technology that has long ceased to be relevant outside educational settings.

There are signs that this paucity of provision may be changing. Whilst the primary sector spent £105million per annum on ICT in 1998 (DfEE 1999) it is estimated that expenditure will rise to £680million by the first years of the new century (Kavanagh 1998). This, it is hoped, will spur the current generation of school children into becoming 'ICT literate' just in time for the twenty-first century's information-reliant global economy. As we saw in chapter four this economic imperative for increasing student use of computers as a 'key skill' in primary and secondary schools has been stressed at every opportunity.

So confident is the government of producing newly information-adept generations of students that they it has explicitly stated the bold intention that every school-leaver will possess a 'good understanding' of computers by 2002 (DfEE 1997a). Yet, throughout the debate surrounding the value of educational computing the place of the *pupil* has been somewhat taken-for-granted. The fundamental focus of the NGfL drive has been on increasing levels of ICT hardware, alongside associated concerns with ensuring the improved provision of quality educational software and raising levels of teacher training. Amidst all this activity, the underlying assumption has been that children will quickly and effortlessly adapt to using the new technology. Nevertheless, a wealth of previous research within adult settings would suggest that not all individuals react to using technology in the homogenous, positive fashion that the government would assume. Indeed, rejection or acceptance of technology is not necessarily dependent on levels of ICT provision but a multitude of individual, social, cultural and economic factors. Although many authors have speculated upon the relative influence of these factors with regard to adult and adolescent users (e.g. Wild 1996, Torkezadeh and Angulo 1994, Igbaria *et al.* 1994) has specifically been paid to how primary school pupils adapt to, and make sense of, computers in school settings from the perspective of the young children themselves.

The Need for a Pupil Perspective of Educational Technology Use

The political assumption that all children are naturally predicated towards using computers has been reinforced by academic literature on educational technology. For example, the computing 'guru' Seymour Papert (1993) has stated that the computer is inherently 'the children's machine' and, as such, concludes that it is up to educators to 'catch up' with their students in adapting to and embracing the new technology. In a similar vein, much of the 'blame' for the low levels of computer use in schools over the last two decades has been directed at both inadequate technological infrastructure and teaching staff; with neither being seen as capable in meeting the demands of a technologically-literate student body (e.g. Brosnan 1998, Yeomans *et al.* 1995).

As Parlo Singh (1997) has reasoned, and as we saw in chapters three and four, knowledge about educational computing continues to be produced and circulated in a multitude of 'official' education sites, including governmental policy texts, curriculum documents, inspection reports, sites of teacher training, parental and community organisations, local education authorities, teachers and school senior management teams. Although all salient sites of production, the prevailing view of primary school computer use has, perhaps, tended to focus closely on such 'adult' arenas of discourse at the expense of the eventual 'end-users' of educational computing; i.e. the pupils. As Buckingham (1999, p.7) continues:

Much of this debate about children's uses of new communications technology has been conducted over the heads of the children themselves. We still know very little about how children perceive, interpret and use these new media ... Children are typically seen here as isolated individuals, who are powerless to resist the negative influences of the media upon them.

Indeed, as Woods (1990) reasons, to understand any school activity it is essential to explore the understandings that children attach to it and whence they arise. In this way more 'child-focused' perspectives can prove invaluable in informing wider understanding of educational issues (Pollard et al. 1997). Thus, whilst the strong influence of the environmental, organisational and cultural contexts of technology use in school settings is recognised, this chapter deliberately focuses on the 'user context' of primary school computer use, defined by Bush (1997, p.164) as 'all the motivations, intentions, advantages and adjustments called into play by [a child's] use of particular techniques or tools'. Exploring the many factors underlying and influencing young children's perceptions and orientation towards using computers within the primary school curriculum also provides a preliminary view of the pupil cohort who are the initial recipients of the Labour government's current technological drive; the first generation of '*Grid Kids*'. In this way, the remainder of this chapter highlights the 'voices' of children in explaining, exploring and rationalising their engagement (or otherwise) with computers in the primary classroom.

Methods

The 'Grid Kids' research study was focused on five schools in South Wales; three primary schools (Years K-6), one junior school (Years 3-6) and one infant school (Years K-2). The sample of schools was stratified to include institutions with markedly different intake characteristics, geographical location and levels of technological implementation and use. Sixty-seven focus group interviews were carried out with children at Grade 2 (aged 6-7 years) and Grade 6 (aged 10-11 years). In total the research covered 267 primary pupils (see Table 6.1).

Table 6.1. Sample Characteristics Across the Five Schools

	Yr. 2	Yr. 6	Girls	Boys	No. Groups	No. Pupils
School 1 – Medium Town Infants	48	-	23	25	12	48
School 2 – Medium Town Juniors	-	49	28	21	12	49
School 3 – Rural Village Primary	10	15	17	8	8	25
School 4 – Sub-Urban City Primary	31	33	34	30	16	64
School 5 – Inner City Primary	41	40	44	37	19	81
Total Pupils	**130**	**137**	**146**	**121**	**67**	**267**

Given the open-ended nature of the inquiry and the age of the children involved, a predominantly qualitative approach was adopted when collecting data. All students therefore took part in focus group interviews moderated by one of three researchers (one male and two females). Although primarily associated with researching older subjects, focus groups have been successfully used with children as young as five and six years (Smith and Keep 1986, Singh 1993, Green 1997, Reay and William 1999) and were therefore considered as a suitable method for the Grid Kids study.

Children were interviewed in groups of three to six at a time; either in friendship or 'work' groups to ensure that they felt comfortable to talk amongst each other. Interviews lasted between 30 to 40 minutes. Although interviewing young children can be problematic, the use of focus groups was intended to overcome or lessen issues of interviewer effect, over-exaggeration or lying. Indeed, the presence of other children acted as a check against the commonly reported problem of young children vastly exaggerating or lying about their contact with computers (e.g. Sanger et al. 1997). On a few occasions during the interviews children making impressive claims about their own expertise or ownership of computers were successfully challenged by other members of the group who were quick to intervene if they felt someone was 'lying'. In this way the focus group format proved an effective form of validation. Headteachers, teachers with responsibility for the co-ordination of ICT across the school and classroom teachers were also consulted to provide cross-referencing to findings. In most cases interviews were carried out in classrooms or resource rooms with school computers present, thus providing a suitable context for the discussions.

Analysis of the interview data elicited a variety of recurring themes which children used to explain, discuss and rationalise their use of computers in school. These can be broadly grouped into: (i) the speed and ease of work processes when using computers; (ii) the extending or curtailing of learners' abilities when using computers; (iii) freedoms and restrictions of the finished product when using computers and, finally, (iv) concerns over originality and authenticity of the finished product when using computers. These themes are discussed in greater detail in the following sections.

The Speed and Ease of Work Processes when Using Computers

An initial element of many children's justification for either wanting to use or not use a computer at school centred around both the time taken and ease of task completion. Indeed, akin to previous research with older students (Schofield 1995) there was a strong sense of an increased motivation for some pupils to use computers when carrying out otherwise mundane or 'boring' tasks in the classroom. Thus, for this boy the apparent speed of producing computer-generated work was one of the 'best' aspects of using computers in school:

> Q: *Can you remember the best time that you used a computer in school? The best thing you did?*

Faezel: Yeah, when we were doing a cats project and I was like able to load up all kinds of like really good pictures onto a disk and I gave it in first and did it really quickly instead of just copying like or drawing them myself
Q: *What sort of pictures were they?*
Faezel: They were photos
Q: *So did you scan these photos did you?*
Faezel: Yeah, scanned them in and I took some off Encarta as well
Q: *Why was that so good then?*
Faezel: Because it was really quick and I just did the project like in a couple of days when most of my friends took ages

[School 5, Year 6 – Group 5]

The attraction to this child of the technological 'quick fix' is clearly linked to the kudos of 'finishing first'; an achievement of significant value within the intensely peer-referential and often competitive micro-world of the primary classroom. Similarly, for these younger children, this technologically-assisted ability to work faster was often translated into desirable non-technological rewards:

Edward: It's easy because you don't have to spend all the time ... because if you know where all the letters are you can just go bbbrrrrrr, [mimes typing quickly] do it really fast
Q: *Why is it better on the computer if it's quicker?*
Oliver: Well, if we finish, well Miss might have some work but if she hasn't we would have to go and look in the unfinished drawer. And if we didn't have anything there we could go and play probably

[School 3, Year 2 – Group 4]

Yet, whilst an increased speed of process and ability to get work quickly 'out of the way' appeared to be a distinct motivating factor for some children to use computers, another recurring theme throughout the interviews was children's consideration of the computer's effect on the *ease* of process. For example, with the younger children, a preference for typing on a computer was often expressed in terms of the physical discomfort of writing by hand with a pen and paper:

Alun: [Writing by hand] my arm would really ache if I thought of a really long story but it wouldn't ache only if I just did it on the computer because I wouldn't be writing it then, just typing

[School 3, Year 2 – Group 7]

Nevertheless, such responses are clearly context specific. For other Year Two children the requisite motor-skills for easily using a computer were conversely presented as a reason for preferring more traditional methods of working – particularly, as in this case, when drawing or producing pictures:

Jack: If you [draw] it on a piece of paper you draw it a bit gooder, cos you've got your hand instead of the computer. Cos on the computer it goes wobbly a bit ... And it's hard

[School 1, Year 2 – Group 11]

Moreover, it was not just the physical process of putting pen to paper that the computer was seen to either alleviate or exacerbate. As this next except illustrates, for some children the often elaborate preparatory processes of physically preparing to carry out work could be avoided by taking the far less 'babyish' option of working on the computer:

> Q: *Would you rather do a picture with pens and paper or on a computer*
> Oliver: Computer, because we're not babies
> Alice: And you don't have to keep getting up and going and getting the colouring crayons and then putting them by [Welsh colloquialism: put away]
> Oliver: It would take longer [by hand] than on the computer ... you could just get the things that you needed, the jug of paint and you wouldn't have to make the paint even
> Alice: Yeah the colours are better you see, you don't have to keep on getting them you just click on them and if you want to choose another colour you just click on another colour
> Oliver: And there's a good bit on there ... there's a question mark and you go on to the question mark and it's a colour
>
> [School 3, Year 2 – Group 4]

Certainly, for these Year Two children, the computer-based attraction of 'doing art without the work' (Scott 1998, p.57) is seen as a distinct advantage. The emancipatory and labour-saving functions of computer-based artwork have been long lauded in an educational context (e.g. Blomeyer 1993) and, for these children at least, would seem to be acting as significant motivating factors in their use of computers in this context. As one of the above children later reasoned, *'You don't have to work as hard!'*. Moreover, it is clear from the underlying tone of most of these quotes that the control that the computer offers (or does not offer) continues to also be an underlying consideration to some young children's decision to either use or not use ICT.

Indeed, both speed and ease of process were often presented as reasons *not* to use ICT. As these older girls argued, now they were more confident and proficient with writing by hand typing on a computer was now seen as a *more* time consuming option:

> Q: *If you had to write a story in class, would you choose to do it on the computer or on paper?*
> All: Paper!
> Q: *Why's that?*
> Sioned: It's quicker
> Claire: It's easier, if you're not really good on computers and you can't write fast'
> Sioned: Because the letters are everywhere
> Claire: If I couldn't write fast I would do it on the computer but because I can't do it fast on the computer, I'd do it on paper
> Sioned: We're not computer experts! I prefer to do it on paper
>
> [School 2, Year 6 – Group 7]

The allure of word-processing for children has often been taken for-granted by academics, with the popular assumption that 'the ability to develop, manipulate and reproduce text is clearly a liberating experience for many children' (Smith & Keep 1986, p.87). However, as these last children intimated, it can clearly be perceived as a constraining experience. Similarly when discussing the possibility of using a computer for artwork, the issue of control was often seen as a restriction by some children:

> Jess: Yeah when you're printing it [on the computer] it turns out like you're not expecting it. Cos I did a painting and I did green grass and it turned out blue on the computer
> Vicki: Um, on paper when you're doing a painting you feel like you've got control, on computer you've got a mouse and it's quite hard to draw a circle or draw eyes or anything, because you don't feel like you've got control of it
> Rosie: Nothing really looks real on the computer
> Jess: If you do the wrong colour then it might be really bright and come out a different colour
> [School 3, Year 6 – Group 2]

Thus, issues of control, speed and ease of process are clearly important factors in children's perceptions of computers; but in both a positive *and* negative fashion. Indeed, this duality of effect pervaded all the themes discussed in this chapter, with children often using similar points to justify opposite actions. Thus the sentiments expressed in these latter quotes appear to be at odds with the early received educational wisdom regarding the inherently motivating nature of educational computing in that it offers students the added 'challenge' of using a computer as an extra motivation (Lepper and Chabey 1985, Lepper and Malone 1987). Instead, it would seem that children are now far more discerning and certainly see beyond any attraction of merely 'having a go on a computer'.

The Extending or Curtailing of Pupils' Abilities when Using Computers

As well as making work processes either easier or harder, the role of the computer in extending (or constraining) learners' 'conventional' abilities was also raised throughout the interviews. Thus, for some children, the opportunity to produce work above and beyond their conventional capabilities prompted a particular enthusiasm for using computers, in this case for artwork:

> Q: *If you were to draw a picture how would you do it?*
> All: Computer
> Darren: Computer, cos you can have the symmetry, you draw it and it will come out on the other side
> Mike: You can have one head and on the other side there's another
> Leah: At Christmas time we made our own calendars on the computer, we had to have like the Christmas things and put Father Christmas and candles

Darren: I do symmetry with planes crashing into each other and the bit where the pilot sits is all gone

[School 1, Year 2 – Group 8]

These children at least provide some empirical basis to the popular notion that 'computers are making unprecedented aesthetic experiences possible and revolutionising the way art is conceived, created, perceived and taught' (Chia & Duthie 1994, p.197) with the computer here being seen as allowing children to produce artwork above and beyond their conventional means. This theme of the computer's ability to affect pupils' abilities persisted throughout the interviews, yet not necessarily in a wholly positive manner. As the following quotes demonstrate, other children held converse views over the ability of the computer to produce better artwork, arguing that the computer restricted rather than extended their abilities when drawing:

Q: *What about if you had to do a picture, would you rather do it on computer or on paper?*
Gurdeep: I'd do it on computer cos I'm not good at drawing
Sinder: If you do it on the paper you can put more details on it
Gurdeep: But if you did it on computer...
Sinder: It would be harder
Gurdeep: Like trying to do a star on it. I tried
Q: *To do a star on the computer?*
Gurdeep: Yeah, I can't do it

[School 5, Year 6 – Group 3]

Q: *So why would you all do it on paper?*
Lewis: Cos it's just easier, you can get the exact ... like you can get the exact shape that you actually want to get
Q: *Why would you do it on paper and not computer?*
Stuart: Because on a computer it takes longer and you've got this mousey thing that moves around everywhere and I prefer it on paper
Lewis: And more detail on paper. You can already do circles and also squares
Stuart: You get more details on paper

[School 4, Year 6 – Group 6]

In both these groups the children focused on more precise matters of 'detail' as justification for drawing by hand. Thus with their ability to produce detailed artwork not being extended or even matched when using a computer, this is seen as hampering their efforts to 'get the exact shapes they want'. Nevertheless, for some children this issue of extending or limiting their abilities was also linked to an added independence when working. As this child (identified by his class teacher as being 'less able') reasoned, when using a computer some of the barriers he usually faced when presented with a blank sheet of paper and pencil were alleviated:

Geraint: Instead of just doing it on a blank piece of paper and like looking at everybody when they're just doing their work and saying 'well how do they do that?' It's easy when you're doing it on computer. Cos it says like if you can't spell something a tiny bit comes up and tells you how to spell it so then you know

[School 4, Year 2 – Group 7]

Here then the computer is clearly seen as fulfilling a scaffolding role for this child; performing a number of supporting tasks to keep the child on task (Wood 1998). Thus, a 'tiny bit coming up and telling you how to do it' would appear to be the stimulus for this child to participate in work which was otherwise inaccessible. Similarly, for other more able children, the computer also gave them independence from other time consuming and routine working practices of the classroom; such as having to queue at the teacher's desk for spellings of words:

Q: *Why do you like the computer then?*
Christina: Cos you don't have to go up to the teachers, in a long queue to get all the spellings right and stuff
Amy: Yeah, you just use spell check

[School 3, Year 6 – Group 3]

Nevertheless, in other cases using a computer in the same circumstances clearly *decreased* children's independence from reliance on external help. Such as in the case of requiring the teacher's assistance to do something that these pupils were not sure of:

Dafydd: It's harder on the computer because you have to do a line and then you have to type it out on the computer, you have to press buttons. Because with the pen and paper you just write, write, write and when you've finished you can go and take it to Mr Lloyd-Evans but then when you do the computer…
Stacey: You have to get the teacher to come
Dafydd: Because sometimes you don't know how to print it off

[School 4, Year 2 – Group 5]

Interestingly, this notion was expanded on by other pupils with regard to the computer making their work (and mistakes) more visible to the teacher; thereby drawing unwanted attention and, ultimately, resulting in extra work:

Keith: Because it's different from writing, drawing is more enjoyable on the computer- you have different qualities of things. But on the writing you have to type and if you get a jagged line Mr Thomas has to come and help you and that holds you up
Dafydd: Then the computer ruins our play [because] you have to keep on typing all through play

[School 4, Year 2 – Group 5]

This last example provides an interesting contrast to Schofield (1995), who in her study of US secondary school computer use, identified the computer as a valued retreat for students during breaktimes from the social pressures of school and play. Here however the reverse view of the computer 'ruining' children's play provides an equally valid reason for some pupils *not* to use a computer for certain activities.

Freedoms or Restrictions of the Finished Product when Using Computers

Until now, most of the children's perceptions of their classroom use of ICT have been centred around issues of *process*. Whilst concerns over the computer's role in the process of producing work provided the focus for many of the younger and less able pupils other, often older, children were also concerned with less practical reasons to either use or not use computers. For example, as these Year Six pupils explain, using clip-art on the computer was of questionable value for conceptual as well as practical reasons:

> Q: *What if you had to draw a picture of something?*
> Bethan: I'd probably go to clip art
> Scott: Yeah
> Kate: I'd do drawing [on paper]
> Q: *Why would you do drawing then?*
> Kate: Because you can't always get the right angle that you're looking for with clip art
> Scott: For me it's both like, because if you can't get something on clip art and you know what it looks like you could draw it out
> Q: *Do you think clip art looks as good as drawing?*
> Kate: In some ways it does and in other ways it doesn't
> Adam: Because if you get to close up you can see all the dots and it gets a bit blurry'
> Scott: Sometimes if you want it coloured in it's not coloured in
> Bethan: And you don't get the choices you want 'cos they don't have 'em
> [School 2, Year 6 – Group 2]

Technology enthusiasts such as Scott (1998, p.57) argue that on-line resources and clip-art are ideal in providing children with a 'risk-free source of ideas'. Yet for these children at least, issues of 'getting the right angle' and 'the choices you want' would seem to outweigh any straightforward ease of using pre-drawn clip-art. Indeed, reactions of this type go against popular notions of the current 'digital generation' of children (Buckingham 2000). Although we are increasingly being seen to live within a 'culture of the copy' (Schwartz 1996) where computer-generated images are part and parcel of everyday life, these children were not content in relying on clip-art. It would seem, therefore, that more subjective issues of aesthetics are coming into play here in informing some children's views of using computers in this particular context.

For example, these children's challenging of the appearance of clip-art suggests a more considered approach to using computers. As Scott (1998, p.55) argues, 'promot[ing] the understanding of the artificial image as the real is one aspect of the everyday aesthetics of computing'. However, as Scott also acknowledges, 'the 'art' of making these images lies in their going undetected' (*ibid.*). If, as in these children's case the 'aesthetic of illusion' is compromised by the obvious computer-generated nature of the image, the computer's 'motivating and engaging character' is fundamentally diminished.

Moreover, this concept of the computer restricting or enhancing freedom to create was not solely related to artwork. As these children from two different interview groups argued with regard to writing stories, the creative opportunities and constraints of the computer were considered as very important:

> Katy: I like doing stories but I don't like doing stories when I've got horrible writing so I do it to make it exciting on the computer to make it like a real adventure ... sort of.
>
> [School 4, Year 2 – Group 7]

> Q: *If I said we're going to write a story now would you choose to do it on a computer or would you choose on paper?*
> Jenny: I would prefer to write
> Lisa: I'd do it on the computer straight away. No I'd actually write it ... it takes quicker to write it
> Jenny: Yeah cos when you write it, I don't know why, it's much more easier thinking cos you got
> Lisa: You don't have to find all the keys and you just know what to write
> Jenny: And like, instead of concentrating what you've done wrong on the computer when you are handwriting like writing, you can concentrate more on the basing story line
>
> [School 4, Year 6 – Group 4]

Again, in general, word-processing has been asserted to be a positive influence on children's story-writing (e.g. Dodorico and Zammuner 1993). Yet, as these quotations reflect, this cannot be assumed to be the case for all children For every child who finds that using a computer makes story writing a 'real adventure' is another for whom the computer detracts from engaging with the story itself This non-uniformity of response is encapsulated in this discussion between four Year 6 girls on their use of the Internet and hyper-text resources in comparison to reference and story books and other paper-based documents:

> Q: *Do you think the Internet will ever replace books in school?*
> All: No
> Sarah: Not for story books ... for facts books [the Internet] might take over
> Q: *Why will people like reading story books then? What so good about them?*
> Sarah: Cos they're interesting
> Lianne: Well, because they have like fun or scary things
> Q: *But you could read stories off the computer like that couldn't you?*
> Lianne: Yeah but... It's just it's not really exciting. Like you want to go over, like, turn the page and find something really scary
> Natalie: Or else you wouldn't get up to that if you didn't do it
> Sarah: And you'll have to press the button down at the bottom every time
> Donna: And there'd probably be a break between the page too. A different page like on the computer you'd be reading it out and when you got to the bottom of that you'd have to um...turn over to the next page and that would probably take like a few seconds to get to that and it would spoil it
>
> [School 4, Year 6 – Group 2]

The inference that computer-based books are lacking in 'fun' or emotion again reflects a more emotional reading of classroom computers than our earlier examples may suggest. As Jeffrey and Woods (1997, p.19) observe, 'fun is a catch-all phrase used by pupils and teachers alike to indicate depth of involvement', and for these children issues of engagement with the text appear to be informing their less than favourable perceptions of the computer as reading medium. For these children at least, the 'ecstasy of pure interface between text and reader' (Cubitt 1998) allegedly afforded by the Internet appears absent.

Originality and Authenticity of the Finished Product when using Computers

An emphasis on the subjective experience of computer-based activities over and above issues of process was an important guiding theme in many children's approach towards using computers in schools, especially with girls. In particular, a desire to lay claim to ownership of the product was a prevalent argument offered by some of the older children. In this case producing written work on a computer severely diminished these children's perceived right to be identified as the unique creative and individual source of that text (Marshall 2000):

> Rhian: And if let's say like you were writing a letter to somebody so it's nice. Like when we had to write to an embassy I did it hand-written
> Lisa: Because it's smarter
> Rhian: And when they flick through it they won't look at that [points to researcher's typewritten notes] When they get to something different it's like outstanding
> Lisa: It looks like that you made an effort and everything
> Hannah: I sent a letter yesterday morning...there was a stuffed horse hanging from this museum ceiling so I decided to write a complaint letter
> Q: *Did you do it on computer or by handwriting?*
> Hannah: Well I prefer to hand write
> Rhian: Because people pay more attention to it when it's hand-written
> Hannah: Because they realise that children have done it
> Rhian: And if you come into an office and it's boring letters and piles and piles and if [a hand-written letter] is there it's different ain't it?
> Hannah: If you decorated it and written it neatly they want to read it
> Rhian: 'If it's not too much either, it's got to be short ... so if it's hand-written they'll notice that
>
> [School 4, Year 6 – Group 4]

These concerns of individuality, differentiation, making your work 'outstanding' are, for these children, the antithesis of using a computer; especially in relation to the 'grown-up' world of word-processed letters and interview schedules. As Zuboff (1997, p.376) argues, computers often make it possible to 'rationalise activities more comprehensibly than if they had been undertaken by a human being' but, as far as these children were concerned, such rationalisation and standardisation of the activity of letter writing only detracted from the effort, emotion and individuality that handwriting was perceived to afford. Such in-depth reasoning was also apparent in these girls' discussion of computer based artwork:

> Natalie: And if then you're on the computer it gets done quicker and I like taking my time doing Art
> Q: *Why do you like taking your time doing art?*
> Natalie: Because it's neater
> Leanne: And then you've got your own, not someone else's
> Q: *So what's the difference with a picture that's been done by hand and something that's been done on computer*
> Sarah: Lots ... [points to two pictures displayed on wall – one a printout and one an illustration from a book] ... yeah that's been done on the computer and that hasn't. Look at the difference
> Donna: Coz there's really good drawers on the computer, they can get all detail
> Sarah: But you can't exactly have a perfect picture can you?
> Donna: Exactly
> Sarah: Coz you have really good pictures on the computer but if you're drawing ... then it's your own, it can never be the same if you draw it yourself
> Q: *What's the difference between those two pictures?*
> Natalie: Well that's your own work [points to illustration], you've done that yourself and you're proud of that and that's [points to computer picture] just like you've just got it off the computer and you've done no work at all
>
> [School 4, Year 6 – Group 2]

In reflecting that 'there's no such thing as a perfect picture' these girls are touching on complex conceptual issues surrounding technology and art (e.g. Baudrillard 1997). Yet, for many commentators the principal drawbacks of computer-based art with children are seen as only being technical issues such as mouse control and the enlarging and reducing of pictures (Chia and Duthie 1994). Nevertheless, the comparisons between these quotes from a group of eleven year old girls and Walter Benjamin's celebrated account of the technical reproduction of art and its effect on the authority of the author are striking. In this case, computer use would not appear to be affording the children any sense of 'aesthetic engagement' (Pateman 1998) with the product and, therefore, not provoking any aesthetic response or, indeed, motivation to use computers to create their own art.

Discussion

Children actively construct their own cultures and it is important to avoid an overtly deterministic reading of the data presented in this chapter. Indeed, as Connolly (1997, p.163) argues, 'no research account of young children's perspectives can ever claim to be the true and definitive account ... we need to accept that there is no one, authentic voice in relation to young children; only a multiplicity of authentic voices'. Thus it is inevitable that much of the data presented in this chapter have been contradictory, especially regarding the different purposes, software and ages under discussion. Yet in identifying a set of distinct themes within which these contradictory discourses take place we have been able to gain a sense of the complexity and varying nature of children's engagement with computers in primary schools.

Above all, this study would seem to suggest that children throughout primary schooling are becoming increasingly sophisticated 'consumers' of technology – yet not necessarily in the unconditionally enthusiastic ways that some policymakers and academics may assume. Whilst there is no doubt that children's exposure to technology is rapidly increasing and diversifying (MORI 1997, Livingstone 1999) it is nevertheless important to recognise the situated nature of children's responses to computers in school settings. As Walkerdine (1998) reasons, there are no norms to children's reactions to computers, they are instead context specific and flexible. Thus, within this chapter the children's varying responses to using computers for writing, drawing and obtaining information often reflected advanced pragmatic and context-driven readings of computers. From this basis it is possible to go some way to concur with Green and Bigum's (1993) assertion that technological change has been coupled with the emergence of new types of student with new needs and capacities. However, Green and Bigum's prediction of the impending estrangement of youngsters from school – alienated from classrooms devoid of the prevailing 'techoculture' prominent in other sites in their lives – appears a little far-fetched in light of the present study. Indeed, these children (at this young age at least) seemed more than willing to adapt, reconfigure and compromise their technological perceptions and expectations when in school.

The gendered nature of the children's responses was also interesting. That the vast majority of comments relating to the aesthetic and moral value of computer based work came from girls is telling and could be interpreted from either the perspective of girls' attitudes towards school-work or girls' attitudes towards technology. It could be that these girls' higher order responses reflect a more considered or 'mature' approach to school work in general. From this perspective, technology may not be an issue *per se*. Indeed, the fact that girls in the sample made equal use of computers whilst in the school and were slightly more likely to have access to a home computer than their male peers (see Selwyn and Bullon 2000 for a full review of the quantitative data collected from this study) suggests that a lack of access or familiarity with ICT does not explain these gender differences. However, it could also be argued that girls' tendency to offer more higher-order readings of classroom computing is a reflection of females' more pragmatic overall approach to computers; concentrating more on the task than the machine (Turkle 1984).

Nevertheless, the overall conclusion that primary children often display complex and detailed understandings of their classroom based activities is not a new contention (Thiessen 1997). However, the range and scope of responses to computer use highlighted in this chapter would suggest that current popular perceptions of school children as eager and unquestioning consumers of technology are ultimately misleading. Thus, in further exploring *how* children are making sense of computers in school it may be possible to suggest ways of more effectively presenting computers to students in classroom settings through both policy and practice.

Clearly, many of the responses discussed in this chapter were related to children's ability to use the computer and the software packages therein. Therefore, responses centring on the usefulness of art-packages in producing straight lines or the speed of word-processing work can, in part, be associated with the children's levels of skill and experiences in using computers. Moreover, the classroom organisation of pupils' computer use was also evidently underpinning some of the children's perceptions of the relative usefulness of using a computer when in class; as apparent in the children in one school allowed to rely on a spell-checker whilst they wrote as opposed to those in another for whom the spell-checker acted as a prompt for teacher intervention.

Nevertheless, it was clear throughout the interview data that some children were approaching computers in the classroom as more that just a means to an end; displaying higher order thinking about their (non)engagement with educational technology. Whilst it is traditionally posited that 'the evaluative assessment of technological innovation is a matter of deciding whether the ends we already have are better achieved by the new means with which we are presented' (Graham 1999, p.49) it can be argued that these children's higher-order assessment of technology use was, instead, based around 'assess[ing] the advantages of technological innovation in terms of the *value* of the ends to which it is a useful means' (*ibid.*). This distinction between viewing technology in terms of value rather than utility is an important one. Instead of viewing technology as exclusively purposive, that is *entirely* a means to an end, the use of technology is based around complex questions not just of efficiency but of style, discovery, experimentation. As Feenberg (1995) argues, such advanced value-driven evaluation of technology in a modern world embodies aesthetic, ethical and cultural domains and not merely pure efficiency. Thus, 'it is a mistake to think that the assessment of technology can rest content with the idea of usefulness; it necessarily passes onto the idea of the valuable' (Graham 1999, p.50).

These distinctions between the valuable and the useful are complex, even with adults. Of course, in many of the views expressed throughout the interviews the value ascribed to the computer by children can be seen predominantly in terms of the 'economics' of the classroom; from the 'free play' benefits of finishing work first to the concerns that the amount of effort put into a piece of work is readily apparent. Similarly, a 'moral' value of originality and 'ownership' was also prevalent in some of the children's responses as were concerns with the aesthetic value of computer-based work. Nevertheless, the fact that some of the children in this study appeared to be thinking beyond issues of simple utility in terms of their use of computers in school is significant – and can be used as a starting point for re-examining the nature of computer use in education.

So, given both this utility and value-driven agenda apparent in children's perceptions of computers in the classroom, how can the integration and use of computing in primary classrooms be 'reshaped' to be more in line with its end-users? Firstly it is clear that children's engagement with computers is dictated, in the first instance, by their level of skill and experience with computers. Therefore, it would appear crucial to ensure that *all* children have the skills needed to use computers unhindered by operational barriers For example, it is interesting to note that UK schools, unlike some other countries, often do not teach typing skills to pupils. Yet whilst this 'skills deficit' observation has been widely made and, indeed, forms one of the central goals of the government's present ICT drive, it can be argued that to see computing purely as a 'key skill' within the primary curriculum may not be the most relevant model of computer use in light of these pupils' experiences and perceptions. Indeed, the economically driven model of solely 'delivering' ICT as a key skill to be gained by pupils would seem to be at odds with the more value-driven and context specific view of computing that this chapter has revealed.

Instead, it can be argued that the development of 'ICT literacy' in pupils that the current National Grid for Learning drive is so focused on is precisely concerned with developing a detailed 'understanding' of computers as well as basic levels of skill upon which to base an empowered use of computers. Thus much of what primary school computing should be striving towards is developing, nurturing and encouraging forms of 'technological sense' (Devon 1987) within children. As Striebel (1988, p. 158) reasons, the dominating 'technological mentality' of computing in education sacrifices any 'understanding and real-life intellectual agency' the learner may have regarding computers. For computers to be effective in schools a mere emphasis on skills is not sufficient, instead learners also need to develop a critical understanding of computing in its social context. Thus above and beyond the basic skills to use ICT the primary curriculum should actively focus on matters of discrimination and informed choice as to whether or not a pupil should be using computers and for what purposes. Indeed, the reduction of computing to a skill which must be covered, belies the capabilities and understanding of computers that primary pupils already have. Instead, it can be argued that the primary curriculum should be empowering pupils to take decisions over whether they should use, or not use, computers during their work and to critically recognise the value as well as the utility of the technology in question.

It is clear, therefore, that teaching staff should be aware of the sophisticated nature of children's engagement with computing Indeed, recent Inspectorate reports in Wales have concluded that 'in half of all primary schools teachers underestimate what pupils can do [with ICT]' (Bower 1999, p.16). This is also borne out by Chalkley and Nicholas (1997) who found a marked difference in primary students' use of computers when they were free to choose their own activities as opposed to the more constrained teacher directed use. However, most importantly, educationalists and politicians must avoid presuming too much on behalf of children, particularly in relation to their supposed enthusiasm for all that is technological. The survival, or even strengthening of non-computerised ways of working highlighted by the children in this study should come as no surprise at all (c.f. Levinson 1997). In the context of the economy of the primary classroom, computers play a complementary or alternative not a wholly displacing role for existing methods of work. When this is recognised by educationalists and forms part of educational thinking about technology then the role and effectiveness of computers in the classroom can be more clearly extended.

Chapter Seven

A-level Students and ICT

Introduction

Having examined education and technology from the perspective of the primary school pupil in Chapter Six, this chapter looks at the same questions from the other end of the schooling spectrum – the 'gold standard' of the A-level student. This comparison is deliberate as, more than any other sector of education, the A-level curriculum has remained conspicuously untainted by the apparent inevitability of information and communication technology. Indeed, there has traditionally been a reluctance among educationalists and the government alike to 'contaminate' the academic purity of the A-level with the notion of any cross-curricular core skill such as ICT use. As Smithers (1994, p.361), one of the leading apologists for the overt academic emphasis of the A-level pathway, argues: 'loading extrinsic objectives onto [A-level] subjects seems to me to be altogether a nonsense. It is the business of the national curriculum to teach you to read, speak, write, count, calculate and measure, and use a pen and a word processor. The point of studying history or physics [at A-level] however, is to study history or physics'.

Indeed, the A-level's apparent technological inertia can be seen as a reflection of a wider imperviousness to change. Since their introduction in the 1950s, A-levels have remained the 'gold standard' of academic qualifications and, in stark contrast to the constant changes to the system of vocational credentialism, remained virtually unaltered since their inception (Bynner 1990) until the recent division into the AS and A2 qualifications. From their conception onwards, A-levels have been primarily focused on providing an academic pathway to higher education, a role they have widely been seen as successful in fulfilling. As Smithers (1994, p.355) again summarises, 'GCE A-levels are the direct descendants of university entrance examinations. They were designed to pick out those who could be educated to a high standard in a short time with few drop-outs. On the strength of such A-levels we have had an efficient and effective higher education system and those young people still in higher education at age 18 perform very well in world terms'.

Yet the considerable expansion of 16-19 education throughout the 1980s and 1990s has led to the A-level being forced to assume roles beyond these original elitist origins. No longer the preserve of the prospective university entrant, there has been considerable pressure for the A-level to simultaneously cater for students *not* wishing to continue into higher education. This pressure has been further exaggerated by a widespread consensus among both politicians and educationalists for a more coherent and unified framework of post-16 education (Richardson 1993,

Spours and Young 1996). However, as Edwards (1983) points out, there has inevitably been tension between the traditional function of the A-level as a means of university selection and its more recent role as a multi-purpose credential. Indeed, as post-16 education has expanded so have the criticisms of the dominance of the A-level pathway. As well as producing an unacceptable wastage of talent, 'A-levels have been criticised for their narrow subject specialism and undue emphasis on content over process. This, coupled with the predominance of terminal assessment, has resulted in a reliance on didactic teaching and passive learning which is often inappropriate for student needs' (Kerr 1992, p.49). With the compromise to many of these problems, the introduction of original 'Advanced Supplementary' levels in the 1980s, widely seen as failing (Fowler 1991) criticism of the A-level system remains; although successful in facilitating university entrance, it has largely failed those students not wishing to remain in education after 16-19.

From this background of discontent a growing argument for a core skills element to A-level education has began to grow in popularity since the 1980s. As Green (1997) contends, 'the concept of 'core skills' – or key skills as some now describe them – has become central to all policy debates around post-16 education and training' (p.88). Attempts to clarify this debate were made via a succession of publications from both the Confederation of British Industry (1989) and the National Curriculum Council (1990) both recommending a series of core skills for post-16 education. As Wellington (1994) points out, despite a lack of tangible evidence that business and industry actually demand such skills, information technology has been consistently prominent in the core skills debate alongside areas such as communication, numeracy and literacy as a central tenet of a work-related post-16 curriculum. Yet, despite numerous proposals over the last two decades, the role of core skills in post-16 education remained 'the subject of prolonged, and as yet, unresolved controversy' (Green 1997, p.88). Thus after a decade of attrition, and the change of government in 1997, it was perhaps inevitable that this situation would eventually alter, especially regarding the role of ICT in the A-level curriculum.

In the first instance, the role of technology in UK education has taken on heightened importance with the Labour government's reaffirmed commitment to promoting information and communication technologies throughout all levels of education. Alongside education-wide initiatives such as the National Grid for Learning this commitment has led to an adoption of the Lord Dearing (1996) proposals to introduce a core skills element for all students following A-level courses. The government's '*Qualifying for Success*' consultation document (DfEE 1997d), building on the Dearing proposals, set out the government's commitment to incorporating ICT as a key skill into the A-level curriculum. To use the government's rhetoric, making ICT a 'normal' part of all A-level students' education will give them a 'solid grounding' and a 'head start in the workplace and beyond'. The government has ruled out integration of ICT into individual A-levels themselves, instead preferring a 'stand-alone' approach (DfEE 1998e), to the point of initially suggesting that attainment in Key Skills could be linked to students' grading of A-levels or, in a very neo-liberal twist, their level of student loan upon progressing on to higher education. Such coercive strategies to include ICT in A-level studies have been reinforced by the proposals to 'persuade' institutions to provide Key Skills via either funding, performance league tables or Inspectorate reports. From this alone, it would seem that A-level courses can no longer afford to ignore ICT. Nevertheless, as Macfarlene (1993: cited in Halsall 1997) argues, the apparent consensus over the desirability of an element of core skills in the post-16 curriculum 'conceals significant differences to the extent to which academic and vocational courses are receptive to the concept of transferable core skills' (p.56). Thus after 40 years of relative solitude will the hither-to inflexible A-levels successfully adapt to the imposition of Key Skills in their syllabi?

To answer this question there is a fundamental need to consider the views and needs of those who are actually expected to implement the policy; in computing parlance the *'end users'*. As Tribe (1996) contests, the concept of core skills have not been subjected to sufficient critical examination, let alone at A-level. The imposition of Key Skills into the A-level curriculum may be attractive to the core skills lobby but what is the reaction of actual teachers and students? For example, after an educational career of compulsory ICT use via the National Curriculum, how will A-level students (groomed as they have been as being an academic 'elite') react to another two or three years of coerced ICT use? Certainly, the notion of compulsory core skills hang uneasily with the notion of the autonomous and independent learner which post-16 studies are alleged to nurture. Furthermore, how will A-level teaching staff cope with the imposition of ICT into the A-level curriculum and the potential 'watering-down' of the most prestigious element of their day-to-day work? In other words, will the enthusiasm of reality match the enthusiasm of the rhetoric?

Methodology

From this perspective the remainder of this chapter reports on interviews carried out with A-level students and teaching staff as part of a larger study into the permeation of ICT into 16-19 education; carried out in five school based sixth forms and three colleges of further education and one sixth form college in the South Wales region. In total 19 focus group interviews were held with a total of 96 students (achieving a gender ratio of 56 male and 40 female informants). In order to obtain a comprehensive picture of students' views of ICT participants in the focus groups were identified as providing a representative sample of the different subject areas identified from a larger stratified sample of 16-19 students (n=983), each of whom had previously completed questionnaires regarding their use of ICT for an earlier research project. Follow-up interviews were then individually held with 20 members of teaching staff in five of the institutions as well as all nine institutional ICT co-ordinators. With both students and teaching staff, all the interviews were recorded (with the consent of the interviewees) on audio cassette and transcribed *verbatim*.

Analysis of the interview data elicited a variety of influences on A-level students' use of ICT. These can be broadly grouped into four main areas of discussion. Primarily, students and teachers were quick to highlight the irrelevance of ICT to both the intrinsic nature of A-level study and much of the A-level curriculum content. This led onto a third area of debate concerning the perceived need among teachers and students for IT as a core skill. Finally, three of the colleges had attempted to pre-empt Dearing's recommendations by introducing compulsory ICT courses for all their A-level students (either the RSA CLAIT or Cambridge ICT Certificates). The effects of these 'dummy-runs' conclude the interview data, providing a valuable insight into how students and teachers reacted to the imposition of a key skills element in their A-level study. These themes are discussed in greater detail in the following sections.

The Irrelevance of ICT to A-levels

It was apparent from the interviews that for the majority of students ICT played little, or no, part in their A-level studies. Furthermore, this rejection of ICT was predominantly based on a perception of A-level work as inherently academic. Many students perceived their A-level courses as essentially abstract and theoretical, thus requiring the comprehension of complex knowledge rather than the superficial niceties of presentation which had previously been stressed in GCSE work:

> I haven't used a computer since I was in school. If I was doing GCSE again then I would be using computers, but A-levels are not really practical and you've got to think for yourself. A-levels are not hands-on, its just theory, so apart from typing essays and reports there's no need for computers [Science Student].

> At A-level its more just really getting on with doing it yourself. You're just concentrating on the exam at the end of it. We've got no need to use the computers [Science Student].

This conception of A-levels as 'not really practical' and 'thinking for yourself' highlights the students' belief that they are now involved in a more serious academic process than GCSEs entailed. Thus A-levels are seen as a 'real' academic pursuit which should not be devalued by relying on ICT. Indeed, teaching staff also saw this nature of the A-level pathway as having a significant effect on students' subsequent ICT use. In the views of staff, the academic and theoretical nature of A-levels was a major constraint to their use of computers. As this ICT co-ordinator argued, A-level students could conceivably use a 'quill and parchment' for their courses and still pass:

> Traditionally the A-level courses have been poor on ICT – reflecting the syllabus. I think at A-level the emphasis is that the ideas are more important than the presentation. You know, you can present your work using a quill and parchment if you like as long as the ideas are good. As a result the more academically gifted are not encouraged to use ICT. They are very advanced in the area of knowledge but not in practical skills [College ICT Co-ordinator].

This perception of the suitability of ICT in the 16-19 curriculum was compounded by the differentiation of the academic and vocational pathways in the eyes of teaching staff. Students following A-levels were seen to have the sole objective of gaining the qualifications and entering higher education. ICT use during their two years of A-level study was therefore superfluous to this goal. Vocational students, on the other hand, were primarily taking courses to immediately gain employment, thus making computer skills a much more relevant aspect of their time in the sixth form:

> If you're doing A-level the priority is to get the A-level – irrespective of how you get it – to go to university. Whereas GNVQ, being vocationally based develops you for a job so they know that if they've got ICT that's going to be a plus when applying. The historical aspect of A-levels is that they get you to university which itself then gets you into a job. How you get there doesn't really matter. A-level students will find that they will be forced to use ICT [in University] anyway [School ICT Co-ordinator].

Nevertheless, an over-riding reason for the marginalisation of ICT in the minds of staff and students was the sole focusing of the A-level courses on the final examination grade. Many students conceptualised their A-level subjects in terms of the final examination, which in many cases counted for 100 per cent of the final assessment. As far as students following examination-only courses were concerned, computer-use was not going to help them improve their final mark and was, for all intents and purposes, irrelevant:

> Now, with A-levels, there's too much work to do that doesn't involve computers. Its not one of my main priorities – especially if you're doing a subject like history where its all exams with no coursework – so there's no need to use computers at all [Humanities Student].

> But they're not in the syllabus are they? ... Well graphs are, but in the exam you can hardly pull out a computer and tap away [Mathematics Student].

The conception of computers 'not being in the exam' is a strong argument as far as many students are concerned. With increasing pressures on all A-level students, both in terms of actual workload and the pressure to achieve good enough grades to (in most cases) progress onto higher education, ICT use is marginalised in the minds of many students as a throwback to the halcyon days of GCSE coursework. As Leggett and Robertson (1996, p.67) argue, the culture of assessment often transcends any other educational objectives, 'education is a serious business, a discipline with a well defined goal: the *grade*'. Nevertheless, if the pressure of the 'grade' loomed large in the minds of students then this effect was intensified for teaching staff. As far as subject teachers were concerned the sole 'job' of teaching A-level was to achieve good examination results. As this teacher explained, this concern precluded any sustained use of ICT with students:

You have to get these kids through the exams – that's the expectation from parents, from kids, from senior staff and heads of department. You've got to do that – that's your job. You therefore can see IT as impinging on the classroom teaching [School Teacher].

This predilection of examination results and league performance tables has an obvious restricting effect on the decision of A-level subject teachers to use computers. These quotations reflect McNeil's (1986) contention that the pressure to perform to exam or other external criteria often exudes traditional or 'defensive' teaching at the expense of more innovative methods of learning. Thus A-level staff seemed to feel that the costs of using IT would out-weigh any marginal (and non-accountable) benefits that computer use may bring. As this teacher elaborated:

The only thing I would have to judge is would [using computers] contribute to improving the course and improving the results? To be honest its debatable whether they would actually improve results – and at the end of the day that's what really matters [School Teacher].

There was therefore a sense among the teachers that their over-riding function was to guide the students through the final process of passing the examination. Thus, whilst areas such as 'the knowledge' and examination technique were fundamental to the content of A-level teaching, other areas such as ICT were inevitably, as this teacher argued, 'left behind':

Its not a matter of pooh-poohing ICT, its a matter of trying to find time to do things ... within the hurly burly of the lessons and the amount of time that you've got to do A-levels here. You have to get a certain content over otherwise the kids haven't got a chance of going into the exam and passing. You've got to have their knowledge, you've got to have their exam technique ... if you haven't got that then the things that are important from a general education point of view like the use of ICT certainly get left behind [School Teacher].

The Nature of A-level Subject Content: An 'ICT Friendly' Area?

Allied to the prevailing feeling that ICT did not fit easily with the concept of A-levels in general, was the notion that computer use was incongruous with the essential nature of many of the subjects that students were studying. There was frequently a feeling that using a computer was completely at odds with the inherent processes involved in particular A-level subject areas:

Our art work is all done by hand – there's not anything that we have to do on a computer. Its not as if we have to do it all up on computer. Its basically 'hands' stuff [Art Student].

Its just sitting down in front of a screen all day – I'm doing P.E, I'm more sporty – I'd rather be active than be sitting on my arse ... What we're doing is healthy for you, like running round rather than sitting in here and going "bom, bom, bom" [on a computer] [Physical Education Student].

This last quotation clearly illustrates the perceived gulf in the minds of some students between their subjects and computers. It was evident that many non ICT-using students were convinced of the incompatibility of the two. Nevertheless, for other students ICT use was also irreconcilable to what they saw as the intellectual essence of their studies. For this English student the crux of her subject was reading 'authentic' literature; an authenticity a use of new technology was seemingly devoid of:

> What's the point of going to look for a book and looking on a computer. Whereas you can go along and find a really nice book and read it – I just don't understand. Its like old literature – why look at it on a computer – its just like a contradiction. Its ugly, its so ugly. On paper its authentic [English Student].

Other students' unease with the 'technofication' of their disciplines was more intuitive. For this student, using a computer ran contrary to the rudiments of A-level English; i.e. subjective interpretation, free expression and personal thinking:

> Q: *Do you think that computers are more suitable for other subjects than yours?*
> It obviously has to be because in science and computers the answer is either right or wrong – there's no interpretation. So computers is a tautology – its right or wrong. You get something wrong and you have to clear it and stuff. But in English, History and Sociology you write essays and its your opinion and as long as you can justify your answer then you're right. And so there is no need for computers at all [Social Science Student].

This last quotation reveals an underlying sense to many of these previous statements that computers lack a personal, human quality which is intrinsic to many subjects. This echoes what Turkle (1995) refers to as the 'modernist computational aesthetic' which dominates our view of information technology. Here computers are commonly seen as being inherently technological, linear and logical – symbolically explaining, unpacking, reducing and clarifying knowledge and processes. Thus computers are 'cold', logical, unfeeling and linear and therefore only suitable for subject areas which share and embody these traits. This view was also reinforced by teaching staff:

> [when teaching Art] There's that unsaid quality ... if you're stood in front of a painting or if you're painting yourself – its a physical process that's not just mechanical... I mean you can draw with a mouse ... but there's almost three disjointed things going on there – your mind and your hand are divorced as its going through the screen. When you're doing it physically you're more in tune with it... I don't wish to sound bloody-minded or anything but if you want to be the next Damien Hirst you don't necessarily need any computer skills [College Lecturer].

As this last lecturer illustrates, to force ICT into some subject areas would radically alter the nature of the subjects being taught, at least in the mind of practitioners. This relates back to the wider question of the exact purpose of A-level courses. Are subjects such as A-level Art designed, as this last quote intimates, to encourage the next generation of Damien Hirst's or to produce an artistically minded cohort of computer users?

The Perceived Need for ICT as a Core Skill in A-level Study

In the institutions not providing a core-skill ICT element at the time of the research the interviews were then directed toward the idea of making ICT a compulsory part of A-level study. Students, on the whole, were dismissive of the proposed changes. Aside from the irrelevance of ICT to students' current situation, many were already confident of their capacity to deal with any future need for ICT. For some students any future use of ICT was not a source of concern, assured as they were with their previously learnt skills from GCSE:

> Yeah, in university they'll be useful, and especially in businesses. You've got a continual use for it there. If you've got a reason for using them, like for work, then they'll be really useful. But not now in college. I've got qualifications to use computers from GCSEs so I'll use them [Science Student].

Nevertheless, other A-level students were doubtful that ICT would play a significant role in their near future, either educationally or vocationally:

> I don't think its that big in university. My sister's at university and she hasn't had to touch a computer now for over a year [Modern Languages Student].

> I don't think ICT will really help me because what I want to do is go into acting and computers aren't used there at all [Art Student].

Indeed, these views were also echoed by teaching staff. Those staff not directly involved with ICT were less assured of the practicality of A-level core skills and the benefits that it would bring to students. As this teacher argued:

> I almost think that being an A-level student most of them will have done GCSEs and ICT and it'd be a waste of their time doing it all again [Physics Teacher].

However, school-based staff involved with ICT provision seemed even more alarmed by the prospect of compulsory A-level ICT delivery. These staff argued that they were already under pressure from the demands of the National Curriculum, thus computer use was perceived by the ICT co-ordinators as more of a priority where the school was directly accountable; in particular to the provision of the National Curriculum at Keystage Three. As the ICT co-ordinator of a recently inspected school argued:

> Our priority at the moment is following the Education Act and that dictates Keystage Three and Keystage Four. We've just been slammed by [the Inspectorate] for not doing enough at Keystage Three and they've got the weight of the law behind them! As far as

Keystage 'Five' is concerned, they're way over the horizon. We don't even consider them [School ICT Co-ordinator].

Those ICT co-ordinators who had considered the implications of the Dearing Report were also disparaging of the proposed changes, arguing that the imposition of ICT onto Years 12 and 13 could conceivably 'break' the already stretched computer provision in many schools:

We had this meeting last night where we were told they're planning to make ICT a core part of A-levels. That's all very well but how can we do that without the bloody resources. The people proposing this were all high-level guys. Its all very well for these LEA and University types to propose these things but they don't know what its actually like down here. I'd love to be in a position to do these things but I haven't got the machines [School ICT Co-ordinator].

Thus it appeared that the imposition of a compulsory element of ICT use into the A-level curriculum was not a welcome proposition among many students and teachers. On the one hand students did not perceive further ICT skills after GCSE as a high priority whilst teaching staff remained preoccupied with the more immediate problem of delivering ICT throughout the National Curriculum. It is therefore interesting to contrast these perceptions against the views of staff and students in the colleges already running ICT as a core skill for A-level.

Delivering ICT as a Core Skill at A-level: Prior Experiences

When talking to the A-level students studying in the three colleges who were already running ICT 'key skills' courses, it was also apparent how many seemed to be resisting, rather than immersing themselves into, these courses. A vast number of students were not regularly attending the courses because they felt the skills being covered were too elementary:

Oh yeah, the thing with the [key skills] classes was that they are too basic. We had a lesson on the mouse ... this is a mouse, there are two buttons, this button does this, this button does that .. and we spent a whole hour talking about computers before we actually switched them on. It just seemed pointless so I didn't turn up to the next one. And when I did go again it took no time to catch up with everyone else and I'd missed five or six weeks [Social Science Student].

I just find it patronising [Humanities Student].
It took them half an hour just to show us how to turn the computers on and then the second lesson we used the mouse... [Humanities Student].
It is hard for them to please everybody but they don't see that some of us have learnt to use them before [Humanities Student].

Indeed, it is evident from these quotes that many A-level students felt that the key skills provision was somehow 'beneath them', merely reiterating what they had previously been taught during their compulsory education. Some students directly voiced this concern, arguing that the key skills sessions should be differentiated between those who were already ICT proficient and those who were still novices:

> They shouldn't teach everyone at the same level, because for some people the [key skills] lessons are too slow, they treat you like you're stupid. I mean a lot of us have done GCSE in it and we're doing stuff that was really basic now. We could be doing something a lot harder but they're still giving us the same as someone who's never used a computer. And they're making us do it [Humanities Student].
>
> I've been to the [key skills] lessons but .... that's just word processing and I don't know what else really. But that's just at a really low level, really low. If you've never used a computer before then you could get something out of it but I had to give it up [Science Student].

This reflects the strong sense among the students that Core Skills had offered them nothing in addition to the ICT provision they had received during their compulsory school careers. Furthermore, other students expressed the concern that the material and skills covered in the core skills sessions bore little, or no, relevance to the work that they were expected to do in their A-level courses:

> Q: *Would could the college do to get you to go to the [key skills] lessons?*
> Introduce more interesting topics. At the moment its all spreadsheets and water pollution and earthquakes ... did you do that? What's that got to do with A-level English? [Humanities Student].
>
> But when you're in [key skills] classes you can't do you own thing anyway [Science Student].
> No you can't [Science Student].
> So you've got to find your own separate time to sit down and do what you want to do [Science Student].

Staff who were also involved with the delivery of ICT as a core skill seemed wholly aware of these short-comings. Firstly, for the approach to be successful with students, staff emphasised that computer use should be integrated and made relevant to students' courses:

> The only way that it can be delivered effectively is in an totally integrated approach... Unless its integrated at source they will ignore the ICT and usually get it through damage limitation and get it through the end of the course – you know, I must word process the report even though I had it marked six months ago [ICT Lecturer].

Secondly, following on from this concern, the danger of delivering ICT as a 'bolt-on' to courses was equally as unproductive, as this ICT lecturer argued:

> It should not be treated as a bolt-on; if you do you lose the students – they are inclined to use your time to go to the library because they've got deadlines and don't see that they

could be using your expertise to provide superior results for their work. So it needs a completely integrated approach to be adopted right from the start [ICT Lecturer].

Similarly, teaching staff also argued against the provision of a homogenous key skills provision, arguing that any delivery of ICT skills should be focused on students' individual ICT needs, rather than a 'blanket' model of skills:

> What we should be doing is to look carefully at the students' needs as far as ICT is concerned and actually catering for those needs. Now, we went for a single key skills qualification for all sorts of reasons connected with funding ... but having a homogenous key skills course I don't think was particularly useful. What I think that we need to be looking at is having an area which looks at an individual's needs and consists of individually accredited units through the Open College Network [College ICT Co-ordinator].

Yet, although agreeing with the sentiment, the logistical impracticality of this was questioned by other staff. As this ICT co-ordinator argued, the relative diversity of A-level courses offered to students by each institution makes integration of ICT into each course a logistical nightmare, especially as A-level students often take a combination of three or four subjects:

> Really the key skills should be part of the subject that you're doing – but that'd be so difficult to manage. Can you imagine the hassle? The thing is, say a student is doing three A-levels – now to do a key skills qualification they've got to come to a workshop. Can you imagine the administration to try and get them to assess work from their subject areas? When they're all doing different subjects? So the way that its going is they're going to learn the key skills completely divorced from the subject area [College ICT Co-ordinator].

As all these quotes illustrate, the general feeling among many A-level teachers was that the introduction of ICT as a core skill had been, at best, fraught with difficulties. Coupled with the students' ambivalence towards ICT, it seems that A-level teachers and ICT co-ordinators are less than convinced of the viability of the creation of a core skills element in A-level education. Thus it would seem that the use of ICT as a core skill was yet to succeed, at least in the eyes of the staff expected to deliver it.

Discussion

It appeared at the time of the research that any imposition of ICT as a key skill into the A-level curriculum would be, at best, greeted with either indifference or hostility – at time of writing this volume in 2002 it is perhaps too early to be judgmental but the Key Skills curricula have certainly not proved to be a universal success. What was clear from the study was that the dearth of ICT use at A-level seems to be primarily induced by the nature of the courses themselves. ICT has little relevance to an A-level curriculum which remains academically specialised and narrowly focused on the eventual examination result as a pathway to higher education. Throughout the interview data there was also a considerable sentiment that provision of Core Skills as an extraneous 'bolt-on' to A-level courses was simply not effective in motivating students to use ICT. This mirrors other recent warning signs that introducing a coercive model of ICT integration into the A-level curriculum will be fraught with difficulty. For example, the Wolf Report (1997, p.8) on the application of GNVQs, highlighted the huge variability in the core skills element of courses, concluding that 'most GNVQ teams find core (key) skills delivery highly problematic'. This begs the question that if core skills were being found 'problematic' in the intrinsically vocational environment of the GNVQ curriculum, how could educationalists expect a better response in the reified, academic culture of the A-level?

Indeed, the intrinsic nature of the A-level, in both its academic content and academic role, would appear to be the principal barrier to the successful imposition of ICT as a Key Skill. Furthermore, there are few signs from the government's interpretation of the Dearing recommendations to indicate that the origins of this 'clash' will be fundamentally altered. With the ever-increasing (and inevitably more pressing) burden on those involved in delivering A-levels to produce 'university friendly' grades and facilitate the government's desired expansion of Higher Education, ICT will continue to be marginalised in the minds of all but the most committed teachers and students. Adding a suite of core skills alongside the A-level curriculum and expecting it to be treated by teachers and students with the same gravitas is, at best, short-sighted. As long as A-levels remain predominantly focused on the 'grade' then the concept of core skills will always be peripheral. The government's concurrent commitment to preserving 'the level of specialisation and achievement in depth offered by A-levels' (DfEE 1997d, p.12) leaves the present Key Skills proposals little chance of becoming anything more than the General Studies of the twenty-first century; resented and ignored by students and teachers alike. As Lawton (1992, p.91) argues, 'there is the danger that core skills might become part of the 'phantom curriculum'... they will become an area of neglect rather than of progress'.

We therefore need to examine some crucial questions that the Key Skills debate has to date circumvented. Fundamentally, we must question the perceived wisdom that all A-level students really need additional ICT skills during their A-level studies. In the first instance, the vast majority of A-level students still progress into a higher education environment which continues to exert very few ICT demands on undergraduates (Dearing 1997, Hesketh 1998). Furthermore, the minority of A-level candidates not participating in university education, are entering a labour market where over-arching personal skills and qualities are valued far more highly by employers than any specific ICT ability (i.e. Harvey 1993, Hockey and Wellington 1994, Osmond 1994, Hesketh 1998). From this background, should we assume that every A-level student needs a compulsory ICT skills element to their post-16 studies? Do we want to be re-training A-level students with skills they will have already gained via the National Curriculum and, in any case, will not necessarily be called upon to use?

We should therefore reassess why we want A-level students to have ICT skills. As '*Qualifying for Success*' primarily asserts, underlying the government's reforms of the A-level curriculum is a desire to prepare all students for the twenty-first century's 'information society'. However, from this perspective it would surely be more beneficial to strive to inject A-levels with an 'understanding' and 'awareness' of using computers rather than an enforced and misplaced instrumental emphasis on skills. Any emphasis of ICT at A-level should therefore concentrate on the '*Why*' rather than the '*How*' of computer use. Such an approach would be far more effective in providing all A-level students with the 'ability to update [skills] through-out life' as the government intends (DfEE 1997d, p.19), fostering as it would effective and appropriate use of ICT. As I have argued elsewhere, an 'understanding' of ICT 'encompasses the ideological notion of a 'sense' of computers; a critical evaluation of the computer, its applications and societal/ cultural effects ... In this way computer 'expertise' must also be coupled with an understanding of ICT in order to be truly effective. Computer use should be compared to any creative process; basic technical expertise is essential, but ineffective without an understanding or sense of what you are doing' (Selwyn 1997, p.55).

This echoes Watkins' assertion (1986) that 'education would be better directed toward equipping students with the more fundamental skills of being able to critique and reflect on the technological changes taking place rather than closely aligning skill to the ephemeral demands of industry'. As this study has shown, students and teachers have widely varying needs and opportunities to use computers and this should be reflected in any imposition of ICT into the A-level curriculum. It is mistaken to assume that forcing an A-level Art student to learn the same array of key ICT skills as an A-level Business student will subsequently result in both using ICT 'normally'. Coerced use of computers will only result in a large number of students 'switching off' from ICT altogether. Via development of an 'awareness' of ICT use all students will at least be making informed, rational choices when they choose whether or not to use a computer. Some will choose to use ICT heavily, others less so, but crucially students will not be leaving the sixth form totally alienated from ICT as many seem to be at present.

In practice, developing a culture of computer 'understanding' in the A-level curriculum is less tangible than a set of 'Key Skills', but ultimately is of far more use to both students and teachers. Understanding is obviously fostered from using ICT, but in an appropriate and useful manner. Reiterating a theme developed in chapter six, students must *want* to use ICT (and perceive it as being of real *utility*) if they are going to develop an effective 'technological literacy' for the twenty-first century. It is also clear from this study that such change would be more effective if integrated from within individual A-level syllabi, rather than the 'blanket' approach currently proposed, thus allowing integration of ICT to be tailored at the level of individual subject areas. Thus students would be able to reflect on, and apply, ICT in an appropriate manner to the needs of their A-level studies.

Nevertheless, it would be naive to assume that such an approach could ever form the basis of ICT provision at any level of education, given the strength of the core skills lobby and the government's view of ICT as an educational and economic panacea. Indeed, the general concept of ICT as a key skill certainly has a large role to play in education, in particular as a cross curricular core skill in *compulsory* education. However, to assume that the same approach will be successful when applied to the A-level curriculum is misconceived. As this study has shown, as they stand at the moment, A-levels cannot be expected to embrace ICT use as other areas of education have. Unless the nature and essence of the A-level is radically re-focused, ICT will always be of marginal concern to both teachers and students.

Chapter Eight

Exploring Accountancy Undergraduates' Use of ICT

Introduction

Of course, schools and colleges are by no means the only educational settings where ICT is used and many of the issues and problems raised over the last two chapters could be argued to be largely specific to the compulsory (or near-compulsory) school setting. This chapter, therefore, rounds off our examination of individual learners and ICT from the very different perspective of the university undergraduate – in particular undergraduates taking degrees in accounting and business and hoping to then go on to train as accountants. Indeed, it has long been confidently asserted that use of information and communication technology (ICT) will be *the* defining feature of higher education in the twenty-first century (e.g. Luehrmann 1971, Walker 1998). Visions of 'virtual universities' and 'cyber-classrooms' continue to proliferate the higher education literature (e.g. Tiffin and Rajasingham 1994, Howe 1998) with little sign of abating. Indeed, if proponents of the information revolution are to be believed, then university education is inevitably following the lead set by business and industry into a computer mediated 'meltdown':

> Developments in multimedia, increased communications and other ICT innovations are obviously key components of the information society. In this new era, managers must be prepared to abandon everything they know – and the same may hold for teachers, educationalists, researchers, students and policy-makers. Maintaining the *status quo* is not an option (Gell and Cochrane 1996, p.254).

Whereas the computer has been used in post-compulsory education for over forty years (Hawkridge 1983) ICT has only recently begun to feature prominently on the higher education policy-making agenda. Spurred on by the success of the Joint Academic Network (JANET) and subsequent development of 'SUPERJANET', the 1997 Dearing Committee of Inquiry formally underlined the centrality of ICT to the UK Higher Education sector, recommending that every student have a laptop computer by 2005, points of Internet access are provided in student accommodation and, crucially, ICT is recognised as a key skill throughout university curricula. Educational ICT in the higher education educational curriculum would seem, at last, to be taken seriously by those outside of the hitherto marginalised educational technology community.

Of course, the wider significance of the computerisation of higher education in terms of national and global economics has been well documented. The pivotal role of the university in producing the levels of human capital required for countries to succeed in the globalised 'information economy' has been expressed in terms of higher education's ability to provide the labour market with information-aware, information-adept and information-literate graduates; i.e. the 'symbolic analyst' cadre seen by Reich (1991) as the driving force of twenty-first century capitalism. In this way, the present emphasis on developing information-literate graduates can be seen as fundamental to the longevity and survival of higher education and the growth of the 'post-modern university' (Webster and Smith 1997). As Breivik (1998, pp.1-3) argues:

> The seemingly abrupt dawn and speed-of-light growth of the Information Age threatens the very existence of traditional higher education ... To address th[e] new definition of an educated graduate, higher education must step boldly forward and acknowledge the fact that the traditional literacies accepted in the past as sufficient for supporting a liberal education are now insufficient. In fact, information literacy must be added to the other literacies because students must be information literate to stay up-to-date with any subject in the Information Age!.

Although ICT is beginning to have a profound effect on the academic activities of university faculty (Gregorian 1996, Okerson 1996, Fuller 1998, Mizokawa 1994) its integration into the day-to-day academic activities of university *students* has been less uniform. Despite the seeming inevitability of the 'computerised campus' during the 1980s (Roszak 1986) many of the predicted visions of ICT-based teaching and learning have been slow in materialising, at least in terms of *use* of computers by students. Despite universities' expenditure on computer resources increasing dramatically over the last decade, students' actual use of ICT has remained inconsistent and highly variable from course to course and institution to institution (Arnold 1999).

That university students may not whole-heartedly embrace ICT use has only ever been of fleeting consideration to most educationalists. Indeed, the main apprehensions of early advocates of educational technology tended to centre around the concern that undergraduates may fall too deeply 'in love' with the computer to the detriment of other aspects of their intellectual development (e.g. Evans 1979). However, as we have seen in the last two chapters, individuals' acceptance or rejection of using ICT is not as straightforward as policy-makers or education technologists may assume and, indeed, is not even consistent *within* individuals from context to context. Extension of work into the 'social shaping' of technology has therefore led many sociologists to now argue that technology can be seen as 'text'; a notion which intimates that the nature and capacity of technology is, in principle, interpretatively flexible (Woolgar 1991). As Woolgar (1996, p.92) continues:

> This version of "taking social dimensions into account" offers the opportunity for giving a new focus to analyses of the problem of the user. When construed as a text, technology is to be understood as a manufactured entity, designed and produced within a particular

social and organisational context. Significantly, this is often done with particular readers in mind – it is fabricated with the intention that it should be used in particular ways. On the consumption side, the technology is taken up and used in contexts other than, and broadly separate from, its production.

In this way, exploring the perspective of the individual student when discussing the use of technology is paramount to beginning to understand the nature of ICT in higher educational settings. From this perspective, the present chapter examines how undergraduate students, as the ultimate 'end-users' of educational technology in higher education teaching, conceptualise the use of educational computing; thereby exploring the varying rationales for either engaging or not with ICT during their time in university.

Methods

Focus group interviews were carried out with groups of between three to eight students in two UK universities as part of a larger research project into ICT and accounting education (see Selwyn et al. 1999, Marriott et al. 1999). The project focused on an established business school in a traditional civic university (Uni 1) and a smaller business department in a 'new' university sector institution (Uni 2). In total 18 group interviews were held with a total of 77 students who had previously completed questionnaires for the study. Of the students interviewed, 50.6 per cent were male (n=38) with the remaining 49.4 per cent female (n=39). Just over two-thirds of the sample were from UK/Eire (n=54) and a third classified as 'overseas' students (n=23). All the interviews were recorded (with the consent of the interviewees) on audio cassette and transcribed *verbatim*.

Analysis of the interview data elicited a variety of influences on students' engagement with ICT in university. These can be broadly grouped into *short-term factors* (i.e. students' immediate concerns with coursework assignments, examinations and other forms of degree work and assessment), *medium-term factors* (i.e. course-related concerns culminating in their final degree classification) and *long-term factors* (i.e. the need and usefulness of ICT in relation to future life and employment prospects). These themes are now discussed in greater detail in the following sections.

Short Term Factors – 'You'll Get the Same Marks Manually'

Students first rationalised their use of ICT in terms of the relevance and utility it had to their present situation, which they tended to see in terms of their various modes of assessment. For some 'fresher' students the educational usefulness of using a computer had been put into stark contrast by their impending end-of-semester examinations; which in the first year of each university accounted for 50 per cent of their overall mark. Students who were less confident with ICT were, understandably, reluctant to jeopardise their examination mark by working throughout the term at a slower pace than they could achieve 'manually':

> Q: *So you came here, like you say, because of the computers, but you don't have to necessarily use them?*
> Faezal: 'I'll use them but it will take me some time because I don't want my marks to go down just because I want to use computers. I can do that in my house also. I don't want my marks to go down in the exam just because I want to use computers. It's basically the same. You'll get the same marks manually'
>
> [Group 2, Uni 1, Year 1]

However, in one of the first year Financial Accounting modules in the civic university students were introduced to both a manual and a computer spreadsheet approach. In the subsequent examination they were allowed to choose between answering manually or on a paper-based simulation of a computer spreadsheet. This attempt, albeit rudimentary, to integrate the computer into the examination process was not, however, greeted with approval by students. Those interviewees who were due to take this examination were reluctant to risk using a less familiar method, having originally learnt the manual method:

> Non: 'One of the exams we've got at the end for financial accounting I think, we're given a print out of a blank spread sheet, as the computer screen would be and we've got to fill it in from the exam paper, I think'
> William: 'We're given a choice whether to do it that way or the manual method'
> Q: *Which way will you choose?*
> Sally: 'Manual'
> Non: 'We've only done the computer for a couple of weeks'
> Ray: 'We did the manual first, and then switching across to spreadsheets now is a bit of a nightmare because you could probably do it quicker manually. Well I know I certainly could at the moment'
>
> [Group 3, Uni 1, Year 1]

Similarly, students in later years who had previously taken this dual-method exam were also dismissive; arguing that a paper-based spreadsheet simulation eradicated any advantage (and therefore purpose) of using a computer:

> Warren: 'In the last exam, you can choose what format you want to answer the question in; either a spreadsheet option or on paper'
> Q: *Did any of you take the spreadsheet option?*
> All: 'No'
> Q: *Why?*
> Warren: 'Well it defeats the purpose really. The whole point of spread sheets is that they add up the numbers for you. There's no advantage to be gained from doing it on a piece of paper mocked up like on a spread sheet. You may as well do it in the conventional method, because the only advantage a computer gives is that if you make a mistake you can adjust it and the computer will re-calculate it all for you, and you can move things around to make it perfect'
>
> [Group 8, Uni 1, Year 2]

Akin to these concerns, students in the 'new' university were also concerned that the compulsory computer modules that they were required to take in the first year would result in them gaining lower examination marks than they would have obtained if taught in conventional classes. Although, as this next quotation intimates, some students did recognise the long-term benefits of compulsory computer classes, these were out-weighed by the short-term jeopardising of the examination grade:

> Raul: 'I reckon that the problem with computer rather than traditional lessons is that ... OK fair enough you learn about computers which may be of value for your job but you may get a lesser grade than you would have. You might get a 2.2 on a computer when you may have got a 2.1 if you had had a proper lesson with a teacher and a blackboard. Computer may be of some value later on in your career, but not starting off'
> [Group 13, Uni 2, Year 1]

Aside from the effect of using a computer on examination performance, a more immediate function of ICT was for the production of coursework; usually essays and reports. In discussing the coursework usefulness of ICT students were quick to discuss the utility of the Internet, although in mixed terms:

> Steve: 'I've done some research stuff on [the Internet], essays, I did some research for one of my essays last term on the Internet and I got some very useful information off it, and I've done that in the past before I was here and it's very useful for research even though you have to search your way through hundreds of pages of absolute crap before you get anything good'
> [Group 5, Uni 1, Year 1]

> Q: *Do any of you use the Internet for assignments?*
> Robin: 'There's loads of shit out there'
> Efan: 'A lot of it is absolute rubbish. You have got to go through an hundred and twenty thousand pages'
> Paul: 'I'd prefer a good old fashioned library myself. You can go in find the book have a look in the index and go straight to the page you want in a minute. With the Internet, you have to wait for the thing to download, then its the wrong information! Because its so easy you go after some other subject and before you know it three hours have passed and you could have done your project'
> [Group 13, Uni 2, Year 1]

Perhaps surprisingly, students' enthusiasm for the Internet as an aid to their assignments was, at best, muted. Some less adept students complained of the difficulty they encountered in finding useful or relevant material. As this First Year student complained, when used without guidance the Internet was not a guaranteed source of assistance:

> Gary: 'I did use it before for assignments and at school and it's always knowing where to look, but at school the teachers always had a vague idea of the best sites to go to. But finding it off your own back you have to be very lucky to find the right sites'
> [Group 2, Uni 1, Year 1]

Other students, although more successful in initially searching were, nevertheless wary of the validity of information found on the Internet and, therefore, its relevance to their coursework:

> George: 'I was doing an auditing essay and I found very good stuff, very good legal stuff. It was really very good but I wasn't sure if I could use it for my essay because we use another system. So you could get good stuff but is it relevant for your degree?'
> Warren: ' I was like that ... I had a marketing essay and we had to find out this thing about life-style changes. And all we could find was American marketing. I mean the American Marketing lifestyles is going to be completely different from the British. So it was just that some bits of [using the Internet] can be completely useless'
> John: 'Exactly, its a hard thing to distinguish between is it actually English based information or is it American or something different?'
> [Group 8, Uni 1, Year 2]

Similarly, on practical terms alone the Internet was not proving to be the convenient source of information that some students had expected, proving again to be more unwieldy and time-consuming than 'conventional' methods:

> Sophie: '[The Internet] doesn't appeal to me at all. We used it a little bit on my work placement last year and I found it so much hassle and it just doesn't appeal to me. I've got access at home but ... no. I'd rather go down the library get a particular book and look it up in the index. That'd take 5 or 10 minutes'
> [Group 18, Uni 2, Year 3]

Thus, the vast expansiveness of the Internet, usually seen as its key strength, was proving to be a deterrent to these students whose criteria of completing assignments quickly and accurately were not always being fulfilled. Of course, a fear of learning or achieving less when attempting to acquire new learning skills is common. As Bronwell & Eison (1991, p.53) reason, '[students'] deviation from established methods invites risk, but offers relatively few rewards'. Thus much of the short-term reluctance to rely on ICT would seem to also reflect a conservatism amongst students eager to find information quickly and accurately in an assessment based culture of learning. Throughout the discussions there was a underlying feeling that in the relatively short life of the modular, continuous assessment degree scheme that there was simply no time to develop new skills at the risk of jeopardising work and, ultimately, final examination grades and degree classifications.

Medium Term Factors – 'Its More a Case of Getting a Tick in the Box'

Aside from students' immediate priorities with examination and coursework performance, a deferred concern with passing the course and achieving a satisfactory degree classification also figured in justifying their present levels of contact with ICT. From an overall perspective, ICT was simply not an essential element of the components that many students' perceived were needed to succeed in their course:

> Warren: 'You could probably safely take away every single aspect of IT except from word processing, and it wouldn't make one dent in the actual degree. You can do it just as well conventionally'
> Carl: 'You could take away the word processing as well, but people like to spell check you know'
> Warren: 'They like us to word-process the essays ... but everything else you could safely take away and it wouldn't effect the student's degree'
> [Group 8, Uni 1, Year 2]

Even those students who had specifically chosen computer courses saw ICT as merely a 'hoop to jump through' on the way to being eventually accredited:

> Amanda: 'Basically it's a tick in a box because if you go on to do the [professional] qualification you get exempt from the first stage if you've done a fair bit of computing at university. So it's more a case of getting a tick in the box than actually taking something [useful] away'
> [Group 9, Uni 1, Year 2]

In part, this perceived lack of importance of ICT through-out the degree courses stemmed from both universities concentrating on ICT at the beginning of the first academic year; presumably hoping to stimulate autonomous student use during the rest of the course. However, as this student again argued, the first academic year was not seen as an integral part of the course, as it did not actually count towards the final degree mark:

> Amanda: 'With the accounting course, the first year you actually do an information systems, accounting information systems course. But doing it in the first year! The first year is, not to be cynical, but people don't necessarily remember much about the first year and to not do anything with IT for the most important two years! I think it's terrible, especially when you're going to go out into your careers. It's going to be, like everything is so computers based now'
> [Group 9, Uni 1, Year 2]

Moreover, for some students the lacklustre nature of these first-year introductions to ICT was raised as providing a tacit indication of the (non)importance of ICT to their degree course:

> Ismael: '[In the first year] there was a lecture where there was overhead projections of the computer screen but there were also workshops where you actually go to. Even those workshops I don't think they were very good because there was one lecturer, one guy going round and there were 20 students so someone like me, I had no idea, I'd never done this before and could just have a set of instructions, do this, and this, it's not very appropriate. For someone who doesn't use a computer much it can be pretty daunting'
> [Group 7, Uni 1, Year 2]

Tracey: 'It can be quite monotonous with the training packages – quite tedious'
Sheryl: 'Yeah just staring at a screen'
Tracey: 'If you're there just reading it for two hours you're like 'Oh God – I've had enough of this' and it just goes over your head then'
[Group 12, Uni 2, Year 1]

Yet, in making these points students firmly blamed their institutions for the low-tech nature of the courses. Despite their current lack of commitment to using ICT, students were disparaging of the lack of ICT-related elements to their courses:

Ismael: 'I think they can bring IT more, I think they can bring more IT into it because they have a teaching method which they've probably used for decades now which is a standard lecture, but the world is changing. It's no longer applicable, they have to bring in computers a lot more. There's got to be a lot more hands-on experience on the computer with 2 or 3 people in the room helping us. It's no good to just have a standard lecture, that has tutorials on it. That's the backward way of thinking now'
[Group 7, Uni 1, Year 2]

Long Term Factors – 'If you can't do the theory you are not capable of doing the job'

Despite the degree-focused nature of their immediate and medium term concerns, students also took a longer-term perspective of their present engagement with ICT; especially in relation to their eventual graduation into the world of employment. Here, unlike their ambivalence towards ICT in university, the majority of students were adamant of the centrality of computers to their future work as accountants:

Ray: 'Everyone uses it nowadays. If you don't have a clue than you've got no chance. Because everyone uses it and people are finding they aren't getting the jobs'
[Group 3, Uni 1, Year 1]

Ismael: 'The thing about teaching in this school is that it is very much based on what you've done decades ago, standard lecture tutorials. Especially with accounting, it's not valid. I've had experience in a couple of accounting firms and they do absolutely nothing by hand'
[Group 7, Uni 1, Year 2]

Many students in later year groups based their view of employment-based ICT use on experience already gained in accountancy firms, either when on placement during their course or on voluntary work taken before coming to university. For these students, such work experience only reinforced their belief in the centrality of ICT as a basic element working as an accountant; as these quotes from students having just completed their year out in industry illustrate:

Glyn: 'I would say that that was where your work was – all day on a computer'
Q: *Was that a shock?*

Glyn: 'No ... not really. I think that we were already that way minded anyway – it was very computer based. I certainly learnt a lot about computers on my year out. Different uses and how you can manipulate around to the way that you want'

[Group 17, Uni 2, Year 3]

Ade: '[My year out in industry] was positive. It seems that everything in accounting now is all into IT and computers. Management accounting is all Excel spreadsheets. Anything you do most of the time is using a computer. Whatever you do is using a computers – you're not doing your t-accounts with credit and debit. Everything is now on computers'

[Group 18, Uni 2, Year 3]

However, whereas students recognised the integral role of the computer in accounting as a profession they still did not necessarily see using ICT whilst in university as a priority. When probed, students seemed confident that above and beyond a basic competency with computers, employers would expect to train graduates 'on the job' rather than expect fully developed skills on entry. Thus, as these students discuss, a basic level of computer awareness is more a taken-for-granted competency than an valuable positioning skill when competing for employment:

Julian: 'Its going to be more useful if you can use a computer, so then [your employer] doesn't have to spend several hundred pounds training you in work
Matthew: 'But in the workplace they can probably sit you down for a week at the most and you'll know it. And you'll carry on using it every day for the rest of your working life. So you'll be used to it!'

[Group 10, Uni 1, Year 3]

Bob: 'I think it's more an additional thing rather than a core thing – computer literacy really'
Tina: 'I suppose [employers] assume that everyone else is doing the same as well and that *nobody* else has that knowledge'
Matthew: '[Employers] are probably used to employing graduates anyway and are probably know what standards their IT literacies are not'
Julian: 'Its not what it should be but its the fact that everyone's at the same level. So [employers] accept that and look for excellent individuals rather than people who are good at one thing'

[Group 10, Uni 1, Year 3]

Indeed, this argument was extended in some interview groups to questioning of employers' real powers of discrimination when asking for 'good IT skills':

Euros: 'I kind of think that we're still at the stage that when [employers] say 'Good IT skills' they're still not too sure what they mean by 'Good IT skills'. And when you get there they do give you training on what they want you to do anyway and its pretty easy to pick up a basic knowledge of IT. They are looking for the personal things like confidence and just being able to do what they want'

[Group 17, Uni 2, Year 3]

As these last quotes intimate, many students saw ICT skills as a basic element of being a good accountant *but* not as an essential element. Thus, when justifying their (non)use of ICT in university, students were quick to highlight the non-ICT based qualities which they felt employers prioritised instead. Primarily, students stressed the need for a deeper 'understanding' of accountancy above and beyond mechanically using a computer to calculate accounts:

Amy: '[In the future] the computer is just going to be able to do it all for you, you know, there's bound to be packages which can more or less do everything. But I think you have to understand what you are doing which is I think is the foundation of what we are trying to learn. And to be able to then solve problems that are going to arise, Just because you know how to work the computer package, doesn't mean that you are going to be able to solve complex problems, in accounting terms'

[Group 3, Uni 1, Year 1]

Feeza: 'You need to know how to use a computer and you need to be able to figure out how to get around with it. But if you don't have the package skill then obviously the employer can show you, as each package is different. Like we are doing Sage here. Back home where I worked Sage is not what we used, it was completely different. But knowing what accountancy is, knowing what a double entry is, knowing what transaction to put where ... You *need* to know what accounts skills are. You could pick up IT skills later on'

[Group 14, Uni 2, Year 2]

Thus students placed most importance on the 'thinking' side of accountancy as opposed merely to the 'doing' side; something which they saw the computer as involved in:

Beth: 'If you can't do the theory you are not capable of doing the job, whether you can use a computer or not. If you have a certain level of knowledge, a certain level of intelligence, then you can use the computer, you can be taught how to use a computer if you can be taught how to do business finance, then you can be taught how to use a computer'

[Group 11, Uni 1, Year 3]

Ismini: 'You do some things manually first and you think about things before you enter them into the computer. So there is the thinking part of accounting and then there is the computerised system. You still need the thinking part'

[Group 4, Uni 1, Year 1]

Finally, aside from the 'thinking' and understanding skills, students also stressed the need for a range of other essential skills in the workplace which they felt they were developing whilst at university; such as adaptability, 'broadmindedness' and confidence:

Q: *So what makes a good Accountant?*
Glyn: 'Well prepared and open minded to the world of accounting. I mean it varies in so many ways – they don't want sort of a tunnel vision student who says that they want to

do this, this and this and they don't like this, this and this. They want more broadmindedness'
Euros: 'Being prepared to go into more than one course of study. They don't want you to just do one certain thing. They may say that 'We need you to do this or we need you to do this'. Its just being prepared to go on with you study and looking into what they want you to study. And confidence as well'
Alun: 'I mean different companies do things completely differently so you've got to be able to adapt to different methods'

[Group 17, Uni 2, Year 3]

Thus even from a longer term perspective ICT was still seen by many of the students as subordinate to a host of other skills and competencies.

Discussion

This chapter has concentrated, primarily, on accounting students' expressed rationales for maintaining only low levels of engagement with ICT. In doing so, I am not asserting that *all* students in higher education are failing to use computers regularly and effectively. Nevertheless, from this sample of accounting students – itself one of the seemingly more 'IT-compatible' subject areas in the university curriculum – the predominant picture from both the interview and preceding survey data (see Marriott et al. 1999, Selwyn et al. 1999) was one of ambivalent and irregular engagement with ICT above and beyond the word-processing of assignments. Thus, in exploring students' rationales for this sporadic use of ICT the chapter has revealed three distinct phases of reasoning.

From a *short term* perspective, the 'consequential validity' of assessment appears paramount on students' engagement with ICT (Linn et al. 1991, Boud 1995, Gibbs 1999); i.e. 'the effect of the test or other form of assessment on learning and other educational matters' (Boud 1995, p.38). For these students at least, the non-integral role that computers took in the assessment demands of their courses, aside from the word-processing of essays, was a clear impetus *not* to make extensive use of ICT. As Knight (1995) argues, students can often view assessment as a 'moral' activity by teaching staff, making it abundantly clear what is valued in the course and by higher education in general. Indeed, for some students, the marginalisation of ICT was starkly illustrated by the optional use of paper-based print-outs of computer displays in one of their exams; a process seen as far more unwieldy and time-consuming than opting for the manual method of accounting. Thus, it would seem that assessment plays an extremely significant role in determining students' immediate (non)use of ICT, acting 'as a mechanism to control students that is far more pervasive and insidious than most staff would be prepared to acknowledge' (Boud 1995, p.38).

Similarly, students' *medium-term* perspectives on successfully completing the degree and attaining a 'respectable' grade were equally as 'ICT-free'. The comment made by one student that ICT could be safely 'taken out' of the degree and make no difference was particularly telling. In this way, as with assessment, many students' present antipathy towards ICT can be seen as purely 'strategic' in the face of the growing external pressures to achieve at least satisfactory degree classifications (Macfarlene 1998). Such behaviour is certainly not a new phenomenon. Three decades ago, Snyder (1971) demonstrated how college students quickly orientated themselves towards the 'hidden' rather than the formal curriculum and tailored their activities to what was tacitly expected of them. Given the purely incidental and conflicting role that ICT appeared to be playing in their degree courses students had little medium-term incentive to continue to use computers.

However, no such preconceptions were held regarding students' *long-term* perspective of establishing careers as accountants. Here students were unanimous in voicing the necessity to have a degree of competence with ICT in order to gain employment with accountancy firms but, nonetheless, were sanguine in where ICT lay in relation to other desirable skills and competencies. Thus ICT was seen as being a basic, but not ultimately essential, element of developing students' 'marketability' to employers (Cryer 1998). Students were, therefore, confident in the levels of ICT skill expected by employers and in their abilities to fulfil these expectations as and when required. As was discussed in chapter eight, this indifferent view of the ultimate value of ICT as a employment skill in fact mirrors a growing body of research into graduate employer demand for skills which portrays a graduate labour market where over-arching personal skills and qualities are valued far more highly by employers than any specific IT ability (i.e. Harvey 1993, Hockey and Wellington 1994, Osmond 1994, Hesketh 1998).

Although higher education institutions are facing the 'information technology challenge' from all directions (Alstyne 1997) the issue of students' use of ICT remains, perhaps, the most exacting. As Arnold (1999, p.49) concedes, establishing routine use of information and communications technology in university teaching and learning requires significant and 'non-trivial' changes to both pedagogic and academic work practices, 'promoting such change is problematic for change advocates and engaging in such change is problematic for participants'. In part, the findings in this study are a reflection of the ever-present tension between the scholastic demands of higher education and the vocational demands of government (Robins and Webster 1999). Yet to merely berate higher education institutions for not reflecting adequately the perceived vocational imperative of ICT in their curricula is to overlook the equally ambivalent attitudes that students displayed towards employer demand for ICT.

Thus, rather than representing the views of misconceived, 'techno-phobic' or short-sighted students, the data presented in this chapter instead point towards a highly rational, empowered and pragmatic student body facing up to both the short and long-term requirements posited by their degree and future employment prospects. In not choosing to presently engage with ICT on a regular or sustained basis, these students appeared to be prioritising the use of ICT against a host of other considerations and then acting accordingly. The fact that sustained use of ICT was neither advantageous or required for the bulk of their degree studies left many students in little doubt over its place, at best a short-term criterion to fulfil and 'box to tick' in the first year before commencing with the 'real' part of the degree.

Similarly, despite most students' belief in the salience of ICT in their future employment, their decisions to place ICT behind a host of other 'desirable' skills, as well as their conviction that they could gain any required future ICT skills 'on-the-job', also demonstrated a very considered and rational 'rejection' of university-based ICT. Indeed, such sentiments can be argued to reflect a key element of information-based employment in the new century; what Castells (1997) refers to as 'self-programmability'. This refers to the capacity to learn and re-learn, train and re-train throughout the lifespan and in direct relation to the short-term demands of the labour market. As Robins and Webster (1999, p.202) describe, 'the requisite for the adaptability and opportunism demanded in the dauntingly flexible world of informational capitalism'. It would seem that for many students *not* using ICT is simply a pragmatic response to the short-term demands of the degree and then gaining employment, rather than a deep-rooted technological inability or long-term ignorance.

It would, from this basis, be all too easy to point towards the whole-sale restructuring of undergraduate education to ensure that students make regular use of ICT. For example, the use of computer-mediated assessment would clearly leave students little option but to use ICT if they are to achieve a desirable degree classification (Miller *et al*. 1998). Yet such a strategy of compulsion can be strongly argued to be of limited long-term effect. As Whitson (1998) argues, the integration of any 'key skill' such as ICT into university teaching and learning requires fundamental reform to curricula *processes* rather than curricula outcomes.

We have to be certain, therefore, about what role ICT is expected to play in higher education if it is to be effectively used by both students and staff. In this way, rather than as a 'bolt-on' key skill, Macfarlane (1998, p.81) argues that the primary role of ICT in higher education should be supplementary and complementary to existing curricular processes; thus 'support[ing] the learning [and] creating access to richly structured instantiated knowledge, and to facilitate and mediate a learner's interaction with it'. Thus, concentrating on facilitating genuinely useful engagement with ICT, such as structured and supported use of the Internet, within the processes of a degree would appear to fulfil this objective without introducing an element of coercion and compulsion which may prove equally as demotivating. Merely to assume either ignorance or apathy amongst students when designing means of increasing the use of ICT on degree courses may prove to be both ineffective and ill-judged.

PART IV
QUALITATIVE EXPLORATIONS OF 'VIRTUAL' EDUCATION

PART IV

Chapter Nine

Perspectives of Adult Learners on ICT and Learning

(With Stephen Gorard & Sara Williams)

Introduction

Having examined ICT use at primary school, sixth form and university level, this chapter addresses one of the current 'boom' areas of education and technology – adult learning. In particular it seeks to examines the claim that ICT can be used to not only increase, but also widen participation in learning amongst the third of the adult population who, at present, do not engage in any forms of learning since finishing formal education. If the rhetoric of 'lifelong' and 'lifewide' learning is to be realised then it is crucial that such individuals are attracted to learning – yet beneath the rhetoric of New Labour's 'learning age' and the National Assembly for Wales' 'learning country' few studies have begun to question the role of ICT in achieving this aim.

The use of ICT to facilitate easy access to lifelong learning for all is one of the central tenets of the UK government's drive to establish a 'learning society'. Advocates in the UK have long highlighted the need to free learning from the traditional confines of educational institutions, and foster instead a culture of lifelong learning based on convenient access to resources and materials. This is seen as a new way of combating social exclusion which, along with improving the skills base of the workforce, are ostensibly the major objectives of recent government policy in the area of lifelong learning.

As we have seen throughout the first eight chapters of this book, a host of moves are being made to provide technology-based learning to all sectors of society, via the predominantly schools-focused National Grid for Learning, the People's Network of libraries and museums and various Digital and Virtual College initiatives such as the Welsh Coleg Digidol Cymru. The key post-compulsory components of this drive come under the umbrella term of the University for Industry (UfI). The UfI has been developed as a framework to stimulate and co-ordinate approved ICT-based lifelong learning training and courses, rather than as an individual teaching institution *per se* (Hillman 1996).

To meet the objectives of increasing access to learning and widening adult participation in lifelong learning, the government has suggested that information and communications technology will be the primary means of overcoming traditional barriers to lifelong learning. For example, it is suggested that the UfI will help negate the barriers facing adults by:

- harnessing technologies to make learning provision more flexible. The UfI will help people find the time to learn;

- stimulating new learning markets. The UfI will help bring costs down and make learning more accessible and affordable;

- offering reliable and accessible information and advice. The UfI will provide a clear route to learning opportunities;

- allowing people to learn at their own pace, in a familiar, convenient and supportive environment. The UfI will take the fear out of learning.

(DfEE 1998f, p. 9)

However, despite these enthusiastic proclamations, the role of technology in widening participation in adult lifelong learning remains untested. Many in education and government, perhaps distracted by the allure of the technology concerned, have tended to treat these new media as relatively unproblematic. This chapter takes a more detached view of technologically-based lifelong learning and ask if it is really capable of widening participation in adult education?

Is ICT Widening Participation to Learning?

In setting out to gauge the effectiveness of such initiatives we need a more detailed picture of those learners currently taking part. What kind of people are they and what are their experiences of 'e-learning'? Are they, as suggested by previous surveys, already educated to a high level and already participating in lifelong learning episodes (Selwyn *et al.* 2001)? Or, has the use of ICT already managed to overcome the barriers of time, space and personal motivation to such an extent that virtual learners now include previous non-participants?

We are already quite clear about the general characteristics of those who currently participate and those who do not, and those who do not make up nearly one third of the adult population. Recent government-sponsored reports, subsequent green papers, and academic studies list the unemployed and others on low incomes, the unskilled and unqualified, ex-offenders, part-time or temporary workers, those with learning difficulties or low levels of basic skills, and some ethnic groups as being the least likely to participate. If extended initial education (apprenticeship, FE, HE etc.) is ignored then women and older people are much less likely to be adult participants in learning. It is therefore these groups within society that the virtual college movement will need to include if it is to be successful in its own terms. These individuals can provide a real benchmark for the success or failure of the current technological initiatives described above. If the various projects are successful they should widen access to learning, and not simply increase it (NIACE 1994). These initiatives could, as their supporters would have us believe, at last lead to a substantial widening of adult participation in lifelong learning. The remainder of this chapter expands on these questions in the light of information relevant to the individuals taking part in a variety of 'e-learning' schemes. In particular we were interested how ICT-based learning was altering the 'learning trajectories' of individuals.

The concept of 'learning trajectories' derives from earlier work carried out in Cardiff on lifelong learning under the aegis of the ESRC-funded 'Learning Society' project based around a representative household sample of 1,104 people and the follow-up interviews with a 10 per cent sub-sample. From these data people's education and training histories were reduced by converting each one into a sequence of episodes (an educational programme, new job, economic inactivity *etc.*) in which participation in education and training did or did not occur. These sequences, in turn, were classified into eleven 'lifetime learning trajectories', which describe almost all of the variations in individual histories. For most analyses, these were further grouped into five broad types. The patterns of participation of all individuals in the survey were therefore encapsulated in these five classes of learning trajectories. A learning 'trajectory' is an overall lifetime pattern of participation which is predictable to a large degree from the educational and socio-economic background of the respondent (Gorard et al. 1998a, Gorard et al. 1998b). The structured interviews attempted to capture all and any episodes of formal learning including one-off health and safety training, leisure reading, and evening classes as well as the more usually reported induction training, and further and Higher Education. *Non-participants* reported no episodes at all despite, in many cases, numerous and varied vocational changes. *Immature* trajectories describe those still in continuous full-time education, and these individuals are not used in the analysis below. *Transitional* learners reported only full-time continuous education or immediate post-compulsory work-based training so far. *Delayed* learners have a learning gap after compulsory school until at least age 21, but then reported at least one substantive episode of education or training. The *Lifetime* learners reported both transitional and later episodes.

As part of a follow-up study looking at ICT and lifelong learning myself and my colleagues were keen to revisit these data and see the role that ICT had played in forming or altering these learning trajectories. However, the household sample of 1,104 people and the follow-up interviews with a 110 individuals revealed very few people learning via the use of ICT (see Selwyn and Gorard 2002). The household survey found fewer than twenty people who were classified as non-participants who reported using a computer for leisure purposes (see Gorard *et al.* 1999d), which primarily entailed games consoles and other machines unlikely to be Internet capable. Where respondents (two in total) described learning experiences via the Internet or software packages they were both already classified as lifelong learners for their other more traditional learning experiences, and they were generally professionals (a lawyer and a mid-wife).

With this paucity of information on ICT-based learners in mind, a change in research strategy was obviously necessary. Still keen to conduct a follow-up qualitative study looking at the learning trajectories of ICT-based learners it was decided to 'sample' deliberately by seeking existing ICT-based learners in the

South Wales region. In this way 36 such technological participants were interviewed from the following contexts:

- Learners taking the Wales Digital College 'On-line for Welsh Learners' web-based course – attracting remote learners from Wales, the rest of the UK, Scandinavia and the United States.

- An elementary 'Introduction to IT' course, lasting four days full-time, and taking place in the 'Enterprise' centre attached to a job-centre in Wales. The student:teacher ratio was 1:7. Each day took the form of semi-structured exercises using a piece of application-free software, followed by unstructured investigation.

- A drop-in centre located in a community centre in a small town in one of the coalfield valleys north of Cardiff. This community-run centre offers a range of leisure and adult-learning opportunities for local residents, including two computer suites where internet and graphic design is taught. One of the local FE colleges also uses the centre as a location for 'out-reach' education provision teaching basic IT skills and the RSA CLAIT qualification.

- An Information Technology & Enterprise Centre (ITEC) in South Wales. Originally set up by the Conservative government in the 1980s as one of the first IT-based drives in adult education and training, this is one of four remaining ITEC centres in Wales offering a range of IT-based training for individuals and businesses. Significantly, this ITEC centre had also been appointed as a local 'learndirect' centre.

Whilst the first group were taking part in a web-based language course which was the primary focus of the larger research project, the others were all taking courses learning about IT by using IT in distributed learning centres. Local interviews were conducted face-to-face, and overseas interviews were telephone-based. A few of these were conducted with pairs of respondents at one time.

The 'Learning Trajectories' of ICT-based Learners

By and large the individual participants in ICT-based learning encountered fell into three discernible groups. First were those who were clearly already lifelong learners for whom the use of ICT was simply a further medium to add to book, radio, television, and face-to-face tuition. These formed the majority of those actually engaged in the web-based course. Second were predominantly young people who had recently left initial education, and saw IT-based learning and IT courses as vocational training in a non-school setting. These formed the majority of learners in the training company and drop-in centre settings. Finally: were those for whom ICT-based learning was a revelation. These few were encountered only on the four-day course at the Enterprise Centre attached to a local Job Centre. Using the nomenclature from the earlier study these are now discussed under the sub-headings of lifelong, transitional and delayed learners. There were, by definition, no non-participants since all were involved in a course at the time. More significantly, very few (much fewer than the 31 per cent in the general population) would be classified as non-participants even if their present ICT-based learning activity is ignored.

Lifelong Learners

A clear majority of ICT-based learners interviewed, proportionately much higher than in the general population, were already on lifelong learning trajectories. For example, in the ITEC centre, there was a very youthful, almost school-type, culture since nearly all of the participants were within a few years of school-leaving age. Jerome was an exception. Aged 50 he had been sent along to the classes from his local Job Centre, and his attendance and travel were paid for by the Training for Work scheme. There he was taking an NVQ Level One qualification in IT which he felt was necessary to find a post in his normal work in warehousing (to which he switched after suffering skin problems as a painter and decorator). As he said in the interview, 'you can't get a job in a warehouse without computer literacy nowadays'. Jerome left school at the earliest opportunity aged 15, found the present course boring 'sitting in front of a computer', had no previous experience of ICT and was having problems with typing. At first sight therefore he was a non-participant in lifelong learning forced by economic changes to take training in order to continue in his line of work. He was on this course with teenagers because no other places were available, having pursued advertisements for training with computer aided design but was told that these were not up and running yet.

However, Jerome described his days at school with enthusiasm and affection remembering his English teacher as an excellent motivator. He left school chiefly because of the financial need of his family following the state execution of his father. He described himself as always an 'avid reader', particularly of biographies, and a fairly regular attendee at evening classes, discussing his O-level in British Constitution, and an RSA qualification. To a large extent these educational interests were related to seeking a posthumous pardon for his father (granted in 1997), rather than stemming from personal development or vocational motives. As part of the same 'mission', Jerome had assisted in the creation of a family website by providing oral histories for some family members. This, therefore, is the story of a 'delayed' or possibly a 'lifelong' learner. Neither the technology, nor the provision of this specific class, had persuaded Jerome to participate in significant later learning. As far as it was possible to glean from this brief biography Jerome was already a self-motivated adult learner – albeit for unusually tragic reasons.

Similarly, Carol, who was at the end of her first week studying an Advanced Software qualification at the ITEC centre via learndirect when interviewed, already had a history of participation in a variety of post-compulsory courses. She had already been studying an RSA course at ITEC, so it also clear in this instance that the learndirect telephone brokering service had made no difference. Carol had stayed at school until 18, and moved to day-release courses, licenceship of the Royal Society of Chemistry, 'a little bit on archaeology and a little bit on Geology'. At the age of 40 she was qualified with A levels, Higher National Certificate with distinction in Business Administration, Advanced National

Certificate, and a degree with the Open University. She had passed Life Insurance Association examinations, taken correspondence courses, and was a member of Royal Society of Chemistry. She had moved around a lot, worked in a variety of jobs – including life insurance sales and working in an architects office – and had an Internet capable computer at home. 'I have always liked reading and have always been interested in books and I suppose I liked school and I suppose I am in a minority there'. 'I am quite happy to go along and learn things on my own and I have got the motivation'.

Even at the Enterprise centre several of the interviewees would have already been classified as lifelong learners. Simon was 44 years old. He was most clearly not a non-participant in later learning who has been enticed into learning by the IT revolution. He ended his initial education with a degree from Cardiff University, and had subsequently received training at work relating to sales along with 'minimal computer training'. He had always worked with computers, and was clearly the most proficient in his class in using the keyboard. He owned a computer at home, with printer and scanner, ostensibly brought for his three children, and learnt his skills on 'a needs must basis'. He had been a Building Society manager until made redundant, and was signed up for the course by his wife who had previously attended the same course. He had qualified as a financial adviser from following a distance learning course in accountancy, and completed a 'night school' course in Navigation. He was studying at home using materials on CD for the Royal Yachting Association examination, with the intention of buying a boat. In a fortnight he was starting a new job in financial services requiring regular use of a lap-top computer.

At the community drop-in centre there were people who were less clearly motivated and certainly less qualified than this, and yet still described numerous previous non-ICT based formal learning episodes. Robert, for example, left school at 16, and went onto 'schemes and was in hospital'. He came to the course as 'it is somewhere to go as we don't have anything up the valleys and it is something to do'. He had a computer at home but no Internet access. Was he a non-participant included by a combination of community learning and ICT? No, for he had completed several paper-based courses at home, at a local college and by correspondence in the last four years. He received an award for scholarship in writing, and now plans to get a job with a local newspaper.

Also at the valleys community drop-in centre, Fiona was now nearly 50. She had a computer at home with Internet access, but only her son used it regularly. She left school at 16 since she was deemed a failure. 'I went to a secondary modern school... If you failed the eleven plus then your life had gone'. However, she moved directly to a secretarial course at a local College, and thence to employment. She had then found work in a bank, and while there completed numerous training courses (not involving computers). However, she was made redundant three years ago. As she was a typist, 'I could see that the computer actually made me redundant. At the end of the day they didn't want typists and secretaries because the clerks could produce their own documents'. She also took a course in Integrated Business Technology at the local College. Since redundancy Fiona had tried numerous courses, but wanted to attend local classes in informal settings with small numbers of people, as she found going back into learning 'terrible'. 'I did do, not last year but the year before, I went down to XXXX College and did GCSE IT, which was a bit horrendous in a class full of seventeen year old boys and girls that did not want to be there'.

She thought that she had found the solution in satellite courses, but has discovered that despite the outreach work carried out by another local FE college, various e-learning schemes, and even learndirect, that in the end she had to attend the institution. 'That is what the people over there [i.e. learndirect] were saying that we're trying to encourage people to learn, and it was going along quite nicely and they do this.' She was doing a course at the Bell Centre with ten weekly sessions per year and a test at the end (at her nearest University). She moved to the present course, in the drop-in centre, as she wanted to know about the Internet, and 'all of a sudden last week they pulled the plug on the course'. 'And what I can't understand is that they don't want to run these courses in the community they want people to go to the University of XXXX, which I don't want to'. 'I'm not the only one'. She had come to the community centre to try as it is so close to home – 'I have nowhere else to go now'. 'Once you get a bit advanced it has to be at the University'. She believed that younger school-leavers did not want the community courses, so it 'is all people of forty plus like me', but that when they get interested they will not go down and do a degree. She had complained but they 'pass the buck....So I am a bit disillusioned really'. 'I spent time through the project nearly crying as you had to do the coursework and I had never done anything like that... I am just clutching at straws now... There is nothing I can do'.

The only totally virtual course involved in this study was based on the 'Online for Welsh Learners' website via the Wales Digital College. At least six of the 'students' interviewed were professional web-site developers needing to work on Welsh translations for their own websites. One worked in computer systems at a local university college of medicine. All had degrees, and they all described further training, marketing diplomas, training in writing business plans, and in Health and Safety.

Another 'virtual' student was already a university graduate, with a masters degree in engineering, and some work-based training, and some 'on-line lectures and courses relating to my job I suppose... Electronic and all that kind of stuff. They've got this thing called Tech On-Line University which has courses'. He had already studied Welsh (the subject of the on-line course) until the age of 13 at school, and had always wanted to continue, since leaving Cardiff to go to a university in England. He had already registered for and followed a course at a university in Wales, and another in the US, and used books, tapes and records. He 'stumbled across the course'. He was only an occasional user of his PC at home since he also used a PC at work all day. Another was a teacher and lecturer of Celtic Studies in the US who was educated to degree level and for whom Welsh is 'my area of scholarship'. She had already taken on-line literature course in Welsh heroic poetry, and 'well I'm currently sitting in on a German class... but other than that I haven't done any courses since I got my last degree'. 'I'm going to be teaching a course myself on the Internet next semester... an English composition class'. She has tried to learn 'with just books and tapes and stuff', and has also discovered and tried the on-line course at the Welsh university.

One older married couple were also interviewed who did their on-line learning together. Originally from Liverpool, both passed their 11 plus examinations going to the local grammar school, and both had degrees (in Mathematics and Physics respectively). Both worked in the Liverpool University Computing Service. One reported 'I was a registered trainer... with the Ceramics and Minerals Products Industrial Training Board and also with the Hotel Industry Training Board'. 'We've also been to the Summer schools'. 'We've been computer professionals for a very long time, so you know the IT side of it doesn't really put any sort of barrier up to us'. 'I actually run evening classes for computing for the terrified'. The female interviewee also read and taught herself craftwork. Her partner reported going on several work-related courses previously, had learnt to rally cars, and had gardening as a hobby. He agreed 'so we were both in computers before you see'. They had moved to learning on-line once in rural Wales (where they moved to on retirement) 'there's always pressure with night school classes with numbers'. 'We also go on Welsh guided walks, we're supposed to walk and talk Welsh at the same time'.

As can be glimpsed from these accounts, many of the participants in learning about IT are already qualified, motivated, and have already been involved in other forms of education or training. The participants in on-line learning are even more highly qualified. Because of the nature of the course they were also relatively privileged economically (given the correlation between Welsh language and economic advantage, see Gorard *et al.* 1997). Several had moved from Wales and described themselves as becoming 'more patriotic' in doing so, while others had moved to Wales and found the minority local language intriguing.

Transitional Learners

That said, a reasonable number of the interviewees on the various courses could be classified as 'transitional', or 'immature', learners rather than lifelong learners. For the most part this is simply because they were very young (all of these were aged 15-18), and by moving from compulsory schooling to some form of training they were mostly lifelong learners in the making. Again, for this group of learners there is very little evidence in their accounts that the use of technology *per se* has broken down any barriers to participation for them.

Josh had left school at the earliest opportunity, and was now 18. He was taking an NVQ level 1 course in IT as he was unable to find a suitable job, and his attendance and travel were paid for by ITEC and via a local government careers scheme. Was Josh the typical non-participant drawn into learning through IT? Apparently not. Josh came from a family in which both of his parents were professionals. His sister was taking a degree course at university. Neither of these are characteristics of the typical non-participant. Josh already had NVQ2 in IT but was doing the more elementary NVQ1 subsequently because nothing else was available and he did not want to do nothing. He enjoyed the social life aspects of the course, found it easy and wanted to help others who were finding it more difficult. He would, of course, have preferred to move on to NVQ level 3, but he described this as being dependent on a job placement. Josh did not appear to be a non-participant drawn into learning by the opportunities available. He was a keen learner, who felt that his impetuous decision to leave school may have been a mistake, and is actually being held back from advancement in his chosen area of IT due to lack of suitable job opportunities.

Patrick was only 18 at the time of the interview, and had been referred to a one week ITEC course on using IT by the Job Centre. He was already able to use a computer with a 'games' computer at home, but was new to the Internet. 'I always liked computers, always fiddling around with computers'. 'The last four days I've been here I've really enjoyed the course'. He had left school at 16 with GCSEs in Maths, English, and Keyboard Applications, subsequently working in a fruit shop, and then as a cleaner in a hotel. Both of his parents were unemployed.

Another interviewee, Alison was aged 16 with no qualifications. She had worked as a receptionist, and was encouraged to attend an IT course by her firm, but promptly resigned and changed her course to Child Care. In doing so she was cut off from her peer group 'as soon as I started coming here they don't want to know me because I've got out of the crowd'. David agreed with this view of his friends: 'most of them says they want to go to college but I don't think they will'. He was also 16 with no qualifications, and wanted to gain some now. After being unemployed for a few months he contacted Career Paths, and eventually found this course (NVQ1 IT). Tracy was 17 and had left school at 16 with no qualifications. She then described her life as hanging around the city centre, and getting into trouble with the police. 'Suddenly reality hits you and realise that you should do something'. Despite her epiphany, she saw the specific course she was on – learning to use IT – as 'a bit of a waste of time'. David, now 18, had left school before taking any GCSEs, took a job and left it as he was being paid more on the current training scheme in NVQ level 1 Retail. He was now studying as 'I don't want to be lowlife scum', but he agreed with Tracy about the irrelevance of learning about IT – 'you don't hardly need it for normal life'. The final transitional learner with no existing qualifications was Mike. He was aged 18, and reported having considerable learning difficulties. He has unsure of which course he was taking.

Delayed Learners

So far the learners encountered in ICT-based courses do not appear to fulfil the category of traditional non-participants (although for some of the younger ones it may be too early to tell). Indeed, for many if not all, their present ICT-based learning followed on from a history of learning. What evidence then was there for ICT-based learning attracting people back to education?

Other than in the course run in the Enterprise Centre, the only example of someone with more than a year break in participation after leaving school at an early age was in the ITEC group. He had contacted them via learndirect, and had heard of learndirect via a newspaper advertisement. Anthony had missed a lot of school, and did not like the idea of more. He left officially at age 16 with no qualifications, and worked in warehouses, as a panel beater, and an upholsterer. In each of these jobs he trained 'by doing'. He also undertook a correspondence course for eight years in electronic repair. Anthony has the same profile as many non-participants, aged 28, having always lived in the same working-class area of Cardiff, with an unqualified mother and siblings who now all work as cleaners. However, like many of the unrecognised informal learners he enjoys reading. He clearly liked the use of ICT in learning because 'you don't have to keep up with the class, you know some people in some cases there are people who are slower or find it too fast', but he had already become a delayed learner anyway through work-based episodes of training, and a prolonged period of voluntary study, neither involving IT in the delivery.

All of the participants in the New Deal introduction to IT course run in the Enterprise Centre were adults. Susan was 32 years old and finding it hard to concentrate on the course. She was not sure whether to finish this one-week course. She left school aged 16 with no qualifications, moved to YTS aged 17 and has not worked since. She reported no subsequent episodes of learning, and was not concerned with gaining any qualifications. When asked whether she read much, she answered 'no, I used to smoke'. She was taking this course because it was one of the few available while her children were at school. Now that all of the children are old enough for school she was considering trying get a job as a 'dinner lady'. She enjoyed the social contact on the course as she 'would normally be doing housework', but had now 'realised there is more'. Susan was clearly less proficient and less confident in the use of a computer than the others in the room, despite having a '[Windows] 3.1 at home' and a partner who has organised to get access to the Internet through the cable TV. Of all the participants in any of the schemes Susan appeared closest to someone whose life might have been transformed by the course. In this way she would already have been a transitional learner, but showed some signs of becoming a lifelong learner. However, it appeared to be neither the organisation of the course, nor the technology involved that was assisting the change to her lifestyle. The barriers she faced were family-based, her children and, above all, her partner. Her intrinsic motivation to look beyond her home appeared, in this instance, to be being fostered by the relatively inspirational nature of the face-to-face teacher in the introductory class.

Gordon was 51 years old, formerly a BT telephone engineer, and now unemployed. He had left school at 16 with O-level qualifications, and then trained on the job with BT mostly by 'sitting next to Nellie'. He explained that he could have taken relevant qualifications at the time but like many contemporaries did not bother as he could do the job of wiring-in exchanges perfectly well, and assumed that 'it was for life'. On being made redundant 15 years ago he worked as a groundsman. Now he would like to take some qualifications but explained that he knew little about them. He was attracted to the IT course as 'everyone is going on all the time about the world-wide web'. He was currently searching the Internet for the themes of the universe and space and was reading a paper entitled 'What is life?'. Gordon would, like Susan, have been classified as a transitional learner before attending this course. Unlike Susan, Gordon presented more evidence of patterns of informal learning prior to attending.

The final interviewee in this category was Jenny, who claimed to have undertaken no education or training since leaving school at age 16. 'I was never there'. She had worked in a shop, factories, and bars (apparently without any retraining). The Enterprise Centre was her first experience since school, and she had this to say about computers:

> Well they're just interesting aren't they? It's been really interesting. I've only been late once... none of us wants to go home, none of us has a dinner break now. It's brilliant because it's your choice isn't' it? When you're in school you had to do it, but now you want to do it. Like the spreadsheets yesterday. I said oh I'm not doing maths, I hate maths. And he said no, you watch and it was really... Once he showed us how to do it and we didn't have to *add* nothing. We've been to Australia this morning haven't we?

Quality of Technological and Educational Provision

Throughout all the interviewees it was apparent that, to a large extent, the quality of individual experience and the potential transformatory effect of each episode on an individual's trajectory was linked to the quality of the technology. This was obvious in their reflections on the nature and value of each course, but must also be considered in terms of their prior learning histories (above).

Many of the 14-18 year-olds at the ITEC centre liked working with computer packages. The exercises allowed them to work at their own pace, and made the experience 'not like school'. They particularly liked not having to wear uniforms, or call the staff 'sir'. In addition, they mostly expressed interest in working with computers, and believed the courses to have vocational relevance. They had previous exposure of working with computers at school, but unlike school they felt that here there was always someone in class to help. Again the human/social contact is a key factor. Despite this relative ease with the technology, all stated that they would be *unlikely* to use the Internet for learning in the future.

Three interviewees were not so keen on their course. Tracy said she was unlikely to finish, and Jerome was bothered by not being able to operate the keyboard. Anthony complained about having to go to the same computer every time, otherwise the teaching software did not remember where they got to last time. In practice this meant that 'some days you can't get anything at all, it don't work at all and some days it takes a long time to work sort of thing'.

The Enterprise short course produced similarly positive comments from Jenny, John, Patrick, Gordon, and Simon, especially about the tutor. 'If we do get stuck we just, well he helps us all the time'. 'Yeah. He's brilliant, isn't he...? If we're stuck like, we just shout oi, over here and he's here'. Susan mostly enjoyed the social contact that the course provided. John felt that there were severe limitations in learning via computer, and had experienced the isolation of trying to learn at home.

> If you're on a campus course, you're there with people working. But if you're at home you'll have the distraction of being at home. A knock on the door – can you take me

down the shop?... The temptation would be, I imagine, oh I'll leave that 'til tomorrow... There's so many distractions... The other thing I think with the course over the computer system if you fully understand it then that's all right. But if you bump into troubles – oh I don't know how to do this – there's no one there to show you... I think also with the college you get motivation off other people.

Fiona felt that the policy of drop-in centres and distributed access learning was a sham. It was being used by colleges to attract traditional paying students, rather than as a valid learning experience in its own right. Her progression course had been cancelled, and she was very angry:

Well, I rang up and complained and spoke to three different people, and what I can't understand is that they don't want to run these courses in the community, they want people to go to the University ... So I am stuck now.

She did not feel able to travel to the local University, a problem that learning via ICT was supposed to overcome, and she was only of several in the same situation. Anyway she preferred to learn in the local community centre, not just because it is closer but because it is not full of youths who 'did not want to be there'.

No, I just think these Universities put these modules on... they seem to make these modules up and send them out to the community. But there doesn't seem to be anything in between... if you want to do a bit more like this then they say that it is a bit too advanced we had better not have that in the community we had better have it taught down in the University. This is the feedback I am getting from the people I have spoken to.

The themes of lack of human contact and problems of technology were perhaps most clear in the online learning episodes. Carol had been using a learndirect course, and like John above found that using the same computer every time is not possible in a true drop-in situation:

I have been here now this morning and I still haven't actually logged on. I cannot get into where I left off yesterday which is really a pain.... If you stay with the same computer stations and it remembers where you were in the process and when you log on again it will automatically go back for that, you can save a stage. If you access from another computer then you can still get into the system but it doesn't remember where you go to.

The problem is coming in and actually connecting into learndirect, and I am told that the problem comes because there are too many people logging onto the system at a time which seems ridiculous to me because they know how many people are registered with them... At the moment as they are having so many problems we are guinea pigs really.

She had no online tutor, because none had been assigned yet due to technical difficulties. She could not get access to the system report, and was unable to print any text which appears on screen with pictures. This was causing serious delays for her course assessment.

Finally, it is worth considering those learners who had used the 'On-line for Welsh Learners' website; perhaps most 'virtual' learners in the sample. During these telephone interviews, some of the learners described initial barriers that they had encountered which had curtailed their use of the site – even after they had paid for the service:

> I approached it with enthusiasm, but I had a lot of trouble getting from the initial web page. The web pages contained too much information. The instructions were much too complicated. I actually forgot the password I was given and found great difficulty in finding out what my forgotten password was. The person at the end of the telephone line I contacted was not at all helpful!. I know they had to be aware of security, but in the end I gave up – even after paying my subscription! [Male 69 – retired teacher, Wales].

For other learners, the limited nature of the learning content and other services which the site purported to offer also discouraged any sustained participation as did the technical quality of some of the site's more innovative features was cited as a problem. As this interviewee described, her professional experience with web design left her unsatisfied with the audio and visual elements of the 'Online for Welsh Learners' learning package. Indeed, this ultimately ended in a decision to stop using the course rather than 'go through the pain barrier' of downloading unwieldy video and sound clips:

> The video clips and the actual spoken asserts...were very poor
> Q: *In what way?*
> Sound quality and picture quality. To a certain extent you think why are they bothering to do a video? ... I think it really did detract, you know I think there would have been a lot cleverer ways of doing it. I mean a bit interactively when you click on the words or as you're hearing the video the words are just popping up you know, there are much simpler ways of doing something like that, which you could do in flash or something, as opposed to a clunky not very nice sounding clip. I mean it's hard enough trying to understand the Welsh as it is never mind trying to understand the other noises they've added. So I think that from a kind of technical point of view ... there are better ways to do it, so I wasn't necessarily that unprepared to sort of go through the pain barrier [Female 30 – IT Operations Director, Wales].

Nevertheless, it was clear that these learners were initially attracted to the website because of its attempts at innovative use of the world-wide web. For example, the same interviewee also described her satisfaction in the more 'interactive' elements of the site, such as the 'test-yourself' sections:

> Q: *Where there any aspects of it that you think were useful ways of learning?*
> Yeah, definitely the bits where you basically have to copy the answers across, you're actually having to type it out. And then you click on it to hear it and it was fantastic because you were interacting with it, you were hearing it, you were instantly rewarded by a kind of 'Yes, that's right', kind of thing and I think that really encouraged you to go along with it, so I found that quite useful [Female 30 – IT Operations Director, Wales].

Some learners were attracted to the prospect of being in contact with an on-line tutor – even though the reality of a 'disembodied' tutor proved unnerving for others:

> Female: Well I mean it's the idea of the site we liked
> Male: Yeah well it's the whole idea of working at home, if you go to night school you've got a tutor you can talk to a tutor and get help. If you've got trouble on the machine at home, providing the machine can talk to you
> Female: It's very important, especially in Welsh because the pronunciation isn't very easy at all especially for English people, and I think it's very important to be able to hear the word being spoken to you and played over again and the sites got to do with that
> [Married Couple 55, 52 – Retired, Wales].

It was clear from all of the interviews that, despite their varying specific experiences of the 'Online for Welsh Learners' site, the current users were enthusiastic and broadly supportive of online learning in general. In this way they could be seen as classic examples of 'early adopters' with many describing other online learning courses which they were also 'experimenting' with. As this interviewee argued, in his opinion the flexible use of ICT 'could only help' with the provision of education in the future:

> Ah, definitely I think that different people pick up things in different ways and with all the different media that you provide them with should be able to do that and it can only help really with making it more available and making it more approachable for people. Some people like classrooms and some people like learning from books then some people like learning from the TV or something. So I think that providing that for everybody, plus in the first place, making it more accessible making it more open to people I think it makes it a bit easier. I think that a lot of people would like to do these kind of learning experiences later on in life, but obviously by that time comes, it makes it a bit more difficult to get involved in these things
> Q: *And the idea of formal learning can be ...*
> I think like a TV is kind of a lot more less intimidating I suppose and your not being forced to be ..... with the times and having to do the lessons every week and so on
> Q: *So you can dip in when you want to kind of thing*
> And come back to it like if you get bored or something then you can leave it and come back to it a bit later kind of thing
> [Male 24 – Electronic Engineer, England].

For lots of the learners, therefore, the 'On-line for Welsh Learners' website was just one of a variety of ICT *and* non-ICT based sources they used to learn to speak Welsh. Many of the interviewees spoke about the need to learn to speak a language with other learners and the associated benefits of learning in a traditional class situation. For many learners, the Internet provided a useful but not essential 'support resource' for their studies; a supplement rather than replacement to 'conventional' methods of learning. Nevertheless, as this interviewee argued, 'learning a language anyway is better than not learning it at all':

Well I think as far as learning a language goes, I think when you have the opportunity I think it's better to learn in a classroom because you can converse with other students and you can practice things that when your working by yourself you can't do. I've tried and I can't get my husband interested in learning this with me, so you know I can say things and practice with me but it's more that if he could ask me words or even quiz me on my vocab but he can't really help me with my pronunciation
Q: *Yeah, right*
So that I think that as far as a language goes when you can I think it's better to learn in a classroom but when you don't have that opportunity then I think that learning it anyway is better than not learning it at all

[Female 32 – College Instructor, USA].

Conclusions

As already stated, not enough people to interview about learning and IT were found in the initial representative sample of 1,104 households, necessitating sampling again purposively in a variety of less formal learning contexts all involving ICT. Of the 36 achieved interviews only one of the respondents (Jenny) could be classified as a former non-participant (discounting the present episode). The other individuals for whom the course about which they were interviewed was their only post-compulsory episode would be classified as 'immature' having experienced less than a year in total not in full-time continuous education or training. The only impressive transformation appeared in a week-long face-to-face course on the use of IT, and was attributed by the participants at least to the nature of the teacher and teaching.

The rush to the Internet, prompted in part by political pressure on the providers, means that much of what makes ICT-based learning special does not actually work. Teething troubles will, of course, be sorted out in time through testing and the use of the first cohorts as 'guinea pigs'. But if the history of IT development has taught us anything it is that by the time existing software systems are relatively bug-free the technology itself, and the software it supports, will have advanced again. As always, absence of evidence cannot be treated as identical to evidence of absence, and of course e-learning was still in its relative infancy in Wales in 2000 when the fieldwork was conducted. Nevertheless, it would be fair to conclude that there is no reason here to believe that IT is significantly overcoming the barriers to lifelong participation in Wales, and it would be unreasonable on this evidence to conclude otherwise.

Chapter Ten

School Teachers' Use of an Electronic Discussion Group

Introduction

Over the last nine chapters one significant group in the learning process have been somewhat conspicuous in their absence – teachers. In part this is a deliberate omission given the preponderance of writing and research focussing on teachers' use of ICT in the field of educational technology. Often such work is nothing more than an extension of personal biography by researchers who themselves used to be ICT-using teachers. Yet the teacher is undeniably an important element of the education/technology equation (although perhaps not as important as the learner) and so it is worth considering the realities of teachers' use of ICT – especially given its prominence within current government thinking. Indeed, much of the National Grid for Learning, at least in the first five-year phase of its roll-out, was directed at teachers rather than learners, with teachers identified as the 'weakest-link' in increasing use of ICT in education. This chapter, therefore, focuses on one emerging aspect of teachers' use of ICT given increasing prominence by the government – the use of computer mediated communication as a means of 'sharing good practice' and forming collaborative networks of collegial interaction. This can be explicitly seen in the NGfL plans which state that once all schools are 'connected' the government aim to develop a 'mosaic of interconnected networks and services' (DfEE 1997a, p.5) giving teachers and students access to shared resources and information as well as the means to communicate with others on a local, national and international basis. To these ends a range of official and commercial 'Virtual Teacher Centres' have been established aiming to 'provide invaluable professional support ... allow[ing] teachers to share issues and expertise from around the country' (BECTa 1999, p.5).

Indeed, of the Internet's three main functions of storage, transportation and communication (Jones 1995), it is perhaps the capacity for on-line contact and dialogue between teachers that has provoked the most enthusiasm amongst educationalists (e.g. Selinger and Yapp 2001, Abbott 2001). Following this lead the UK government have been actively promoting the Internet and e-mail as a means for teaching staff to share their knowledge, experience and good practice with others around the country and the world. As the then Secretary of State for Education asserted soon after the launch of the National Grid for Learning:

We need teachers to be in the vanguard as we move into the information age .... These tools enable teachers to share ideas and good practice, to learn quickly from each other, and find out which schools are doing well and why (David Blunkett in DfEE 1998c).

In this way on-line communication between teachers has been positioned as a cornerstone to the sustained success of the NGfL policy. Indeed, as Hargreaves (1994) argues, collaboration and collegiality are widely viewed as ways of securing effective implementation of externally introduced change amongst the teaching profession. Successful on-line communication amongst teachers can be seen, therefore, as a 'key factor' contributing to the implementation of a centralised educational reform such as the NGfL initiative.

In practice, a host of on-line forums are being set up within the National Grid for Learning to enable teachers to communicate with each other. An ever-expanding range of on-line discussion groups and bulletin boards are being made available, often in the guise of 'Virtual Staffrooms,' to entice teachers to participate. Yet in what ways are teachers using these new and often unfamiliar forums of communication? Is the prevailing hope of the NGfL facilitating a host of 'virtual communities' of teachers an accurate one? Amidst the hyperbole that has quickly enshrouded the NGfL it is very easy to overlook the limits of the technology and, it follows, the validity of the many claims surrounding the Internet as a communication medium. This chapter examines how teacher discussion groups are 'working out' in practice. Moreover, how accurate are the claims being made regarding the Internet's capacity to create virtual communities of teachers?

Computer Mediated Communication and the Formation of 'Virtual Communities'

The enthusiasm surrounding the Internet's role as a platform for on-line educational forums has been fuelled by wider societal excitement surrounding computer mediated communication (CMC) and its potential for altering and creating new forms of social relations. Following this line of thought, many authors have been enticed by the democratic potential of the Internet and CMC. In theory, it is argued, the Internet allows each user an equal voice, or at least an equal right to speak (Foster 1996). For example, it has long been speculated that computer-mediated communication will reduce the barriers to communication between people working at different hierarchies within organisations (Sproull and Kiesler 1996). This has also led many to extrapolate the capacity of the new 'cyber-technologies' in leading to new forms of social interaction and relationships:

> Communications networks offer the prospect of greater opportunities for seeking advice, challenging orthodoxy, meeting new minds and constructing one's own sense of self. Entirely new notions of social action, based not upon proximity and shared physical experience but rather on remote networks of common perceptions, may begin to emerge and challenge existing social structures (Loader 1998, p.10).

In the eyes of its many enthusiasts on-line communication is a powerful medium for specialist but disparate groups of like-minded individuals to form democratic 'virtual communities', providing mutual support, advice and identity (e.g. Rheingold 1993, Gates 1995). According to Rheingold, virtual communities can be defined as 'the social aggregations that emerge from the Net when enough people carry on those public discussions long enough, with sufficient human feeling, to form webs of personal relationships in cyberspace' (Rheingold 1993, p.5). As well as acting as electronic mediums of exchange the burgeoning popularity of on-line discussion groups has also prompted many commentators to reach more extravagant conclusions. As Wooley (1992, p.135) claimed:

> The experience of using such services powerfully reinforced the collective imagination of computer users that there was another 'world', a world where much of their social intercourse might take place, where much of their information would come from ... could this be where the denizens of the global village truly belonged? Could this be a *new* reality?

Whether or not we share the zeal of these latter authors, it is clear that this concept of creating virtual communities of teachers is an integral part of the National Grid for Learning and, therefore, provides the focus of the present chapter. In particular by examining *how* teachers are using this new technology the chapter aims to ask whether the resulting interactions really be seen as constituting a *new form* of educational community?

Studying On-Line Teacher Discussion Groups – the Case of the 'SENCo Forum'

The vast majority of on-line teacher forums take the form of discussion groups, mail-lists or bulletin boards. Here participants can 'post' messages to all other subscribers to the group (and any other interested Internet user) which can then be responded to over a period of time. This will usually lead to the emergence of 'threads', or discussion topics, where a number of contributors will provide responses and counter-responses to an original posting; thus forming a dialogue. Although discussion groups tend to have an over-riding common theme and an inferred shared interest there is no one specific intended outcome. As Savicki *et al.* (1997) point out, the context of Internet discussion groups is one in which membership is usually large, members probably do not know all others in the group and the task is not to produce a specific result, but rather to generate ideas and discuss them. In this way, on-line discussion groups have often been idealised in terms of a magazine where all readers can become writers (e.g. Feenberg 1984).

Although less immediate than forums for 'real-time' communication, such as the Multi-User Domains and 'chat' channels, these forms of discussion groups are argued to be equally as furtive in their capacity for the formation of virtual communities via, what Levinson (1992) terms, 'interactive asynchronicity'. As Tepper (1996, p.44) reasons:

Any user of [the Internet] can tell you that virtual communities arise in these non real-time arenas as well. Although a discussion composed of discrete postings lacks the immediacy that many find alluring about real-time sites, it has an advantage over these latter in that the membership of the community is not constrained by the logistics of who can log on when. Time lags in the conversation allow for the formation of E-mail back channels between group regulars that help promote conversational intimacy among the regulars.

With this in mind the study presented in this chapter focused on one of the longest established and most heavily subscribed UK teacher discussion groups at the time. The 'SENCo Forum' is specifically orientated towards Special Needs Co-ordinators (commonly referred to as SENCo's); the title given to teachers and professionals in the UK supporting students with special educational needs (the current UK terminology for 'learning disabled' students). At the time of writing the SENCo discussion group boasted over 900 subscribers. The concept of a Special Needs Co-ordinators' electronic discussion group was the focus of early work by the then National Council for Educational Technology (NCET) into the viability of on-line teacher forums and this particular group has subsequently been highlighted as an example of good practice in this area (NCET 1995, 1996, Parker & Bowell 1998). As Wedell *et al.* (1997) note, the concept of an e-mail based Special Needs Co-ordinators' discussion group was initially developed because of the very complex responsibilities associated with the role, coupled with a lack of appropriate further professional development. It therefore aimed to replicate earlier use of computer networks to foster a sense of community between similarly organisationally disparate or geographically isolated professionals such as librarians (Ladner and Tillman 1992). As perhaps the longest running UK 'virtual arena' for teachers it was considered an ideal forum to study.

From this basis, and in the light of earlier work on non-educational Internet groups (i.e. Wellman and Gulia 1999, Smith and Kollock 1999, Roberts *et al.* 1997, Schoch and White 1997, Savicki *et al.* 1996), the study sought to examine the following questions:

- What role was the forum taking on for its participants – what were the functions it was fulfilling for teachers?

- Were on-line relationships between participants broadly supportive or narrowly specialised?

- Was a shared sense of 'community' emerging amongst participants – was there any evidence of attachment to on-line communities?

- What were the patterns of participation in the Forum and the diversity of its activity – was discussion equal and 'democratic' or dominated by a 'virtual elite' (Jordan 1999)?

In order to gain a representative picture of teachers' use of the SENCo Forum, on-line exchanges and discussions from a period of 24 months (October 1996-October 1998) were examined in the light of these questions. The 'live' development of the discussion was followed over a six month period with the prior eighteen months of archived messages also examined. These data took the form of 3654 messages with a total of 734 developed threads. As can be seen in Figure 10.1, the membership and amount of activity on the forum grew over the two year period from an average of around 50 contributors per month in the first year to nearly 100 per month across the second year. Similarly, the number of messages being posted effectively doubled from the first year to the next, reaching a monthly maximum of 434 postings towards the end of the second year of study. Although the SENCo Forum is by far the most active teacher forum in the UK, this level of use is dwarfed by the size of 'regular' (non-educational) discussion forums on the Internet which can regularly attract anything between 200 and 1000 postings per day (Burkhalter 1999). Moreover, the structured nature of the academic school calendar was mirrored by teachers' use of the SENCo Forum, with natural dips in on-line activity coinciding with the traditional vacation months of August, December and April.

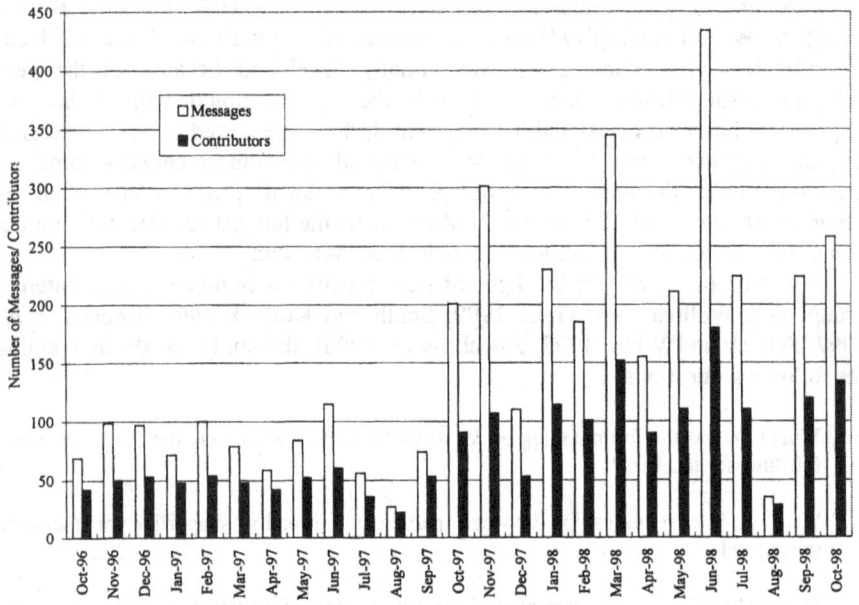

Fig 10.1. Numbers of Messages Posted and Active Contributors to the SENCo Forum between October 1996 and October 1998

Having established this quantitative background, a grounded theory approach was taken in order to analyse the content of the SENCo Forum further. To this end all themes discussed in this chapter were generated from the data themselves. These are now discussed in more detail.

Use of the Forum as Information Exchange

Over the two years of postings covered by the study, discussion on the SENCo Forum covered a wide range of topics and took many forms. However, throughout the three and a half thousand postings dominant forms or types of interaction between teachers emerged. One such recurring form of discussion involved participants using the Forum as a discursive information environment. The topics of these threads ranged from the mundane (such as 'the availability of sloping desks for six year old students') to the more serious (e.g. 'the legal implications of physical contact with students'), but was dominated by requests for information and queries regarding specific disabilities, resources, implications of recent policies and other practice-based teaching concerns. Tellingly, requests for information and advice on computer software and hardware were also a recurring feature, as could be expected amongst an implicitly 'computer-active' population of teachers.

Indeed, collaboration between teachers in this way and the formation of collaborative cultures is a crucial part of education (Nias *et al.* 1989) and in the very visible role of special needs co-ordinator the need to ask for advice is crucial. As Sachs and Smith (1988) argue, teachers typically work in isolation from their peers and the prevailing professional and bureaucratic expectation is that they achieve a level of competency on their own. As a means of overcoming this professional isolation, on-line discussion groups could assume an important role as information exchange between teachers (Bakkenes *et al.* 1999). For example:

Mon, 13 Jan 1997 15:08:38 -0500

Does anybody know where I can find out more about: Tourettes syndrome; Asperges; Prader-Willy (or could anybody tell me anything about them?) I know roughly what the first two are but the third I've *never* heard of. They've all come up at school recently and the SENCo and I could do with a bit of help!

Any info would be greatly appreciated.

Cheers,

Chris

Re: Asperges, tourettes, prader-willy
Tue, 14 Jan 1997 09:31:45 PST

Chris,

A really good site for Asperger Syndrome is http://www.udel.edu/bkirby/asperger/ which has a number of useful articles on the educational implications but also see the links on Autism, Tourette's etc. at the Xplanatory's transit station which has links to many useful sites.

regards
Paul Hopkinson

Tue, 14 Jan 1997 12:11:00 +0000

Caused by chromosome abnormality. Severe obesity, mental retardation, small hands and feet, small genitalia. In infancy, problems with poor muscle tone, feeding, and body temperature control. With time tone improves but obesity follows. Short stature, behavioural difficulties -scoliosis -diabetes mellitus in 2nd generation.

Robert Farr

The willingness for individuals to co-operate with each other and exchange information in this way was typical of many of the examined threads. Indeed, it is this use of CMC that has led proponents of the Internet to make claims for its capacity for on-line community building. Rheingold (1993), in typically hyperbolic manner, refers to the aggregation of knowledge in computer-mediated spaces as 'computer-assisted groupmind' or 'on-line brain trusts'. As the above exchange demonstrates the Forum did appear, in a limited way, to be approximating this notion.

If we are to accept this notion of the SENCo Forum as an 'on-line brain trust' then the above exchange, in theory, could also be seen as indicative of Goodson and Hargreaves' (1996, p.20) notion of teacher professionalism in a post-modern age. This sees a 'commitment to working with colleagues in *collaborative cultures* of help and support as a way of using shared expertise to solve the on-going problems of professional practice, rather than engaging in joint work as a motivational device to implement the external mandates of others'. However, to broadly characterise all use of the Forum in this way would be misleading, as the extent of on-line collaboration between participants clearly had its limitations. For example, not all motives for offering assistance on the Forum were purely altruistic, as this later response to the original plea illustrates:

Tue, 14 Jan 1997 11:37:13 GMT

Hello Chris. It may be helpful if I draw your attention to THE XXX DIRECTORY OF SPECIFIC CONDITIONS AND RARE SYNDROMES IN CHILDREN WITH THEIR FAMILY SUPPORT NETWORKS. This is a large loose leaf Directory which is updated twice annually and contains over 200 entries covering almost 800 defined conditions affecting children. The particular criterion for entry in this Directory (given that there are thousands of medical conditions affecting children) is that there should be some form of parents support group or information network in existence in the UK for each entry.

Please note that if you have an information need relating to a condition which is not in THE XXX DIRECTORY it may be worth writing to BaP Parent Advisers. We have a database of conditions for which no support group currently exists and for some of these conditions we have parents actively seeking links to other affected families.

THE XXX DIRECTORY has entries for all three of the conditions you name (the usual spelling is Prader-Willi) and if you care to send me a postal address I will mail you a flier containing full details. We are currently working on an electronic edition and if all goes well there should be a subscription service to THE XXX DIRECTORY on the Internet before Easter.

Best wishes. Philip Cook. Director XXX.

This thinly veiled advertisement sits in stark contrast to the first two offers of advice. Presumably it may have been more helpful if this respondent had actually listed the details of Prader-Willi from his directory, yet this apparently was not an option. Here, at least, the concept of the Internet as a 'free' information exchange clearly founders. Indeed, early on in the Forum's life several debates on the use of the Group for advertising were raised. Eventually, it was decided that no advertising would be allowed. However, this in turn was a cause for concern and reticence in the minds of some before genuinely coming forward for help with his school's effort to collect vouchers in a nation-wide supermarket promotion to provide ICT equipment to schools:

Those vouchers schemes!
Wed, 21 May 1997 17:54:24 -0400 (EDT)

You are all probably collecting these so my plea will not be in the right direction, but if you know of anyone/organisation/way of obtaining more vouchers I would be pleased to hear from you either by Email or Snail Mail. We are aiming to collect for 2 multimedia systems and being a small school need to generate a lot of the vouchers from elsewhere. If you can help contact:

Stuart Mills

P.S. If this is considered as advertising or wrongful use of the forum. I do apologise and hope you are not offended by receiving this Email.

It was interesting to note that this particular thread remained undeveloped, as the last two examples suggest, help was available to participants on the Forum but only up to a point. Indeed, the members of the group seemed quite selective in responding to requests for help. Although this sometimes was indicative of an inability to assist it also seemed to reflect a lack of interest among the group – especially when requests for help were coming in from 'outside' the Forum. Indeed, teachers have often been found to define school matters outside of their own teaching concerns as a distraction or source of frustration (Golby 1996). In this way, over the two year period of study, over a third of the postings (n=1381) remained unanswered. Moreover, requests deemed as irrelevant were treated quite acerbically, especially when coming from 'non-members' who were sometimes seen as asking naive or irritating questions:

> Can you help me with a presentation I'm giving next week?
> Wed, 25 Feb 1998 04:03:38 -0800
>
> As the professionals most likely to be aware of the needs of children with hearing impairments in your schools, (particularly focused on those using hearing aids, but also including unilateral hearing losses and those who have recurring bouts of glue ear) would you please answer the following question. The response will help me in a talk I am giving to teachers of the deaf at the end of next week.
>
> Do you think that the acoustic environment of the classroom has a detrimental impact on the learning of this group of children in mainstream classrooms? If you could press reply, delete this message (but leave the subject heading unchanged) and then type either 'yes' or' no', I'll be able to sort the replies and get an indication whether or not you feel this to be a problem.
>
> Many thanks you for your help.
> Luke Port
>
>
> Wed, 25 Feb 1998 13:13:00 -0000
>
> Yes
>
> Nick
>
>
> Wed, 25 Feb 1998 13:21:00 PST
>
> But why ?
>
> Paul H.
>
>
> Wed, 25 Feb 1998 21:05:47 -0000
>
> Yes – are you going to tell them how to suck eggs also?
>
> Iain

As these three different examples of information exchange show, the on-line sharing of expertise amongst teachers is not as straight-forward as its proponents would contend. Moreover, through-out the three and a half thousand postings it was interesting to note that a hardcore of participants regularly responded to requests for help and were generally known and referred to within the group as active members. Indeed one such participant (Paul H) provided responses for both of the previous threads – once with relevant information and once with a less helpful comment. Such activity reflects Donath's (1999) argument that people's motivation to actively participate in newsgroup discussions often transcends mere altruism or selfless goodwill and has more to do with the establishment and maintenance of a reputation as an integral member. Thus, to be seen to be answering is sometimes as important as the answer itself; as the irrelevant responses to the last thread would suggest.

'Making Sense of SENCo' – Empathetic Exchanges

However, the exchanging of information was by no means the sole form of interaction which the Forum was used for. Another use involved teachers swapping experiences and comparing personal situations. Thus, gaining a sense or orientation of 'professional self' also appeared as an important use of the Forum for many of its users. The topics of these more empathetic exchanges ranged from the comparison of personal teaching experiences to subjective – and often heated – discussion over the nature and importance of the SENCo role in schools. Thus, participants were keen to exchange tips and anecdotes, often evolving into quite unrelated and informal discussions of their shared profession. In this way a regular use of the list was to discuss, juxtapose and make sense of what it is to be a Special Needs co-ordinator, as this opening gambit typifies:

SENCo responsibilities
Thu, 18 Jun 1998 17:22:21 EDT

As a school SENCo my job description is as laid out in the Code of Practice. However, along the way I have picked up other duties. I would be interested to hear from those in the Primary sector to know whether they also co-ordinate the 'more able' under the SENCo umbrella or whether this is regarded as a separate responsibility. (No mention of able in the C of P) I also have to spend much of my time dealing with Emotional and Behavioural difficulties which involves head/teacher/support assistant/lunchtime supervisor liaison. Because several children on the SEN Register are registered with social services I have to spend a chunk of time liasing with social and other support services.

I also run parenting support sessions for a variety of needs, such as families in crisis. As SENCo I'm involved in Literacy Hour discussions, Numeracy Hour discussions, Assessment etc. I find myself trying to juggle too many balls. The format of my IEP's is the very least of my problems! Is it like this for all Primary SENCo's?
Your comments, please!
Nicky B

As this posting infers, the UK 'Code of Practice' (or 'C of P' as Nicky B refers to it) in the 'Identification and Assessment of Special Educational Needs' (DfE 1994) formed, for most of the Forum members, a significant part of 'teacher's problematic' (Dale 1977) – major constraints on the work of teachers which they have very little control over. In this way much of what was being discussed within the group was firmly focused on the ambiguity and negotiated nature of the SENCo role. Thus teachers were using the SENCo Forum as a source of support. This search for reciprocal reassurance was illustrated as this particular 'thread' developed:

Re: SENCo responsibilities
Fri, 19 Jun 1998 14:51:07 EDT

YES YES YES and more! I am a full time SENCo; I don't know how those with class responsibilities cope.
Sioned

Fri, 19 Jun 1998 23:29:40 +0100

Definitely all this and more! As well as being a full-time SENCo at my two-form Primary school, I am ICT Co-ordinator, and 'Senior' teacher responsible for Child Cruelty (dealing with it – not dishing it out!) Just like Sioned, I don't know how the classroom teachers cope.
Vera

Sat, 20 Jun 1998 08:04:48 +0100

I am SENCo, ICT Co-ordinator, KS1 Co-ordinator and have full time class responsibility for Year 2. Coping isn't an option. I seem to spend most of my time fire-fighting !
Helen Jones

It was quickly noticeable that rather than offering positive support and providing a 'celebration' of being a SENCo such discussions more often than not adopted a negative or a self-deprecatory tone. Yet this is, of course, by no means purely an on-line phenomena. As Kainan (1994) notes, 'grumbling' has long been an integral part of teacher's presentation of self to their peers and the outside world. Complaining is a means of highlighting that things are difficult and highlighting things that nobody intends to change, but above all teachers are careful to present themselves as competent. Thus grumbling helps teachers stress their hard work and the status of their profession. This use of grumbling was certainly prevalent within the Forum:

Re: SENCo responsibilities
Sat, 20 Jun 1998 10:30:24 +0100

I think we are all in similar boats. I am part time only and I think that is the only reason that I cope. I am IT and ICT co-ordinator (yes there is a difference – but the ICT bit is very new and is not much more than a title at the moment), SENCo in an MLD school with statemented 120 children (probably a different role to mainstream, easier in parts, harder in others), responsible for academic reports, data protection, copyright and supermarket vouchers/promotions. I suspect most of us use vast quantities of hair dye (to cover the rapidly increasing grey) and a few glasses of wine of a Friday night!

Regards
Kim

Fri, 19 Jun 1998 21:49:51 +0100

I work in a range of schools as a support teacher and unfortunately I would say that this is quite common. A great deal of my time is also wasted because the SENCo has at the last minute been off loaded with other commitments and had to cancel. This last year has been very difficult for some, for example SENCo's who have been given higher teaching commitments, above their other responsibilities, and have only an afternoon if they are lucky for their 'SEN duties'. If we are looking at inclusion etc. etc. then the role of the SENCo has to be fully understood, appreciated and costed. There are lots of glossy booklets that say what should be done but my experiences would suggest that there is still too little support and recognition of the SENCo's role. All the SENCo's I have contact with are very highly committed individuals.
Louise

However, whereas many of the observed threads on the Forum quickly dwindled away, in this particular case the discussion did not. As Nias *et al.* (1989, p.87) contend, teachers' chat is often a 'high-level activity' and the rapid development of this thread provided an, albeit infrequent, example of the fast-moving nature of on-line debate with participants quickly moving over a variety of topics. In response to the common technological theme in the postings from Vera and Kim the next participant then focused on ICT:

Re: SENCo responsibilities
Sat, 20 Jun 1998 18:14:16 +0100

Having read a number of SENCo replies I wonder if responsibility for ICT comes as a package with that of SENCo, or is it that to be a SENCo you have to be the type of person that does not know how to say no.

Regards
Tim Young

The reason for this question is not made explicit and may even have been intended as rhetorical. Nevertheless, once in the 'public domain' the main point of Tim's posting remained undeveloped as the latter half of the statement and more throwaway remark that then led the discussion first onto the personality characteristics of those teachers who become SENCos:

Re: SENCo Responsibilities
Sat, 20 Jun 1998 22:11:43 +0100

Dear Keith,
I just wanted to say that it is not necessarily that SENCo's don't know how to say 'No'. I was actually taken on as SENCo and Assessment Co-ordinator, but our OFSTED inspection said that several members of our staff had too many responsibilities, and I was one of them. I was asked what I would like instead of Assessment (almost anything, actually!) and I REALLY wanted ICT. I love it to bits, and it's made my whole job much more interesting, as I have a lot more control over the differentiation of software in the school. I wouldn't have it any other way!
Best wishes,

Vera

... then suddenly taking on a more gendered dimension:

Re: SENCo responsibilities
Sun, 21 Jun 1998 08:17:49 EDT

Tim, have you noticed how few men are SENCos?

Nicky B

Sun, 21 Jun 1998 11:42:57 EDT

Ha!! Red rag to a Bull time! Too true, most blokes have more sense and opt for cushy numbers like deputy head or senior teacher – pastoral... Could it be that because men can only do one thing at a time they are not able to cope with the co-ordinating, multi-roled, super human requirements implicit in being a SENCo?

Whoa there: I'm a man (shades of 'Some Mothers Do Have Em') and I do the job because although it is mega stressful it is the most worthwhile, enjoyable and above all self motivating thing there is in school, CoP not withstanding. But you're right – it is mainly women doing it. I have a few ideas why but I'll keep them to myself for the moment – over to anyone else.

Mark Williams

These particular examples of use of the discussion list clearly approximate Schoch and White's (1997) functions of *orientation* and *solidarity*, whereby messages are used to orient the list to participants' situation who then reaffirm their own orientation by empathising. However, although these messages were concerned with empathy and solidarity they were also intentionally or not concerned with presentation of self, often through the guise of complaining and grumbling. Thus the 'talk' here between staff can be seen as a means of negotiating and establishing participant's identities as SENCos. As Nias (1989) argues:

> Talking [is] then, an essential tool for the creation of a shared reality within staff groups, and it [is] this reality which in turn enable[s] individuals to seek and find, through interaction with others, confirmation of their 'selves' (Nias 1989, p.208).

When an essential element of a teacher's 'self' is a role which is isolated from that of other staff (such as SEN co-ordinator) then discussion groups such as the SENCo Forum would seem to provide an empathetic platform and ready audience for a legitimate means of formation of self.

A Haven in Stormy Seas? The SENCo Forum as 'Virtual Respite'

This 'need to be seen' in both empathetic and information exchanges would suggest some participants were approaching the Forum as more than just an detached electronic 'question and answer' session. Given this suggestion of a more social dimension, to what extent could the Forum be seen as more than a detached bulletin board for disparate professionals. Indeed, not all of the content of the Forum was focused on overt requests for information or eliciting support; as was reflected in the sporadic outbreaks of 'humorous' postings. As Woods (1984, p.190) argues, teacher humour is a vital aspect of the profession 'to resolve the great conflict and discrepancy between the appearance on the one hand, and the reality on the other'. This was apparent in the earlier quotes regarding gender imbalances in the number of SENCos. In the same vein entire threads were sometimes initiated and carried on in an apparently humorous manner:

A letter to Santa
Mon, 9 Nov 1998 22:31:36 -0000

Dear Father Christmas,

I have tried to be a good SENCo and class teacher all year round and dutifully written out my IEP's for 53 children. So please may I have:

1. a personal secretary
2. a special needs ECO for the school full time on a permanent contract
3. a class helper for every teacher
4. less than 30 pupils in each of our classes. (Therefore the magic number of no more than 6 children in each literacy group.)
5. a lot less paperwork

Thank you ever so much

Suzy
KS1 & SENCo

Tue, 10 Nov 98 19:41:35 PST

Dear Father Christmas, New batteries for my magic wand please. PS: Those long lasting ones would be best, it gets heavy use

John P. (Leeds UK)

Tue, 10 Nov 1998 22:56:45 +0000

An extra couple of hours in a day would be useful!

Vera
Leeds

Thu, 12 Nov 1998 19:21:35 -0000

Two hours or two days less please? (and a new box of water colours)

Gareth Scott

Wed, 11 Nov 1998 11:37:42 +0000 (GMT)

I would be happier with a couple of extra days, please!
How good do you have to be for Santa to give you what you want?

Sharon

This discourse would appear to indicate a more relaxed and trivial discussion yet the underlying theme of positive presentation of professional self remains the same. From the initial justifications of how hard the first teacher was working ('*I have tried to be a good SENCo and class teacher all year round and dutifully written out my IEP's for 53 children*') to the latter disagreement whether teachers would rather have more or less time to work, such initially humorous exchanges often reverted back to a projection of professional self. Pollard (1987) draws attention to the predominantly trivial and un-intellectual nature of 'real-life' teacher chat, arguing that it serves to form and reinforce a sense of unity among staff rather than any more professional purpose. Yet this was rarely, if ever, the case on the SENCo Forum which, even when lapsing into seemingly low-level discussion still maintained a sense of professional identity and positive presentation of self. This underlying agenda is perhaps best illustrated in the occasional posting of participants' 'beautiful moments' as were termed:

Beautiful Moments!
Thu, 14 Nov 1996 22:03:52 GMT

In the course of work as an educational psychologist increasingly tuning in to the essentialness of the goal of full inclusion I am beginning to notice beautiful moments in the everyday course of my work. This may sound a little bizarre and confirm some worst suspicions about Ed psychs but please bear with me.... I wonder if anyone else shares these experiences in such a time of horrendous rejection, segregation and exclusion? These moments have increased since I have been involved in creating circles of friends around vulnerable and challenging individuals and being increasingly aware of the importance of a child's natural community, their peer group. Take two recent moments....

A The warmth of a family
Ian a 15 year old with no spoken language and cerebral palsy adored by his 2 year old sister and playing with his 5 month old baby sister during a transition plan meeting at a special school....beams when she accepts the furry toy he offers... and when we all agree to meet again to create a PATH for his future life outside school in the real community.....this is the first time his mum has been in the school for 8 years....

B A circle supporting
Darren's circle struggle to ask him who he can speak to for support in his family... what can they do to help keep him out of hassle at school and with his mum....

Small moments, nothing special perhaps and yet beautiful in there (sic) own way and in potent contrast to so much of the day to day scrudge and battles of work in the special needs world. Anyone else out there caught a moment to share...I would be very interested(nice to know you are not the only crazy one)? Apologies to those in the SENCo forum who feel this is not what its all about cos I increasingly think that these moments are exactly what it is all about!!

All the very best

Hugh Price

One of the most important functions of real-life shared educational arenas is a means for teachers to engage in a form of 'collective stocktaking' on the pupils and classes that they will face in the school (Hammesley 1984, Burgess 1983). Nevertheless, the participants here are giving quite detailed personal details of children that other readers are very unlikely to have come into contact with. Quite who the intended audience are for these descriptions is therefore ambiguous. It could be that this intended listing of personal 'triumphs' is a form of individual, reflective stocktaking resulting in a cumulative but not necessarily cohesive collection of personal perspectives. Indeed, the tendency of such postings on the Forum to create on-going 'collections' of stories and jokes in this manner was interesting and undoubtedly associated with the retrievability of such stories when told on-line. Thus, themes such as the 'beautiful moments' recurred over the two year period of the study; suggesting a continuity to this more social dimension of the electronic forum not obtainable in 'real-life' interactions.

Nevertheless, within such public stock-taking there is also a clear element of self-promotion. As Peterson (1964) argued career teachers want recognition as they grow older – recognition for having dedicated their lives to other peoples' children and for the peripatetic educational psychologists this would appear to be even stronger. A trend which was apparent in subsequent postings.

Re:Beautiful Moments!
Fri, 15 Nov 1996 06:54:33 GMT

Hugh's mailing arrived like a warm fire on a cold winter's evening! I fully support what you are saying about such moments being exactly what it is all about. I teach a primary nurture class (Y5/6) of 12 SEN children. Mostly EBD's. At times I feel very weighed down by the requirements from paperwork, and it can be hard not to lose sight of what I am doing. To add a few moments to those that Colin gave us...

A Being sorry.
Jason had been shouting and swearing at a member of staff on playground duty. He was required to write an apology letter. He proceeded to and remained on task for 10 minutes (a first!). The letter had a picture of Jason holding out a bunch of flowers to the member of staff under his writing.

B. I can...
Matthew refused to draw a Santa on his card. 'I can't do them' he crossly states. This went on for 20 minutes with many, many tears. Encouraged, and left on his own, he eventually holds up a drawing. 'I like the way you've drawn him fat and jolly' I interject. Matthew beams from ear to ear. Kerri starts to get cross... 'I can't draw Santa's', and Matthew says 'I'll do it for you. I can'.

...just so far this week...and I've still to up-date my daily records and think about next terms planning...meet with a couple of parents... organise some IT inset...

...but I know what really keeps me going :-)

Neil Chandler

As Woods (1984) describes, in a school the staffroom acts as a 'main arena' for staff to indulge in humour and relaxation – a 'haven in stormy seas' – but the overall tenor of these postings were all more self-referential than group directed. The 'expressions given' by the authors of the postings (Goffman 1959) throughout all these 'beautiful moments' are explicit in their reaffirmation of their individual professionalism. This was especially noticeable in the penultimate sentence of Neil Chandler's posting (*'just so far this week...and I've still to up-date my daily records and think about next terms planning...meet with a couple of parents... organise some IT inset...'*). So, even less formal discussion was charged with a more formal undercurrent. Yet, this too can be seen as contiguous to teacher communities in 'real-life'. As Kainan (1994, p.287) argues: 'The inner purpose is the competition. Like the peacocks in the jungle, teachers compete with each other' (Kainan 1994, p.287).

A Sense of Community – How Participants 'Imagined' the SENCo Forum

Despite the ever increasing volume of postings on the Forum during the two year period could these exchanges be seen as constituting anything more than disparate communiqués between individuals at different times? Can it be reasonably asserted that the SENCo Forum was in anyway a 'community'? Benedict Anderson (1983) argues that all communities are imagined. In this way 'communities are to be distinguished ... by the style in which they are imagined' (p.6). Therefore, how did the participants in this particular teacher discussion group 'imagine' or view their on-line community – if at all? Sporadically, throughout the exchanges a sense of some participants' attachment to the SENCo Forum would emerge:

No emails received
Fri, 26 Jul 1998 23:34:50 +0100

I have not received emails since Wednesday and wonder why all has gone quiet.

Trudi

Bearing in mind that this message was referring to a two-day period at the end of the academic year, a lack of activity on the Forum would not be surprising. Yet this plaintive message suggests that contact, rather than content of contact, was most important to this participant. This sense of 'disconnectedness' was also apparent in this posting by a member who had been unable to participate due to technical problems:

'Back from Hols!!!!'
Tue, 12 Nov 1997 09:37:44 GMT

Hello colleagues who have tried to make contact with me. I feel like Star Trek returned, we have had numerous technical problems and I have not been able to make contact with anyone; receive or check messages, unless contacted personally by post or phone. It has been very lonesome.

Anyway we are back on line; I have cleared off 172 messages, collected since last July, my bedtime reading has risen slightly and not the same as the old Mills and Boon!! My apologies to colleagues who may have felt that I was no longer interested in the project or making contact with other SEN staff.

Best Wishes, Eryl P.

Both these postings could be seen as reflecting some form of attachment to the Forum. Yet similar indications of a shared sense of community or collective community identity were few. Moreover, when more group-focused messages were posted they seemed to lack a feeling of cohesiveness and genuine attachment. The festive posting from this regular contributor at first indicates a shared sense of community:

Subject line – what subject line?
Fri, 12 Dec 97 19:27:15 +0100

Dear all
Please accept this email as our Christmas Card. Merry Xmas and a successful new year's learning for all!

Roger and co

PS Thanks you for the card you sent me. If you didn't send it because I offended you then I am very sorry and will try to make amends in 1998.
PPS Thanks to the NCET team for helping us communicate so effectively. Looking forward to meeting again.
PPPS My new year resolutions will include trying to insert subject lines in my emails so people can, in future, delete them because of the subject matter rather than just the name of the writer!

Yet the apparent friendliness of this posting belies an insincerity or at best a laziness from this particular participant. Just as a circular letter or memo carries a different significance, here any sense of collective identity appears a little hollow. Indeed, more often than not, there were clear signs from members of the boundaries of the Forum. In the next message a member apologises for inadvertently posting more personal message to the group; a transgression he obviously feels outside of the Forum's remit. Yet in apologising this message reaffirms a view of the narrowly specialised rather than broadly supportive role of the group:

RE: Waaaahhhhhh Rraaaahhhhhh Whooommm
Tue, 17 Jun 1997 21:07:09 +0100 (BST)

Sorry everyone for the unrequested details of my holiday and comments on a Canadian friend's emails that reflected her struggle with cancer. I was emailing too late on a Sunday night! Whoops!

Hugh

Thus it would seem that, despite some teachers' extensive use of the Forum, any manifestation of a 'community-spirit' was infrequent. Whether this is purely a reflection of the relatively short time that the teachers spend on the Forum when compared to heavy users on other (non-educational) arenas is not certain. Nonetheless, to claim a sense of community among members would be to greatly exaggerate the bulk of the on-line activity.

Discussion

From a purely quantitative viewpoint, the SENCo Forum was certainly an example of the burgeoning popularity of on-line teacher discussion groups; with the amount of postings increasing steadily over the two year period of study. However, on closer inspection this use was limited. Much of the generated discussion noticeably emanated from a 'hardcore' of participants. Indeed, well over a third (n=1347) of the total messages over the two year period were posted from a clique of 26 members who were regularly contributing to the Forum, as often as ten times a month. Interestingly, in contrast with the traditionally male picture of the 'heavy'

Internet user (Griffiths 1997, 1999), the gender composition of this 'hardcore' of participants generally reflected the balanced nature of the wider membership with eight female, thirteen male and five gender-undisclosed members. These members were prominent in developing and sustaining threads as well as attempting to negotiate and give the Forum an identity and initiating more empathetic exchanges with other members. As such, they could be seen therefore as providing much of the 'soul' of the Forum.

Thus, significant caveats remain as to the nature of teachers' use of the Forum – especially in relation to the surrounding rhetoric of the medium. Firstly, it is clear that the official construction within the National Grid for Learning of on-line discussion groups as 'staffrooms' is somewhat misleading. Despite the apparently less formal exchanges, the SENCo Forum did not appear to be replacing, or even replicating, the staffroom's function of an arena in which to 'unwind' and relax (Burgess 1989). Neither could it really be seen as fulfilling Hargreaves' (1982) notion as a 'backstage' for staff. As this chapter has shown, on the whole a professional and rather formal air characterised the exchanges between Forum participants, a situation not usually found in either most 'real-life' staffrooms or other on-line discussion groups. Indeed, the SENCo Forum noticeably lacked the predominance of in-jokes, shared references and idiosyncratic use of language that characterise other on-line discussion groups (Tepper 1996). There was a distinct absence of many of the usual practices involved in on-line discussion – such as flaming and flamebaiting or the ritual belittling of 'newbies' (Millard 1997, Stivale 1997). Indeed, apart from the occasional 'humorous' interjections, the subject and tenor of the debates reflected a more serious and professional side of teacher discourse.

Yet, whilst not fulfilling the social functions of the staffroom, it would seem that the SENCo group represents a salient form of Nias' (1989) 'extra-school reference group', which Nias argued are an important means for teachers to share and gain experience with colleagues. Certainly, as this chapter has discussed, the SENCo group was being used by its participants as a professional forum for both sharing information and providing support. It can be argued, therefore, that the on-line group was being treated by its members as a *bone fide* 'teacher context' along the lines of a professional conference with on-going discussion groups. Keddie (1971) makes distinction between the two contexts where teacher knowledge is displayed and applied: the *Teacher context* concerns the practical, pragmatic nature of teaching – what they actually do in the classroom – based on common-sense thought and action. The *Educational context* based on the ideals of educational policy as explained and justified to outsiders – a 'professional face' even if it is not necessarily the reality. Despite the very public nature of the Forum and the considerable numbers of non-SENCo members, participating teachers clearly felt comfortable enough to treat it as a teacher context. However, that is not to argue that the adoption of the discussion list as a teacher *context* is contiguous with the formation of a teacher *community*.

That said, adopting Mackay and Powell's (1998) criteria of *mutual support* as constituting a sense of community among Internet discussion groups, the Forum would seem to be based around providing such support for its members. This would lead some authors to argue that on-line support can be seen as developing a 'critical community' for teachers, dissolving the professional isolation of the reflective practitioner (Sellinger 1998). Certainly the Forum displayed more signs of being what Hargreaves (1994) terms a 'collaborative culture' rather than merely representing a sense of 'contrived collegiality'. Indeed, by their very nature on-line discussion groups are voluntary, spontaneous, development-orientated and unpredictable – they are generally anything but contrived. However, upon closer inspection any sense of 'community' or 'collaborative culture' was often, at best, transitory. A willingness to extend help outside the carefully negotiated boundaries of the group was rare with much apparently collaborative discussion really taking place for personal and individual means.

The individual focus throughout much of the SENCo Forum dialogue was not surprising. Teaching is, in itself, a profession demanding considerable levels of autonomy and self-initiative (Little 1990). Moreover, as Foster (1996) argues, computer-mediated communication tends towards solipsism due to the very nature of the technology – engendering an 'egotistical self-absorption' rather than communication with others. Indeed, it has been argued that use of the Internet to ensure a positive self is the norm rather than the exception to the rule (Miller 1995). At most then this can only lead to a very artificial sense of 'community'. Extending Toennies' (1957) notion of *Gemeinschaft* and *Gesellschaft*, Foster (1996) argues that the question of the formation of virtual 'communities' is best viewed by asking whether such groups are based around personal identities or communal identities. In this case, the SENCo discussion group was very much based around personal identities with only occasional expressions of any kind of shared, communal identity. As Foster (1996, p.29) continues:

> The spirit of community is essential to the vitality of virtual communities. That which holds a virtual community intact is the subjective criterion of togetherness, a feeling of connectedness than confers a sense of belonging. Virtual communities require much more than the mere act of connection itself.

This lack of a sense of community was exacerbated by the tendency of most members to only sporadically contribute, leaving a lot of the discussion to the 'hardcore' of regular participants. As Ogden (1994) points out, the fact that meaningful dialogue only takes place between relatively few members of discussion groups or mailing lists, with the vast majority preferring to 'lurk' or passively participate, means that such social spaces are more accurately 'transcendent' communities. Thus, at best these on-line discussion groups should only be classed as 'pseudo' educational communities with less diversity than is immediately apparent. This is compounded by the fact that such 'relationships' are not pervasive across time or space with participants ultimately having no shared obligation to each other. In all, discussion groups such as the SENCo Forum cannot be expected to be more than sites of information and empathetic exchange amongst disparate professionals whose sense of 'community' lies elsewhere.

As we have seen, although still in their infancy, on-line discussion groups such as the SENCo Forum would appear to be developing into sites of professional exchange and discussion for teachers. However, in order for such groups to grow into the major sites of teacher participation and action that the NGfL model obviously envisages, it is essential that they are as inclusive as possible, proving attractive to all teachers and not stagnating into closed communities of enthusiastic but inward looking 'cliques'. Of course, as the increased government funding of ICT begins to reach the level of the classroom, teacher participation in such groups can be expected to increase, but it would be wrong to assume that this will automatically lead to meaningful majority use. In reality, for most individuals the possibility of constructing and developing patterns of participation in virtual forums will continue to depend on their material situation. It is likely that, however well established on-line forums become, there will continue to be a persisting continuum of user types from the 'phobic' to the 'fully integrated' teacher participant (Leask & Younie 1999), with a sizeable proportion of teachers failing to make full use of such resources. Despite the empowering rhetoric to the contrary, information and communications technologies look likely to continue to most appeal and be used by a minority similar to those who developed them (Poster 1995, Jordan 1999, Robins 1999).

Moreover, it is important to recognise that however useful on-line forums prove to be for some teachers it is unrealistic to expect them to provide the revolutionary panacea for the teaching profession that many proponents of educational technology would have us believe. As this chapter has shown, the SENCo Forum was still limited in the degree of support and help that was offered outside of its membership and, in many ways, mirrored the distinct professional boundaries that could be expected in a disparate 'off-line' community of like-minded teachers. There was certainly little evidence of the radical formation or reshaping of 'post-modern' communities of teachers that some commentators assert that computer mediated communication will lead to. Indeed, as Poster (1997) contends, the Internet should really only be seen as extending pre-existing identities and institutions and, therefore, as avowedly modern in the sense that prevailing modern cultures transfer their characteristics to new domains. Certainly throughout this study more 'post-modern' use(s) of the Forum, such as individual's re-invention and reshaping of their identity (Coates 1998), was scarce and perhaps is always going to be in what is essentially a fairly conservative, professional arena. Those seeking for examples of post-modern 'virtual community-building' are best looking elsewhere on the Internet. Nevertheless, on the basis of this preliminary exploration, on-line discussion groups can certainly be seen as offering a fertile but *complementary* arena to real-life communities and networking amongst teaching professionals.

PART V
LESSONS TO BE LEARNT?

Chapter Eleven

The Dilemmas of Critically Researching Technology and Education

Introduction

Given the 'whistle-stop' tour of the previous ten chapters – from primary school to business boardroom and back again – it makes sense to pause for reflection on the process of carrying out such research on education and technology as well as the implications and conclusions that we can draw from doing so. Before we go onto consider the implications of all the preceding research in chapter twelve, this chapter takes some time to reflect on the process of qualitatively researching and reporting on education and technology. In particular it offers a personal account of the ethical dilemmas encountered as a doctoral researcher when adopting a more questioning, qualitative approach to researching (and reporting on) the state of educational computing in UK schools and colleges over the second half of the 1990s.

Having completed a first degree in 1995 where I had first dabbled in educational technology research via a final year dissertation, I found myself in the (some would say enviable, some would say terrifying) position of winning a scholarship to undertake a piece of doctoral research. Committed to designing a research project focusing on educational use of ICT in 16-19 education the need to adopt a more critical approach became quickly apparent (as I have already discussed at the beginning of this book).

On a purely personal level, as I began to feel my way around the relevant literature very little of the optimistic rhetoric therein resonated with my own experiences of educational ICT use. whether in compulsory or post-compulsory settings. Furthermore, the bulk of education technology literature I came across failed to reflect, or even acknowledge, the bleak picture of schools' ICT use as painted by countless 'official' government and Inspectorate reports. I found myself reading numerous accounts of the potential benefits of using 'virtual reality' and 'hypermedia' in the classroom in the same breath as official statistics were telling me that the majority of computers in schools at the time were incapable of running Microsoft Windows – let alone sophisticated multimedia applications. It was from this basis that I began to construct my own research project.

As a nascent 'social scientist' I was keen to move the research project beyond the view that educational computing is distinct from society in either its cause or effect. Instead I made a conscious effort to eschew the positions of either technological determinism or 'techno-neutralism' and move towards a perspective that avoids drawing a 'technology'/'society' distinction and, instead, focused on the *social contexts* where technologies are used. Yet, in doing so I quickly found myself at odds both with the closed culture of educational practice I sought to examine and the academic body of knowledge I ultimately sought to position my findings in; raising a number of unforeseen and unexpected ethical considerations. It is this struggle that the remainder of this chapter reflects on – how I attempted (and often failed) to 'tell tales' on a technology as deified as the computer in education and make my voice(s) heard.

The Research Project: 'The Permeation of Information Technology into 16-19 Education'

My three year doctoral project sought to examine the use of ICT in full-time 16 to 19 education in Welsh schools and colleges (i.e. 'Sixth Form' and 'Further' education spanning Years 12 to 14). Despite the burgeoning significance of the 16-19 sector in the UK, the use of ICT in this phase of education had tended to be overlooked by previous researchers, leaving my project starting from somewhat of an empirical wilderness. Because of this, it was decided to split the project into two distinct phases – an initial 'quantitative' phase to map out a preliminary 'snapshot' of ICT use in the sector which could then be used to inform the second phase of qualitative research – designed to unpack and extend the trends highlighted from the quantitative data. It is this latter phase of qualitative investigation that this chapter will concern itself with.

In particular this chapter shall explore the ethical problems that arose in qualitatively examining such a closed area of education and the subsequent dissemination of findings back to a traditionally 'techno-utopian' educational community. Aside from more 'conventional' ethical problems encountered when carrying out qualitative research in educational settings (see White 2002), an unexpected element of ethical 'ambiguity' was particularly prominent in 'pre' and 'post' data-collection contexts; both in terms of negotiating access to participants and, then, disseminating the findings back to stakeholders.

Gathering the Data

Gaining Access to Institutions and Students

Gaining research access to educational institutions is becoming a notoriously difficult affair. As Troman (1996) observes, schools and teachers are increasingly reluctant to participate in education research projects for a number of wholly understandable reasons, not least their ever-expanding administrative workloads. It was therefore with low expectations that letters of access were drafted to ten local 16-19 institutions in the expectation that, at best, four or five would be amenable to a request for assistance. In the event such worries were unfounded. All but one institution immediately agreed to participate in the research project. In fact, a week after requesting access, this remaining institution was the focus of a national media investigation into the alleged expulsion of low-achieving pupils to increase its performance indicators – in retrospect an unfortunate time for an unknown 'outsider' to be seeking research access.

Aside from this single school, gaining access to the institutions was more akin to the experience of Burgess (1985a) who reported his surprise at being *invited* to carry to out his research in the school with very few hurdles and questions asked. My similar ease of access was quite unexpected and ran contrary to the concurrent experiences of research colleagues with other schools in the same locality. Given my unfamiliarity with all the institutions concerned I could only conclude that it was the focus of the project that seemed to be opening so many doors for me. For these institutions at least, ICT was turning out to be a seductive proposition.

Having been granted initial access by the Senior Management Teams I was then directed further down the institutional hierarchies to more permanent contacts. In all but one case I was steered towards the school or college's ICT co-ordinator – invariably an information technology or mathematics teacher who was charged with the day-to-day running of the technological infrastructure. This would appear to be the logical point of access but, in theory, could have presented a potential barrier for a project primarily focusing on the social and cultural shaping of ICT through-out schools and colleges. Indeed, when trying to research the 'social' aspects of technology a 'fobbing off' of social science researchers is not uncommon with access often restricted to more technical contexts (see Woolgar 1990, Rachel and Woolgar 1995). Although this is often not an overtly conscious or punitive arrangement on the part of the 'researched' – borne more often of an assumption that one is automatically more interested in technical rather than social arrangements – it was an immediate cause of concern for me. What if I was only granted access to the machinations of the ICT department and the closed world of the computer lab? How could I gain access to those who were maybe not engaging with ICT in such an enthusiastic manner? Upon entering the research sites, these concerns soon proved to be as unfounded as any problems of access were earlier.

Indeed, the ICT co-ordinators appeared to be just as enthusiastic as their Headteachers and Principals in assisting the research process, and any concern about my access being limited to strictly ICT-related activities was soon dispelled. During my initial meetings with ICT staff it was continually made clear to me that *anything* I required could be arranged. In this spirit I was regularly offered far more access than I could ever have physically managed. For example, when asking for a batch of 100 questionnaires to be administered to students, individual schools instead demanded on three separate instances that the entire Sixth form should be covered, often 200 or 300 students, and that the school would be more than happy to administer and deliver the completed forms themselves. For an underfunded and overworked single researcher this all seemed too good to be true. Despite all my earlier worries, requests for the qualitative research phase were treated in the same way. When discussing my wish to carry out focus group interviews with around 20 students in the school one ICT co-ordinator offered, in all seriousness:

We can send a mini-bus load of them [students] down to you for an afternoon if you want [Research Diary October 96].

This concept of students as chattels is an interesting one, especially when you consider that the seventeen and eighteen year-old students concerned were under no obligation to attend lessons let alone being transported ten miles into a university department to be 'experimented on'. Nevertheless, although I stopped short of accepting this last offer I was generally mindful of making the most of my unprecedented good fortune.

The expressed motives for this general willingness amongst staff to go well out of their way to help me were manifold. The ICT co-ordinators seemed genuinely pleased that some-one was taking an interest in the school's ICT. The presence of an outside researcher therefore gave the ICT department a legitimacy within the school. Often the research was framed by the co-ordinating teachers in terms of reaffirming the position of ICT with the school hierarchy, particularly with reference to use of the study's findings. On other occasions the research clearly took on a more cathartic function for the ICT staff, serving as a form of 'punishment' on an otherwise un-interested body of students:

Q: *Its not an inconvenient time to be doing this is it?*
T: Yeah ... but its not a problem. It'll serve them right filling this in. They pay bugger all interest to IT when they're here so at least this'll focus their attention on it for a bit. Probably the only time all year [Research Diary March 97].

The notion of research as a form of 'revenge' on pupils was also not one that had occurred to me during the design of the project, but nonetheless teachers sometimes acted in this, sometimes tongue-in-cheek, manner. Throughout the fieldwork period students who were regularly 'supplied' to me who, upon questioning, turned out to be participating under a certain degree of duress – plucked from free lessons under threat of some alternative ICT-related activity or, in the case of vocational students, the promise of a credit on their National Records of Achievement. How much this was genuinely due to a sense of retribution or merely teachers' desire to provide representative numbers to live up to their earlier promises was not clear, but the question of students' free and informed consent was generally not considered to be an issue. Although teachers' 'compulsory' volunteering of students as participants is commonplace (Ball 1985) this inevitably leaves the researcher in an ethical compromise. Although students were always asked once the teacher had left the room if they were indeed happy to participate by then it was often too late, as my power-relation as 'the man from the university' would presumably preclude many from declining.

These concerns aside, now 'in the field' everything appeared to be progressing smoothly. As the fieldwork got underway I had much to be pleased about; extremely easy access into schools, staff who were almost over-zealous in their desire to help and a plentiful, if sometimes ethically dubious, supply of interviewees. However, as I began to collect more data my role as researcher, at least when constructed in the eyes of the participating institutions, began to become more apparent.

Emerging Motivations

Schools and colleges understandably resent being seen as 'research fodder' and more often than not negotiate a 'research bargain' aimed at advantaging them as well as the researcher (Hammersley and Atkinson 1995). As Phtiaka (1994) reiterates, the question of 'what's in it for us?' is now of paramount importance to educational institutions when negotiating participation in research projects and often extends beyond general reports of the research findings to demands for more 'market-sensitive', school-specific feedback. Although this had not been immediately apparent when negotiating access for my research it slowly emerged as the project wore on. In anticipation of the schools demanding some form of 'payback' I had initially made vague illusions to writing up a report of my findings if the schools so requested – deciding to wait upon the weight of demand before finally deciding what form this should take. Despite foreseeing the need for some form of feedback at the end of the project I was soon taken aback by the ferocity of some of the institutions' desire for this privy information and, more importantly, how this eventually shaped their reaction and reading of the data.

Throughout the fieldwork I was constantly approached for reassurance that a report would be forth-coming which would crucially include details of other schools' situations. This, to an extent, reflected the general lack of co-operation between institutions in the area. One ICT Co-ordinator was very keen for me to recount even the basic levels of provision in other schools as he had no legitimate means of discovering himself. My role was clearly reversed in this situation to being *his* 'key informant'. Indeed, in most cases, the desire for knowledge was of a distinctly competitive nature.

As the project progressed schools became more open about their motivations for participating. The more competitive institutions wished to confirm their advantage whilst the less 'well-endowed' wanted 'ammunition' to press their governing bodies for extra investment in ICT. Thus, it was quickly apparent that the recent 'marketisation' of post-16 education had forced institutions to make a commitment to ICT in terms of the educational marketplace and their ability to compete for students. As this college ICT co-ordinator argued;

> One of the things that we're always saying is look, we've got to get our IT facilities sorted. Because when kids come from schools they're going to come from a background where they've got lots of dinky equipment. So the facilities that we've got here in college have got to be at least as good, if not better, than the facilities in schools otherwise it'll be 'why go to [the FE] College? The hardware is out of date. The machines are far too slow'. Its a sexy thing at the moment to have [College ICT Co-ordinator, July 1997].

In response to this I decided that the quantitative section of the reports would include composite data for the school sixth form and college sectors, neatly avoiding any breach of confidentiality between schools. Yet upon presenting the data back to institutions the conditions of my research were quickly defined as much more than was made apparent during the laissez-faire introductory encounters.

Disseminating the Data

Once the fieldwork period was over I had to decide how to disseminate my findings, especially in light of the institutions' explicit wishes for detailed market-driven feedback. Indeed, as Hodkinson and Sparkes (1993, p.125) contend, one of the core ethical problems facing the researcher in this situation is what nature the school-specific feedback should take, in simple terms 'what to feed back to whom'. Seeking a period of grace, I decided to wait until the data had been analysed before arriving at a decision.

It quickly become apparent that, in general terms, the conclusions of the study may not be as positive as some of the institutions had perhaps hoped. The study was reaching several conclusions. Primarily, the level and nature of ICT use in 16-19 education was extremely sporadic and heavily shaped by students' qualification pathways and subject areas. The findings painted an overall picture of educational computing being very much shaped by the cultures and contexts that surround its use with only a restricted sub-culture of 'high-ICT' students and staff making any sustained and extensive use of computers. Moreover, the interview data suggested that the rationales behind students' rejection of educational computing were often more to do with school based factors than an 'inability' or 'deficiency' to use ICT. Although a sizeable minority of students felt unable to use computers effectively, a noticeable number of students also saw ICT as wholly inappropriate to the nature of their work and therefore chose not to use it actively. A further section of students also viewed computers and computer users with a disdain and even stigma which also precluded them using ICT in school and college. On the whole, teaching staff also felt constrained by the pressures of qualification pathways, especially the emphasis throughout the A-level curriculum on the final examination, rather than extraneous 'extra-curricular' activities such as ICT.

So, having successfully completed the supposedly hardest part of the research process (that of gathering the data) the project was faced with a potentially bigger challenge – how was it best to present this critical reading of educational computing to the institutions concerned? As Hodkinson and Sparkes (1993) argue, at the crux of this 'dilemma of dissemination' is what the researcher hopes to achieve by feeding back data to participants. Simply trying to 'tell it like it is' and disowning yourself from any consequences may lead to as many dangers and unethical problems as it seeks to avoid. Yet, in settling on an approach I had to be clear as to *what* the project was trying to achieve: increased equity of access to ICT or improved facilities? Moreover, *who* was the project seeking to empower or aid? The students themselves, their subject teachers, ICT co-ordinator or senior management teams? As Hodkinson and Sparkes (1993, p.127) conclude, 'any such decision predetermines the nature of what we feedback, the way in which it is done and to whom'.

In the end it was decided to produce a short twenty page report summarising the specific quantitative and qualitative data for each institution with the qualitative section taking the form of aggregated student data encompassing five of the recurrent themes of the study: area of study; qualification; gender; access and teaching staff. The use of a report as part of the research bargain is now common practice in educational research (Burgess 1983, Simons 1987) but still raises ethical concern of what to feedback to schools and internal confidentiality. In this way, to preserve the integrity and anonymity of my sources, it also was clear that feedback would have to be restricted to student data as the limited number of staff members interviewed would leave many of them instantly recognisable to their colleagues and senior management (Riddell 1989).

Feeding Back the Reports to ICT Co-ordinators

Throughout the feedback process I was very aware of preserving the 'fragile' and 'provisional' triangle of trust between researcher, senior management and teaching staff (Simons 1989), and aware that, despite their acquiescence with the carrying out of focus-group interviews, many of the ICT co-ordinators may not have necessarily expected a report based on qualitative data. Nevertheless, keen that the students' 'voices' were heard, I persevered.

Upon presentation, all the ICT co-ordinators received the reports eagerly and generally seemed enthusiastic about the broad-level quantitative data. However, upon reaching the interview sections of the reports the mood of some noticeably changed, with the ICT co-ordinators readily accepting the quantitative findings (however damning) but questioning, challenging or dismissing the interview data as 'not representative' and 'just the students' opinion'. In one case, a college ICT co-ordinator dismissed the entire qualitative section because it was raising issues that had 'not been found in the survey'. Thus in some, but not all, cases there was a clear unwillingness to believe students' voices as readily as trust was put in the quantitative data – which in many ways were only cruder summaries of students' opinions and perceptions! The tendency among educators to see quantitative data as providing 'the facts' and, therefore qualitative data as almost irrelevant is well documented (Finch 1985, Burgess 1985b) and, therefore, was not in itself that surprising. However, the subsequent (mis)application of the qualitative findings by the institutions was as telling as the initial disinterest.

Revisiting the research sites a few weeks after the feedback sessions, it was soon apparent that virtually the only finding that the senior management teams and ICT co-ordinators had picked up from the qualitative data was a sub-section of the report on students' complaints concerning lack of teacher awareness of computers. This in itself was only one element of a much larger analysis which highlighted many perceived shortcomings concerning the provision, resourcing and organisation of ICT in the schools as well as a lack of curricular commitment and importance. Yet, despite these many other salient points the one factor constantly focused on was students' views of apparent staff deficiencies. One institution went as far as circulating a leaflet after the project to members of staff proclaiming that 'the one main finding' of my project was a 'lack of skill and knowledge amongst staff' – and thus urging them to attend ICT training sessions. As Phticka (1994) argues, one of the principal disadvantages of offering written feedback is that data may be taken out of context or used for unintended purposes. Nevertheless, the lack of attention paid to the overall qualitative picture was disappointing and at worst distorting the perception of the project among those what had participated. However, such a reaction to the qualitative findings proved to be just a prelude.

Feeding Back to the 'ICT Committee'

One of the most helpful and amenable institutions had asked whether it would be possible for me to address my findings to their newly established 'Information & Learning Technologies' working party – consisting of staff members from across all departments. This was to be an 'informal meeting' after college hours designed to hopefully give the committee 'food-for-thought' for the rest of the term. Despite the slightly foreboding atmosphere the evening started well enough and my initial presentation of the quantitative data was politely received.

However, once the presentation progressed onto the data collected from the interview focus groups then the mood of some of the staff quickly altered. As Jackson (1993) quite rightly asserts, qualitative research is primarily 'conclusion-orientated' rather than 'decision-orientated' and, as such, my presentation of the data was offered with no expectation of directly improving practice or provision. Yet, it was not long before the validity of the interview data was challenged and then most emphatically and from an unexpected source; namely a group of relatively young GNVQ lecturers, including one who had earlier in the fieldwork period talked to me about her MA research project on educational computing and desire to expand this work into a PhD. As the following excerpt from my field notes illustrates, for this particular member of staff, the interview data were not something that could be engaged with:

NS: As you can see from these quotes, some of the students obviously felt this [lack of contact with ICT] was in some way linked to their gender ...
pause for all to begin to read quote
T1: I don't believe you
pause
NS: ... in what way?
T1: Gender's got nothing to do with it. I teach all day long and there's never any problem with the girls using ICT. You didn't watch any of my lessons so how do you know that?
NS: I'm not saying that this is generalisable across *all* classes ... so, how would you explain what these two students are referring to?
T1: They're just making it up or over-exaggerating. It's nothing to do with IT
[Research Diary November 1997]

This incident certainly coloured the rest of the evening and again raised yet again the perennial problem of 'whose side' the educational researcher is 'on' (Becker 1967). Throughout the research I had been at pains not to present myself as any sort of 'ICT expert' but as a researcher who was interested in how students use computers – hoping to be seen in Hammesley and Atkinson's (1995) role of 'acceptable incompetent'. Indeed, for most of the research project I had successfully achieved this. Yet in relaying my findings back to the ICT staff I was thrust into the role of 'unacceptable incompetent' masquerading as 'expert' which was this particular teacher's first line of rebuttal against my data.

A fundamental clash between ICT research and ICT practice is, unfortunately, well-established within the teaching profession. As Clark and Estes (1998, p.5) reflect, there is:

> [an] increasing number of [ICT] colleagues who not only ignore the lack of research evidence to support technology enthusiasm but simply do not trust research ... Much of this distrust comes from a lack of support one finds in the research for people's intuition about the benefits of educational technology. Their reasoning seems to suggest that if research does not find evidence for something that *seems* so powerful, then research as an inquiry strategy *must* be flawed.

However the incredulity and totality of this particular teacher's denial of the data also suggests that it was not just my dubious status that they resented but the inference from the quotes that gender was in fact an issue in ICT use. That the teacher concerned then went on to question the plausibility of the students' opinions itself reflects an unwillingness, perhaps inability, to consider alternative perspectives outside of their own ICT orthodoxy.

Feeding Back to the Academic Community

However, the difficulty I was encountering to persuade people to engage with my qualitative data was by no means confined to educational practitioners. Perhaps the most resistance I encountered was not from the educators themselves but from those in the *academic* education technology community. As the following excepts from one referee's report of a summary paper from the qualitative element of the project exemplify, fellow members of the education computing research community had perhaps the most problems accepting that I or the students who I interviewed were 'right':

> The paper would be immeasurably better if it contained a real debate about the extent to which these data reveal that [education] is inappropriate to a modern age in which social sciences (as well as scientists) use computers as indispensable tools. At present the paper reads like a polemical piece against change of any kind. It makes the author sound rather dinosaur-like!
> [...]
> I think the following findings from the data should be identified and addressed as a matter of grave concern:

the misconception among many of the interviewees about the use of ICT – apparent lack of any awareness that ICT can assist learning in all subjects, and that it is an amazing resource for learning (the web, CD-ROMs etc.)

I can't believe I'm the only ex-English graduate and English teacher who sees some role for ICT in both life and learning. I think the data provides the opportunity for a very interesting paper indeed, but it is not the one that has currently been written

[August 1998]

This extreme academic reaction was not isolated and was generally evident from the more technology-orientated journals rather than the more enthusiastic sociology/policy titles. Another referee in 1998 accused me of using data that was 'obviously' five years out of date judging by the picture of ICT provision I was reporting. At the time of its writing the paper was actually based on data collected four months previously and described a far rosier picture of schools' Internet use than 'official' government statistics would have suggested. Elsewhere, my analysis of interview data 'must' have been flawed and rooted in my own personal misgivings – which could be taken as either a lack of understanding of grounded theory or an accusation of me fabricating data. Or, as the above comments imply, the data merely reflected 'misconceptions' amongst students of school ICT. Again, as with the ICT teaching staff, the underlying response from these quarters of the educational technology academic community was, at best, far from encouraging and seemingly inflamed by the use of qualitative data to tell more critical stories on educational use of ICT.

Discussion

As Hammersley and Atkinson (1995, p.285) contend, although reflexivity is a vital part of qualitative research in the social sciences it is important to retain a sense of limitation:

Some discussions of the ethics of social research seem to be premised on the idea that social researchers can and should act in an ethically superior manner to ordinary people, that they have, or should have, a heightened ethical sensibility and responsibility. There is also a tendency to dramatise matters excessively, implying a level of likely harm or moral transgression that is far in excess of what is typically involved.

Thus it must be borne in mind that discussing the ethics of social research is often little more than discussing the ethics of day-to-day life. All the teachers, ICT co-ordinators and senior managers had jobs to do, external market-driven pressures to respond to and understandably saw me as a legitimate means of helping them do just that. As I have already hinted, this had become quickly apparent at the beginning of the fieldwork period.

In retrospect, it should come as no surprise that the introduction of market forces and open competition into the post-16 sector have increased the symbolic importance of ICT to 16-19 institutions. Kenway (1995, p.52) highlights the growing trend of using technology to market education; after all the idea of 'high-tech sells schools [and] attracts customers'. Thus institutions are increasingly feeling the pressure to be seen as 'high-tech' from a variety of sources, particularly from potential students fresh from experiencing a computer enriched National Curriculum education. As Kingston *et al.* (1992, p.10) continue:

> More and more students will present themselves at colleges at 16-plus having had considerable experience of ICT ... With the increasing emphasis on the 'customer' ... colleges must ensure that both the systems and trained staff are in place to cater for a relatively more demanding clientele coming through from schools.

Thus, the initial ease of gaining access to schools, colleges and students could be seen as part of institutions' on-going need to be seen and confirmed as being 'high-tech'. As Simons (1995) concedes, in these increasingly market-led times one should expect data and findings to be manipulated and selectively treated by both sponsors and participants. In this way, who was actually in control of the research process was unclear. Having entered an ethically ambiguous pact with the institutions to do what I liked with as many students as possible, did I have the right to then feel concerned when crucial elements of what I had found were ignored, refuted or glossed over because they failed to fit into this underlying celebratory agenda?

In many ways I had expected a degree of selectivity, even incredulity, from practitioners when presented with the research findings – after all, one of the first rules of social science research should be to always bear in mind your unimportance in the relation to what you are researching. Nevertheless, the degree of hostility from different quarters of the academic education technology community perhaps took me by more surprise.

Yet on reflection, the whole tenor of this reception to my data could be seen as being indicative of a wider malaise amongst many education computing 'enthusiasts' – namely lack of consideration for any dissenting voices. There is a certain arrogance in suggesting that students who are less than enthusiastic about ICT are 'misconceived', and a myopic determinism in believing that ICT will inevitably 'take over' education. A history of failed educational technologies should serve as a warning against taking this view – yet time after time the same weary predictions and prophecies are used to justify the future ubiquity of something that is presently of minority concern amongst many students and teachers.

ICT may well be permeating society in general, but research consistently has shown that it has failed over the last two decades to take a similar hold in the classroom (e.g. Pelgrum & Plomp 1991, Watson *et al.* 1993, Stevenson 1997). There is a similarly vast body of research which shows that when ICT is used in schools such use is unequal and the preserve of certain students over others (e.g. Sutton 1991, Schofield 1995, Singh 1993). Both these observations were well documented by my own research so, in a sense, I was saying nothing radically new – yet still encountered a 'closed' negative reaction. Instead of blindly ignoring this fact and assuming that ICT will eventually 'come good' it surely would make more sense to try and examine some of the factors underlying this lack of use, rather than dismiss them out of hand.

Nevertheless, at the end of the day, what was there to worry about? My research was warmly academically received outside of the narrow educational technology community. Numerous journal articles were published in more 'scholarly' and 'theoretical' journals which are, in these RAE days of 'hackademia', considered far more 'prestigious' and bankable than the specialist technology journals who were so opposed to the findings. So what if the noses of some 'techies' were put out of joint along the way?

Yet, it is precisely the technologists' resistance to any hint of criticism that leaves an empty, nagging feeling that the research process is, in some way, incomplete. If everyone *but* the subjects of your research are taking notice then you cannot be satisfied by the fruits of your labours. As a social science researcher I did not set out to find, or indeed even want to find, the bleak picture that I did and I certainly would not hope to find it again in ten years time. Yet, I encountered little suggestion or indication from the educational technology community that they were receptive of any (hopefully constructive) criticism.

As ICT becomes more ingrained into educational settings so too will more researchers from a variety of disciplinary backgrounds be attracted to study it. Hopefully this will go some way to further breaking down the present technicist stranglehold. In the meantime those of us already involved with educational computing would do well to heed Bryson and de Castells' (1994, p.217) conclusion:

> The most important job for researchers concerned to understand the scope and limits of the educational uses of technology is to seek out those stories that are not being circulated, to stop *making sense*, to look for educational technology's version of Foucault's *subjugated knowledges* within which the complications, contradictions and complexities of this new educational domain are most likely and most productively to be discerned. For it will most likely be in the *these* tales, we suspect, that radically innovative possibilities for the transformation of hegemonic practices might best be found.

Chapter Twelve

Conclusions

Introduction

Education and learning are messy businesses, drawing on many different influences and party to many shaping factors. Perhaps the main conclusion that should be drawn from the studies described in this book is that, unsurprisingly, educational technology is no different from the rest of education. From this perspective the gulf between the rhetoric and reality of educational technology pervades all the empirical chapters of this book and, therefore, forms a recurring theme to all the examples of educational use of ICT. Yet the role of the academic researcher is more than just throwing stones into small ponds and then running away. Pointing out the inevitable short-comings of practice and policy when set against their rhetorical origins is all very well – but ultimately not a very constructive or fulfilling pastime. In this spirit, and to go some way to addressing the 'so what?' question that all academic researchers inevitably face when examining the social, this concluding chapter attempts to make some sense of the last eleven chapters and offer some pointers for future practice, policymaking and research in the area of education and technology. To do so we first need a consolidation of the pessimistic/optimistic viewpoints that usually beset discussions of technology and society and edge instead towards a realistic perspective of the relationship(s) between education and technology.

A Pessimistic Perspective: Education and Technology as a 'Consensual Hallucination'

To play devil's advocate for one moment, the tales told about technology and education by learners, politicians and business-people throughout this book expose the fact that educational technology is little more than a 'game' for many concerned. This is not to deny that in the short term, for learners, educators, politicians and the IT industry alike, the use of ICT in education is now very important. Yet it could be argued that in the longer term many of the technological developments, ICT-based learning applications, political drives and initiatives are of very little sustained practical consequence at all. It could be concluded that educational technology remains very much as it did before Margaret Thatcher, Kenneth Baker and assorted IT companies began constructing and selling the myth of 'educational computing' and 'information technology' at the beginning of the 1980s. In the final analysis educational technology remains a diverting pastime and 'add-on' to the curriculum for some teachers and learners (as it was for the 'hobbyist' pioneers of the late 1970s) whilst for most in education its impact has been slight.

Of course, although the 'game' may remain the same the stakes have been raised beyond all recognition from the halcyon days of the BBC Micro, and it is here that educational technology has gained its short-term importance and current notoriety. Thus, educational ICT has been seized upon by governments and politicians as a short-term 'fix' for a variety of educational problems and issues. Extensive initiatives such as the National Grid for Learning have been developed which place ICT at the heart of educational policymaking. These initiatives position ICT as an integral part of every teacher's and learner's practice – at least on paper – providing a raft of 'benchmarks' and 'competencies' that must be developed, displayed and assessed. For the IT industry, compulsory and post-compulsory education now represent major and lucrative marketplaces in which to sell their wares. On the face of it educational technology is a major element of education.

Yet throughout the studies that have been presented in this book the disparity between the short-term, rhetorical importance of ICT and the less illustrious realities are all too striking – and it is here that ICT is a 'game' that is currently being played by all in education. As we have seen, in the long term educational technology is perhaps not as important at the 'chalkface' as its supporters would like to believe. Few people appear concerned that there is little evidence that ICT leads to sustained and widespread 'gains' in learning or increased educational 'standards' (however you choose to define these nebulous terms). Few people appear concerned that 'groundbreaking' and 'innovative' initiatives such as the National Grid for Learning have significant conceptual and structural similarities with a host of previous technological initiatives and programmes that failed to make any noticeable or lasting impact throughout the last two decades. Few people appear concerned that for all the bluster of the new ICT-based syllabi and curricula in schools, colleges and universities, for many learners and teachers ICT remains just another 'tick in the box' in a long line of 'core' competencies and key skills that dominate the current educational landscape. Few people appear concerned that the multinational and national IT firms that are currently so visible in the educational marketplace are displaying a less-than public spirited approach to selling their products to learners, parents and school administrators – even less acting in a manner that suggests a long-term commitment to educational technology. Few people appear concerned that computers in the classroom remain 'over-sold and under-used' (Cuban 2001, Reynolds 2002).

From this pessimistic perspective education and technology could therefore be characterised as all style and no substance; as a 'consensual hallucination' (c.f. Gibson 1982) that all stake-holders in education currently feel obliged to espouse the 'benefits' of, spend high-profile amounts of money on and devote more time writing and talking about that actually practising. As Robertson (1998, p.6) argues 'the futuristic associations of multimedia technology appear to have been a substantial attraction to politicians: affordable and accessible [education and] training can be offered in a Millennium wrapper, 'on-demand' and 'on-line''. In other words ICT offers a ready and convenient technological sheen to otherwise insipid educational policymaking. This 'Emperor's New Clothes' thesis can be applied at any levels of education that you choose to examine. As far as many teachers are concerned educational ICT is something that will be of *future* benefit to their students. As far as many students are concerned educational ICT is something that their teachers expect them to do whether it is of benefit to them or not. For many educational 'stakeholders' ICT lends an ephemeral and rhetoric gloss as a 'technical fix' to educational 'problems' as diverse as falling standards, lack of resourcing and inequalities in participation, regardless of the mundane realities.

In this way educational technology is by no means unique. Although longstanding, the use of technological fixes in public life has increased immeasurably with the rise of information technologies. Now, for example, information technologies are being heralded as solutions to a variety of social problems – from increasing political participation via Internet-based voting, to reducing doctors' workloads by making health advice and information available on-line. Vast sums of money are being spent around the world to apply ICT in a variety of settings with the intention of 'improving' society. However, a little consideration shows that reliance on technology as a ready solution to non-technological problems such as those faced in education can be a dangerous stance to adopt. Even if a technology is seen to 'work' it is very difficult to understand why – especially when the application of technology has been accompanied with other non-technological interventions. Technological fixes tend to produce uneven results – very rarely ending in the same outcomes for all of the population – and often merely replace one social problem with another. Technological fixes can also be criticised for only dealing with the surface manifestations of a problem and not its roots. Indeed, social problems are quantitatively and qualitatively different from technical problems. They tend to be less specific with many different causes and do not operate within a closed system like many technological problems. The roots of social problems are social in nature and therefore ultimately require social solutions. This, of course, is a far more difficult, timely, expensive and often imprecise course of action – hence the enduring attraction of the almost instant technological fix.

Thus the over-riding danger of the technological fix in education is that it raises initial expectations among the general public *and* educational community which are often dashed when such 'wonder technologies' do not end up having the desired beneficial effects. This can lead to a cycle of initial hype and eventual disappointment as new technologies are quickly introduced into educational settings, only to fade away whilst social problems continue to persist. In educational terms, the gap between the rhetoric and reality of ICT should come as little surprise.

An Optimistic Perspective: Education and Technology as a Burgeoning Panacea

As was suggested by the subtitle of that last section, such viewpoints are perhaps a touch too pessimistic and even cynical to be of any lasting use. Surely education and technology is not such an open and shut case of political and economic dishonesty? Indeed there have also been indications throughout all the studies outlined in this book of the beneficial effects of educational technology. Although the chapters examining primary school, sixth form and university students highlighted their pragmatic and highly selective use of technology, there *were* examples of students using ICT to extend their capabilities, gain access to resources and information and generally improve their learning processes. Although not a substitute for face-to-face collegiality the teachers using the online SENCo forum in chapter ten *were* on occasion experiencing a virtual form of professional support – sometimes overcoming the limitations of their physical location and individual experience. Also, the adults engaging in ICT-based learning *were* participating in transformative activities – the main limitation of which was that they were the type of people who would have been learning anyway. Leaving such criticisms of social justice aside for one moment, in all these cases technology *could* be said to be having a *positive* impact on some of the learners and educational settings.

Indeed it would be churlish to work as an academic researcher and teacher and claim that ICT has no positive or beneficial role to play in education. In my own teaching the process of presenting many of the issues raised in this book to undergraduate and postgraduate classes is greatly enhanced by using ICT. Moreover, the process of gaining access to and researching educational settings has been greatly enhanced by technology. Interviewing adult learners from America, Sweden and even Liverpool was made immeasurably easier via e-mail and the telephone. Searching for and retrieving all manner of information has been made relatively straightforward via the world-wide web. ICT has had a great impact on my role as a researcher and my role as a teacher. My final analysis is, therefore, not a neo-Luddite one by any means. Any conclusions should be located firmly between the 'pessimistic' and 'optimistic' viewpoints outlined above. Yet any analysis must also consider more than just the 'success' stories and, crucially, must consider all the guiding forces beyond what goes on in the classroom. The chapters covering the political and economic construction of educational technology at the macro level suggest that there are wider forces at play than just the provision of technology in educational settings. Thus I would advocate a wide-reaching analysis of education and technology which draws on all these levels resulting in a picture of technology and education which is never pessimistic or optimistic – merely realistic. Sketching out such an analysis therefore forms the remainder of this chapter.

Towards a Realistic Perspective: Unpacking the Mundane and Messy Realities of Education and Technology

In developing a realistic perspective of education and technology we need to revisit the areas outlined in Chapter Two as forming a broad, balanced and wide perspective of education and technology. In this way we can identify various factors which have recurred throughout this book's examination of education and technology, namely: the technological; the social; the educational; the cultural; the economic; and the political.

Technological Concerns

The most obvious area of contention could be that of the technology itself. Indeed, many people would point towards technological issues as a primary cause of discrepancy between the rhetoric and reality of education in the 'information age'. From a practical perspective even the most cynical commentator would have to admit that there is weight to this argument. Although on paper the concept of developing an ICT-based pedagogy in a primary school classroom sounds attractive, in practice the realities of implementing such ideals entail often insurmountable technical challenges. The sheer technical scope of establishing and operating ICT learning centres in geographically remote or economically deprived communities, developing computer networks in schools which often have far more pressing concerns such as employing teaching staff or repairing decaying buildings, belies the rhetoric of the seamless 'network society' and the provision of 24 hour on-line learning 'anytime, anyplace, anywhere'. As always, technology is not perfect.

The impact of technical shortcomings on technology-based education were amply illustrated throughout the empirical chapters in this book. Yet such problems are often dismissed as 'teething troubles' by educational technologists who are more concerned with looking for the next 'perfect' learning technology rather than the one currently being 'imperfectly' used. This is currently evident in the most recent ICT-based learning initiatives which are being sold around access to learning via third generation mobile telephones; a technology which, at the time of writing this book, has barely moved beyond the prototype stage of development. One likely scenario is that once the technical difficulties of learning and providing learning via mobile telephones are apparent, the technologists, politicians and other interested parties will simply move their attention and efforts onto the 'next big technology' – always chasing a moving target.

This illustrates a weakness of relying wholly on technology as a solution to educational problems. Golding (2000) reasons that there are two types of technology: 'type I' technologies such as the Internet, which have the capability to do things that we could already do before but more quickly and more efficiently; and 'type II' technologies such has the telegraph and bio-technologies which have the capability to radically transform our ability to do things which were previously impossible. Because of the success of type II innovations we are in danger of putting too much faith in type I technologies such as the Internet, digital television and mobile telephony which can only offer to streamline rather than fundamentally transform activities such as education and learning. Illustrating this argument, Toulouse (1998) observes that so-called 'interactive' services via the Internet can only ever be at best participative. Visions of ICT providing learners an individual responsive 'hotline' to new or 'better' forms of learning therefore grossly misrepresent the present-day technology. At best, ICT can offer an 'improved means' to 'unimproved ends':

> [ICT] has not brought about any obvious improvement in the information provided to citizens. Sure, it has brought virtuoso technologies, but these – to paraphrase Thoreau – have led to improved means for unimproved ends (Webster 2000, p.86).

Recognising the Social and 'Educational' Basis of Technology-Based Education

To point solely towards the short-comings of technology is, of course, to overlook many other real issues faced by ICT-based education. As has been highlighted throughout the empirical chapters, the crucial issues of ICT-based education are not just technological – they are social, economic, cultural and political. The 'cyber-guru' Nicholas Negroponte could not have been more misguided in asserting that in the information age 'all that is solid melts into bits'. Although still in its infancy, it is clear that technologists cannot assume that ICT on its own will necessarily lead to 'better' forms of learning and education. For a host of technological *and* non-technological reasons, many learners remain unwilling or unmotivated to participate in ICT-based learning.

Developing our discussion of the non-technological issues, we can identify a host of educational reasons underlying the effectiveness of ICT-based learning primarily that many of these 'new' approaches to learning are faced by established 'old' problems. For example, we have seen how the content of much ICT-based learning could not be described as a genuinely 'new' form of education provision; more a 'pseudo-new' form of learning. There are, for example, very few features of the online courses experienced by our 'virtual' adult learners in chapter nine that could be classed as genuinely 'transformative' or 'revolutionary'. Moreover, those features that could potentially offer interaction with tutors and other learners or provide access to interactive, multimedia resources were, more often than not, conspicuous by their absence in practice. Of course, the term virtual education is 'widely and indiscriminately used around the world' (Jurich 1999, p.35) and should perhaps be seen as nothing more than a contemporary reference to most forms of computer-based distance learning. As Mayes (2000, p.3) argues, for reasons of cost alone the interactive pedagogical opportunities offered by information *and communications* technology are often overlooked by educators, leaving ICT-based pedagogy rooted in more 'old-fashioned' linear and restricted models:

> There are really two pedagogies associated with ICT. One is the delivery of information – this is predominantly the pedagogy of the lecture or book, and emphasises the 'IT' – the other is based on the tutorial dialogue and involves conversations between tutors and

students, and mainly emphasises the 'C'. Of course, successful teaching is underpinned by both – and the rapid interplay of the two is ideal – but in the context of lifelong learning policy the real problem is that 'IT' is cost-effective and the 'C' is not. Unfortunately, in terms of pedagogic effectiveness the second is better than the first.

This point is reinforced by the comments of some of the school, university and adult learners, bemoaning the lack of human and social contact when participating in ICT-based provision. Learners through the Internet and other online resources may feel isolated when presented with the unstructured nature of the data and its sheer quantity. This could be the biggest barrier for on-line learning as the present government envisage it, for as Williams (1999) argues, 'education is a fundamentally conversational business'. It is, or should be, critical and emancipatory rather than about the transfer of information, and of determinate skills. Yet it is the latter which dominates current ICT-based education thinking. As Holmes (1997, p.3) contends:

> The expanding use of the Internet as an imagined means of total knowledge in a globalised world empties out the identity of its participants and, therefore, the 'social' context in which the pursuit of knowledge can be thought of as a shared goal.

ICT should not necessarily be seen as providing *better* educational contexts, but *different* contexts for learning. When discussing the educational application of ICTs we have to weigh up the benefits of increased access to information and artefacts at the cost of the *nature* of this access. As Zuboff (1988, p.376) reasons 'Information technology ... produces a voice that symbolically renders events, objects and processes so that they become visible, knowable and sharable in a new way'. However, should this 'new way' of experiencing events, objects and processes always be treated as an adequate substitute for face-to-face experiences and the other 'social' elements of education?

Education and Technology – a Clash of Cultures?

If ICT can be seen to clash with the social processes of education then it can also be seen to clash with the many educational cultures and sub-cultures that it comes into contact with. As Goodson and Mangan (1995, p. 613) note from a schools perspective, educational technology research has generally lacked 'a developed analysis of the challenge which micro-computers in classrooms may present to the well established cultures and sub-cultures of schools, and in particular to subject sub-cultures'. A noticeable exception to this trend, of course, has been their own work regarding the effects of subject on educational computer use. Here Goodson and Mangan (1995) explore how the computer demands a much more individualised teaching environment than some subjects usually permit; causing an inevitable 'culture clash' between the computer and subject area. They argue that only certain areas of the curriculum, such as Technological studies and Art & Design, have cultures compatible with the pedagogical and organisational changes that computer use dictates. These findings reiterate Eraut (1991, p. 37) who argued that, 'the insertion of a computer rarely affects either the curriculum or normal classroom practice: its use is assimilated to existing pedagogic assumptions'.

Similarly we have seen throughout all the eight empirical chapters of this book that educational technology is not neutral but socially constructed. If these two social constructions overlap then ICT will be readily used by learners. Thus we have seen how learners construct their 'computer identities' very much in terms of the subjects and courses they are following or teaching. These 'computer identities' are obviously shaped by many influencing factors, including an individual's own personal interests (which may or may not include ICT use) and crucially, as has also been highlighted in this book, the structures of curriculum, pedagogy and evaluation (Furlong 1991).

Educational technology could therefore be seen itself as a distinct culture, more congruous with some areas of education and learning environments than others. Paechter (1995) highlights how some staff (and it would seem from the studies in this book students as well) 'retreat' into their subject sub-cultures when faced with another sub-culture to adapt to. In these areas of education therefore, ICT are battling with existing, deep-rooted norms and values whilst in other areas of education they are easily assimilated. Thus, as Schofield (1995) concludes, the pre-existing structures and attitudes that define many educational cultures often prove to be insurmountable obstacles to technological use taking place. For example, in the case of the school and university students in this book, ICT could be seen as being more congruous with some subjects' histories. Computers and other new technologies are more integrated into some subjects' practice than others; both in their development and use. One can see the history of ICT in an area such as Business Studies for example. However, its tradition of use in a subject such as Art and even English is less obvious. As Lave and Wegner (1991, p.101) conclude:

> Participation involving technology is especially significant because the artefacts used within a cultural practice carry a substantial portion of that practice's heritage ... Thus understanding the technology of practice is more than learning to use tools; it is a way to connect with the history of the practice and to participate more directly in its cultural life.

Recognising the 'Economic Imperative' of ICT and Education

Yet educational and technological processes alone do not account for the whole story of education and technology. As we saw in chapters three, four and five the political and economic foundations of educational technology also exert a telling influence on its eventual use and effectiveness at the level of the learner and classroom. Indeed, from the evidence presented in the first three empirical chapters, if governments and policymakers seem to believe in any long-term effectiveness of ICT in education it is in terms of using educational technology as a delayed means of increasing economic competitiveness. Thus underpinning most if not all of the educational technology policies over the last twenty years has been a powerful rhetoric regarding the use of technology-based learning to re-skill and up-skill the workforce and increase the country's economic competitiveness. This perceived economic function of educational technology could be seen as pervading and over-riding all others. For example, beyond broad statements regarding the 'digital divide' in education, it is clear that the present lifelong learning agenda is almost exclusively economically focused in practice, and that any concern with the socially excluded can be more accurately seen as a concern with the economically excluded (Bynner 1998, Tight 1998).

The effects of this economic component to technology and education can also be extended to the role of private sector interests in the public concern of education. Indeed ICT-based education is proving to be big business around the world. In the USA alone, it is predicted that over two million students are taking online courses as part of a world-wide online learning marketplace expected to be worth US$50billion by 2005 (Dumort 2000). With multinational corporations such as Microsoft beginning to become actively involved in such programmes, ICT-based education does not look set to fade away quietly just because it may not be fulfilling its societally inclusive or educational aims.

Developing Realistic Expectations of Policy and Practice

Given all these factors it is obvious we need to rethink that way that ICT is approached by both politicians and practitioners if it is to be effectively integrated and used in education. Above all there is a need to move beyond the short-termist reliance on the rhetoric of ICT as a technical fix and the associated continual cycle of 'hype' and 'disappointment' that accompanies it. The need for a more measured and realistic approach is more urgent than ever as too much time, effort and resourcing has already been invested in ICT-based learning for future governments of any political persuasion to deviate substantially from the approaches described throughout the book. Indeed, whilst the New Labour government regularly proclaim their new ICT policies to be 'breaking new ground' (Blair 2000) we have seen in chapter three that the political predilection for using ICT as primary means of establishing a learning society was set as far back as the first term of the Thatcher government.

Thus if ICT *is* to be successfully and effectively used for educational purposes in the twenty-first century then it is essential that the myth of omnipotent teaching and learning technologies is challenged by those within the educational community and ICTs are (re)constructed and (re)contextualised along more appropriate and realistic lines. Of course, such a recontextualisation of technology will undoubtedly be a difficult process. As with many instances of innovation and change, the educational community has demonstrated a willingness towards 'historical amnesia' when it has come to educational technology. Nevertheless, if the myth (and associated expectations) of the omnipotent 'educational' computer can themselves be reconstructed in the minds of politicians, practitioners and parents towards a more realistic vision of what ICTs can *and cannot* do for education, then it may yet be possible for technology to play a widespread and sustainable role in learning (Gold 2002, Smith 2002). Until then, the legacy of the 1980s discursive shaping of 'IT' looks set to continue to blight the societal use and expectations of 'educational' technology for years to come.

Such a change in the mindset of politicians and practitioners will be by no means an easy task as the last three decades have left many people convinced of the centrality of the computer to society's lurch into the twenty-first century. Yet we have seen how such promises have not been translated into effective policies. This suggests a radical rethink of the political approach to ICT and education. There is a danger in seeing ICT as a single solution to all educational problems. Instead technological initiatives and interventions should be seen as complementing rather than replacing other 'conventional' forms of education policymaking and practice. In policy terms ICT needs to be afforded a more realistic billing than its current over-inflated prominence.

From this basis it can be argued that the practice of using ICT should be changed. In practice ICT should be made as *accessible* and *easy* as possible for all learners (and teachers) to use. As Wenger (1990) theorises, for technology to be used effectively in a learning process it must be *transparent* to learners; an epistemological role which is 'intricately tied to the cultural practice and social organisation within which the technology is meant to function' (p.102). Therefore, for ICTs to be successfully used in educational settings their significance as effective learning tools must be highly *visible*, whilst simultaneously their role as mediating technologies supporting visibility of the subject matter must be highly *invisible*. Without a good balance between these two interacting requirements effective use of the computer cannot, and will not, take place. But in 'technology resistant' areas of education the role of transparency is reversed. ICTs are highly visible as mediating technologies (thus getting in the way of the process of learning when used) and highly invisible as learning tools (hidden away/ given no prominence in pedagogy of department). Here, the focus is very much on the technology, not the education.

At the individual level, adoption of instructional innovation depends on a number of factors: *congruence* (how easily the changes fit in with existing practice); *cost* (estimates of the needed extra time and effort needed to implement the innovation); as well as individuals' perception of *importance* and *difficulty* of implementing innovations (Ghaith and Yaghi 1997). Similarly, educational managers and facilitators can strive to foster a culture of ICT use throughout all areas of educational organisations. Dunlap and Goldman (1991) highlight the role of 'facilitative' leadership; with an emphasis on articulation of vision, provision of resources, conflict resolution, team building and co-ordinated feedback. In practical terms educational institutions should therefore strive to manipulate both the formal organisation and symbolic cultural intent of the institution and adopt a strong 'value' system of ICT use.

It is clear from the studies in this book that the reasons for the huge variations in use of educational technology are varied, but that the influence of educational cultures and processes of 'doing' education are highly salient in determining both students' and teachers' use of educational technologies. Although, as Goodson and Mangan (1995) hypothesise, these effects may soften as ICTs become more established in educational settings, it is unlikely that technology will ever be totally integrated into every area of education. Nevertheless, awareness of the reasons underlying these different reactions to ICT will help to reduce the 'clash' between education and technology.

Developing a Realistic Research Agenda on Technology and Education

We need now to finally consider how academic research into ICT and education can be advanced over the next decade. Here in particular, we need to resist and reject the recently mounting political pressure on educationalists to 'prove' technology's worth after the last twenty years of apparently ineffectual use. For example, there have been growing calls in the UK from central government for educational research to 'prove once and for all' the cognitive benefits of ICT use for the learner. More worryingly, there are as equally as coercive calls from the Department for Education and Skills for teachers to use ICT to raise educational standards and levels of achievement or face obsolescence in the 'modern' teaching profession. It is a worrying and ultimately fruitless trend for researchers and educators to be cowed into adopting this approach and respond to political pressure to affirm that ICT does somehow lead to unproblematic advantages in the classroom. Instead what we need above all is research that engages with the messiness of educational technology and 'tells it like it is' – further exploring all the themes touched upon in this book.

However there is a real concern that a desire for realistic, objective and careful research is being pushed to the sidelines as the Department for Education and Skills and other quasi-governmental bodies exert an increasing influence on the ICT research agenda in the UK. There is now an explicit and implicit emphasis towards 'proving' that ICT effects school processes and providing relevance to ICT-using practitioners. Worryingly educational technology researchers are all too often proving to be happy to work within such confines, which often coincide with their own biases, beliefs and ultimate faith in the 'value' of educational technology. Yet, as has just been contended, we need research which engages with the messy realities of technology and education without any preconceptions that what will be found will be 'good', 'bad' or even 'indifferent'. The danger is that the current education research climate is so charged and the stakes for funding success are so high that any concern with accuracy and impartiality will be discarded in the endless stampede to affirm what many people have 'known all along' about technology and education. Yet, as Gorard (2001) reminds us, producing 'research' which is nothing more than a thinly disguised endorsement for a personal belief in the benefits of technology in education is not what social science research is about:

> Surely, unless researchers can greet all possible outcomes of their empirical investigations with at least equal respect, and they are prepared to be surprised by what they find, and they apply the same standards of rigour to other people's work regardless of whether the approve of the findings or not, then they are not behaving as researchers but as political agents .... Some 'researchers' explicitly advocate taking sides *before*

collecting the necessary empirical evidence. But the researcher cannot afford to 'take sides' with anything but the truth. When a researcher has an agenda this should make no difference to the research ... Research cannot be simply subordinated to the needs of policy-makers and political agitators without being in danger of becoming contract 'research' which may be used to justify already-prepared programmes of action (to benefit either the government or a political pressure group).

Indeed, the over-riding message from the studies in this book should be that educationalists have no right to expect the accounts of learners, teachers and other stake-holders in education to correspond with their own notion of what is 'correct' or indeed what is deemed as acceptable in the wider educational technology field. To the contrary, as Bryson and de Castell (1994) argue, there is every need for researchers and teachers to become privy to peoples' real-life understandings of education and technology in order to make sense of the actual public practices and outcomes which are manifest. To ignore this is to negate the entire practice of objective qualitative research and instead attempt to impose a contradictory and dogmatic technicist regime onto the realities of education. Instead, as Bryson and de Castells (1994, p.216) again point out:

> There is *no* 'master narrative' to be found or made in educational discourses about educational computing. There is no *true story*, no *grand synthesis*. There is instead a *set* of stories, each with its distinctive scope and limits, each of which imposes, in different ways, a different system of constraints, prescriptives and prohibitions, a different set of limit situations defining the boundaries beyond which teachers and learners cannot go.

If nothing else I hope that the studies in the book have helped to contribute to muddying the waters of educational technology research a little bit more. The further that we can move away from the master narrative of an all-conquering 'educational technology' towards a recognition and understanding of the inconclusive and messy nature of ICT-based education the better. There are many good, bad and indifferent tales that need to be told about technology – we should not feel guilty in telling them.

Bibliography

Abbott, C. (2001) *'ICT: changing education'* London, Routledge/Falmer
Adams, J. (1982) 'The BBC literacy project is launched' *Educational Computing*, January 1982, p.21
Adamson, I. and Kennedy, R. (1986) *'Sinclair and the sunrise technologies'* London, Penguin
Agalianos, A. (2001) 'Logo in mainstream schools: the struggle over the soul of an educational innovation' *British Journal of Sociology of Education*, vol. 22, no. 4, pp.479-500
Alstyne, M. (1997) 'Higher education's information challenge' *Executive Strategies*, vol. 2, no. 4, pp.1-14
Anderson, B. (1983) *'Imagined communities'* London, Verso
Anderson, R. and Ronnkvist, A. (1999) *'The presence of computers in American schools'* California, Centre for Research on Information Technology and Organisations
Apple, M. (1979) *'Ideology and curriculum'* London, Routledge and Kegan Paul
Apple, M. (1987) 'Teaching and technology: the hidden effects of computers on students and teachers' *Journal of Education Policy*, vol. 1, no. 1, pp.135-157
Apple, M. (1992) 'Constructing the captive audience: Channel One and the political economy of the text' *International Studies in Sociology of Education*, vol. 2, no. 2, pp.107-131
Apple, M. (1997) 'The new technology: is it part of the solution or part of the problem in education?' in Hawisher, G.E. and Selfe, C. (Eds) *'Literacy, technology and society: confronting the issues'* New Jersey, Prentice Hall
Apple, M. and Jungk, S. (1990) 'You don't have to be a teacher to teach this unit: teaching, technology and gender in the classroom' *American Educational Research Journal*, vol. 27, pp.227-251
Arnold, M. (1999) 'Mainstreaming the digital revolution' *Higher Education Quarterly*, 53, 1, pp.49-64
Baker, K. (1993) *'The turbulent years: my life in politics'* London, Faber & Faber
Bakkenes, I., de Brabander, C. and Imants, J. (1999) 'Teacher isolation and communication network analysis in primary schools' *Educational Administration Quarterly*, vol. 35, no. 2, pp.166-202
Ball, S. (1985) 'Participant observation with pupils' in Burgess, R.G. (Ed.) *'Strategies of educational research'* Lewes, Falmer
Ball, S. (1999) 'Labour, learning and the economy: a "policy sociology" perspective' *Cambridge Journal of Education*, vol. 29, no. 2, pp.195-206
Ball, S. and Bowe, R. (1992) 'Subject departments and the "implementation" of National Curriculum policy: an overview of the issues' *Journal of Curriculum Studies*, vol. 24, no. 2, pp. 97-115
Bannister, N. (1998) 'IT firms set to net schools profits' *The Guardian*, 30th November, p.18
Barber, M. (1998) 'The future is now on the internet' *Times Educational Supplement*, 2nd October, p.21
Barber, M. (1999) 'Why it is smart to be well-connected' *Times Educational Supplement*, 4th June, p.21

Bardini T. and Horvath A. (1995) 'The social construction of the personal-computer user' *Journal of Communication*, vol. 45, no. 3, pp.40-65

Barthes, R. (1973) *'Mythologies'* London, Paladin

Baudrillard, J. (1997) 'Objects, images and the possibilities of aesthetic illusion' in Zurbrugg, N. (Ed.) *'Jean Baudrillard: art and artefact'* London, Sage

Becker, H. (1967) 'Whose side are we on?' *Social Problems*, vol. 14, no. 3, pp.329-347

Bell, D. (1973) *'The coming of post-industrial society: a venture in social forecasting'* New York, Basic

Bennett, F. (1999) 'Education and the future' *Educational Technology & Society* vol. 2, no. 1, [http://ifets.ieee.org/periodical/vol_1_99/fbennett_short_article.html]

Bennett, R. (1995) 'School-business links: clarifying objectives and processes' *Policy Studies*, vol. 16, vol. 1, pp.23-48

Berdayes LC and Berdayes V (1998) 'The information highway in contemporary magazine narrative' *Journal of Communication*, vol. 48, no. 2, pp. 109-124

Besser, H. (1995) 'From internet to information superhighway' in Brook, J. and Boal, I.A. (Eds) *'Resisting the virtual life: the culture and politics of information'* San Francisco, City Lights

Beynon, J. and Mackay, H. (1989) 'Information technology into education: towards a critical perspective' *Journal of Education Policy* vol. 4, no. 3, pp 245-257

Bigum, C. (1997) 'Teachers and computers: in control or being controlled?' *Australian Journal of Education*, vol. 41, no. 3, pp.247-261

Bigum, C. (1998) 'Solutions in search of educational problems: speaking for computers in schools' *Educational Policy*, vol. 12, no. 5, pp.586-601

Birch, D. (1998) 'Communication policy in Asia: limited democracy and the public sphere' *Media International Australia*, vol. 86, pp.87-102

Blair, A. (2000) *'Speech at the knowledge 2000 conference'* March 7th 2000, [http://www.number-10.gov.uk]

Blomeyer, R. (1993) 'A case study of microcomputers in art education' in Beynon, J. and Mackay, H. (Eds) *'Computers in the classroom: more questions than answers'* London, Falmer

Blunkett, D. (1997) 'On the starting grid' *Educational Computing and Technology*, December 1997, pp.11-12

Boud, D. (1995) 'Assessment and learning: contradictory or complementary?' in Knight, P. (Ed.) *'Assessment for learning in higher education'* London, Kogan Page

Bower, M. (1999) 'Half of all primaries let pupils down on IT' *Western Mail*, 15th March 1999, p.16

Bowles, S. and Gintis, H. (1976) *'Schooling in capitalist America'* London, Routledge and Kegan Paul

Boyd-Barrett, O. (1990) 'Schools' computing policy as state-directed innovation' *Educational Studies*, vol. 16, no. 2, pp. 169-185

Boyson, R. (1981) 'Computers the key' *Times Higher Education Supplement*, 13th March 1981, p.3

Breivik, P. (1998) *'Student learning in the information age'* Phoenix, Oryz Press

British Education Communications & Technology Agency. (1999) *'Making the most of the National Grid for Learning: an introduction to the National Grid for Learning'* Coventry, BECTa

Bromley, H. (1992) 'Culture, power and educational computing' in Bigum, C. and Green, C. (Eds) *'Understanding new information technologies in education'* Geelong, Deakin University Press

Bromley, H. (1995) *'Engendering technology: the social practice of educational computing'* Unpublished PhD Thesis, University of Wisconsin, Madison

Bromley, H. (1997) 'The social chicken and the technological egg: educational computing and the technology/ society divide' *Educational Theory*, vol. 47, no. 1, pp. 51-65

Bronwell, C. and Eison, J. (1991) *'Active learning: creating excitement in the classroom'* ASHE-ERIC Higher Education Report #1, The George Washington University, Washington DC

Brosnan, M. (1997) 'The fourth 'R': are teachers hindering computer literacy in school children?' *BPS Education Section Review*, vol. 21, no. 1, pp.29-38

Bryson, M. and de Castell, S. (1994) 'telling tales out of school: modernist, critical and post-modern "true stories" about educational computing' *Journal of Educational Computing Research*, vol. 10, no. 3, pp.199-221

Bryson, M and de Castell, S (1998) 'New technologies and the cultural ecology of primary schooling: imagining teachers as luddites in/deed' *Educational Policy*, vol. 12, no. 5, pp.542-567.

Buckingham, D. (1999) 'Superhighway or road to nowhere? children's relationships with digital technology' *English in Education*, vol. 33, no. 1, pp.3-12

Buckingham, D. (2000) *'After the death of childhood: growing up in the age of electronic media'* Cambridge, Policy

Buckingham, D. and McFarlene, A. (2001) *'A digitally driven curriculum'* London, Institute for Public Policy Research

Bunting, C. (1999) 'Retailers log-on to profit in education' *Times Educational Supplement*, 7th May, p.18

Burgess, R. (1983) *'Experiencing comprehensive education: a study of Bishop McGregor school'* London, Methuen

Burgess, R. (1985a) *'Field methods in the study of education'* Lewes, Falmer

Burgess, R. (1985b) *'Strategies of educational research'* Lewes, Falmer

Burgess, R. (1989) 'Something you learn to live with? gender and inequality in a comprehensive school' *Gender and Education*, vol. 1, no. 2, pp.155-164

Burkhalter, B. (1999) 'Reading race online: discovering racial identity in usenet discussions' in Smith, M.A. and Kollock, P. (Eds) *'Communities in cyberspace'* London, Routledge

Bush, C. (1997) 'Women and the assessment of technology' in Teich, A.H. (Ed.) *'Technology and the future'* (Seventh Edition) New York, St. Martin's Press

Bynner, J. (1990) 'Education and training: provision and training' *British Journal of Education and Work*, vol. 3, no. 2, pp. 5-11

Bynner, J. (1998) 'Youth in the information society: problems, prospects and research directions' *Journal of Education Policy*, vol. 13, no. 3, pp.433-442

Carey, S. (1985) *'Conceptual change in childhood'* Cambridge MA, MIT Press

Carr, A., Jonassen, D., Litzinger, M. and Marra, R. (1998) 'Good ideas to foment educational revolution: the role of systemic change in advancing situated learning, constructivism and feminist pedagogy' *Educational Technology*, vol. 38, no. 1, pp.5-15

Castells, M. (1989) *'The informational city'* London, Blackwell

Castells, M. (1996) *'The information age: economy, society and culture. volume I - the rise of the network society'* Oxford, Blackwell

Castells, M. (1997) *'The information age: economy, society and culture. volume II - end of millennium'* London, Blackwell

Chalkley, T. and Nicholas, D. (1997) 'Teachers' use of information technology: observations of primary school classroom practice' *ASLIB Proceedings*, vol. 49, no. 4, pp.97-107

Chia, J. and Duthie, B. (1994) 'Computer-based art learning: primary children's responses' *Computers and Education*, vol. 23, no. 3, pp.197-209

Clark, R. and Estes, F. (1998) 'Technology or craft: what are we doing?' *Educational Technology*, vol. 38, no. 5, pp.5-11

Clinton, W. (1998) 'Education is the global priority' Speech to the *Education World Congress*, Washington - reprinted in *The Independent*, Section 2, 6th August, p.4

Coates, G. (1998) 'Chat rooms and the art of being there while somewhere else' paper presented to the *British Sociological Association Annual Conference*, Edinburgh

Coen, D. (1998) 'The european business interest and the nation state: large-firm lobbying in the european union and member states' *Journal of Public Policy*, vol. 18, pp.75-100

Cole, G. (2002) 'Digital dilemma' *The Guardian*, 8th January 2002, pp.2-3

Confederation of British Industry (1989) '*Towards a skills revolution: report of the vocational education and training task force*' London, CBI

Connidis, I. (1983) 'Integrating qualitative and quantitative methods in survey research on ageing: an assessment' *Qualitative Sociology*, vol. 6, no. 4, pp.334-352

Connolley, P. (1997) 'In search of authenticity: researching young children's perspectives' in Pollard, A., Thiessen, D. and Filer, A. (Eds) '*Children and their curriculum: the perspectives of primary and elementary school children*' London, Falmer

Cryer, P. (1998) 'Transferable skills, marketability and lifelong learning' *Studies in Higher Education*, vol. 23, no. 3, pp.207-217

Cuban, L. (1986) '*Teachers and machines: the classroom use of technology since 1920*' New York, Teachers College Press

Cuban, L. (2001) '*Computers in the classroom: oversold and underused*' Cambridge MA, MIT Press

Cubitt, S. (1998) '*Digital aesthetics*' London, Sage

Dale, R. (1977) '*The structural context of teaching*' Milton Keynes, Open University Press

Dale, R. (1989) '*The state and education policy*' Milton Keynes, Open University Press

Davis, A. (1994) '*Telecommunications and politics*' London, Pinter

Davis, F. (1993) 'User acceptance of information technology: system characteristics, user perceptions and behavioural impacts' *International Journal of Man-Machine Studies*. vol. 38, pp. 475-487

de Vaney, C. (1998) 'Will educators ever unmask that determiner, technology?' *Educational Policy*, vol. 12, no. 5, pp.568-585

Dearing, R. (1993) '*The National Curriculum and its assessment*' London, Schools Examinations and Assessment Council

Dearing, R. (1996) 'The review of qualifications for 16-19 year olds' Summary report. London, SCAA Publications

Dearing, R. (1997) 'Higher education in the learning society - report of the national committee into higher education' London, HMSO

Denzin, N. (1978) '*Sociological methods: a sourcebook*' (2nd Ed.) New York, McGraw Hill

Department for Education (1994) '*Code of practice on the identification and assessment of special educational needs*' London, HMSO

Department for Education and Employment (1995) '*Superhighways for education: the way forward*' London, HMSO

Department for Education and Employment (1997a) '*Connecting the learning society*' London, Stationery Office

Department for Education and Employment (1997b) '*Excellence in schools*' London, Stationery Office

Department for Education and Employment (1997c) '*Survey of information technology in schools*' Statistical Bulletin 6/97

Department for Education and Employment (1997d) '*Qualifying for success*' London, Stationery Office

Department for Education and Employment (1998a) '*Open for learning, open for business: the government's NGfL challenge*' London, Stationery Office

Department for Education and Employment (1998b) 'Information and communication technology key to getting europe back to work' *Press Release 204/98* London, DfEE

Department for Education and Employment (1998c) 'Blunkett announces details of biggest ever investment in schools information and communication technology' *Press Release 184/98* London, DfEE

Department for Education and Employment (1998d) '*Numeracy matters: the preliminary report of the numeracy task force*' London, Stationary Office

Department for Education and Employment (1998e) 'Blackstone announces A-Level improvements' *Press Release 170/98* London, DfEE

Department for Education and Employment (1998f) '*The learning age: a renaissance for a new Britain*' London, Stationery Office

Department for Education and Employment (1999) '*Survey of information technology in schools: statistical first release 13/99*' London, DfEE

Department for Education and Employment (2001a) 'Wills welcomes OfSTED report on impact of government ICT initiative in schools' *Press Notice 2001/0255* London, DfEE

Department for Education and Employment (2001b) 'Digital TV and the internet to help pupils tackle pythagoras and boost GCSE standards' *Press Notice 2001/0190* London, DfEE

Department of Education and Science [DES] (1987) '*New technology for better schools*' London, Department of Education and Science

Department for Education and Skills [DfES] (2001a) 'Virtually all schools are now connected to the internet' *Press Notice 2001/0334* London, DfES

Department for Education and Skills (2001b) 'Survey of information and communications technology in schools 2001' London, DfES

Devon, R. (1987) 'In praise of computer illiteracy' *Bulletin of Science, Technology & Society*, vol. 7, pp.338-343

Dodorico, L. and Zammuner, V.L. (1993) 'The influence of using a word processor on children's story writing' *European Journal of Psychology of Education*, vol. 8, no. 1, pp.51-64

Donath, J.S. (1999) 'Identity and deception in the virtual community' in Smith, M.A. and Kollock, P. (Eds) '*Communities in Cyberspace*' London, Routledge

Doring, A. (1999) 'Information overload?' *Adults Learning*, vol. 10, no. 10, pp.8-10

Downey, J. (1999) 'XS 4 all? "information society" policy and practice in the european union' in Downey, J. and McGuigan, J. (Eds.) '*Technocities*' London, Sage

Dumort, A. (2000) 'New media and distance education: an EU-US perspective' *Information, Communication & Society*, vol. 3, no. 4, 546-556

Dunlap, D. & Goldman, P. (1991) 'Rethinking power in schools' *Educational Administration Quarterly*, vol. 27, no. 1, pp.5-29

Durndell, A. and Thomson, K. (1997) 'Gender and computing: a decade of change?' *Computers and Education*, vol. 28, no. 1, pp. 1-10

Dyson, E. (1998) '*Release 2.1: a design for living in the digital age*' London, Penguin

Education Week (1999) '*Education inc: the business of schooling*' Special reports, November/December 1999 [www.edweek.com/sreports/business]

Edwards, A. (1983) 'The re-construction of post-compulsory education and training in england and wales' *European Journal of Education*, vol. 18, no. 1, pp.7-20

Eraut, M. (1991) '*The information society - a challenge for education policies? policy options and implementations strategies*' London, Cassell

Ergas, H. (1987) 'Does technology policy matter?' in Guile, B. and Brooks, H. (Eds) *'Technology and global industry: companies and nations in the world economy'* Washington DC., National Academy Press

Erickson, F. (1987) 'Conceptions of school culture: an overview' *Educational Administration Quarterly*, vol. 23, no. 4, pp. 11-24

Esland, G. (1991) *'Educated labour: the changing basis of industrial demand'* Wokingham, Addison-Wesley

Evans, C. (1979) *'The mighty micro: the impact of the micro-chip revolution'* London, Coronet

Feenberg, A. (1984) 'Utopia and dystopia' on-line Seminar conducted for the Western Behavioural Sciences Institute, June 1984 cited in Levinson, P. (1997) *'The soft edge: a natural history and future of the information revolution'* London, Routledge

Feenberg, A. (1995) *'Alternative modernity: the technical turn in philosophy and social theory'* Berkeley, University of California Press

Finch, J. (1985) 'Social policy and evaluation: problems and possibilities of using qualitative research' in Burgess, R.G. (Ed.) *'Issues in educational research: qualitative methods'* Lewes, Falmer

Flores, J. and Alonso, C. (1995) 'Using focus groups in educational research' *Evaluation Review*, vol. 19, no.1, pp.84-101

Foster, D. (1996) 'Community and identity in the electronic village' in Porter, D. (Ed.) *'Internet Culture'* London, Routledge

Fowler, G. (1989) 'In Defence of A-levels' *Education and Training* November 1989, pp.3-4

Fransman, M. (1990) *'The market and beyond: co-operation and competition in information technology in the Japanese system'* Cambridge University Press, Cambridge

Fuller, S. (1998) 'Why even scholars don't get a free lunch in cyberspace' in Loader, B.H. (Ed.) *'Cyberspace divide: equality, agency and policy in the information society'* London, Routledge

Furlong, J. (1991) 'Disaffected pupils: reconstructing the sociological perspective' *British Journal of Sociology of Education*, vol. 12, no. 3, pp. 293-307.

Furlong, J., Furlong, R., Facer, K. and Sutherland, R. (2000) 'The National Grid for Learning: a curriculum without walls' *Cambridge Journal of Education*, vol. 30, no.1, pp.91-110

Garfield, M. and Watson, R. (1998) 'Differences in national information infrastructures: the reflection of national cultures' *Journal of Strategic Information Systems*, vol. 6, pp.313-337

Gates, W. with Myhrvold, N. and Rinearson, P. (1995) *'The road ahead'* London, Penguin

Gell, M. and Cochrane, P. (1996) 'Learning and education in an information society' in Dutton, W. (Ed.) *'Information and communication technologies: visions and realities'* Oxford, Oxford University Press.

Ghaith, G. and Yaghi, H. (1997) 'Relationships among experience, teacher efficacy and attitudes toward the implementation of instructional innovation' *Teaching and Teacher Education*, 13, 4, pp. 451-458

Gibbs, G. (1999) 'Using assessment strategically to change the way that students learn' in Brown, S. and Glasner, A. (Eds) *'Assessment matters in higher education'* Buckingham, Open University Press

Giddens, A. (1998) *'The third way: the renewal of social democracy'* Cambridge, Polity

Glaser, B. and Strauss, L. (1967) *'The discovery of grounded theory: strategies for qualitative research'* Chicago, Aldine

Goffman, E. (1959) *'The presentation of self in everyday life'* New York, Doubleday

Golby, M. (1996) 'Teachers' emotions: an illustrated discussion' *Cambridge Journal of Education*, vol. 26, no,3. pp.423-434

Gold, K. (2002) 'Vision of the future at an e-school' *The Sunday Times*, 20th January 2002, Section 4, p.10

Golding, P. (2000) 'Forthcoming features: information and communications technologies and the sociology of the future' *Sociology*, vol. 34, no. 1, pp.165-184

Goodson, I. and Hargreaves, A. (Eds) (1996) *'Teachers' professional lives'* London, Falmer

Goodson, I. and Mangan, J. (1995) 'Subject cultures and the introduction of classroom computers' *British Educational Research Journal*, vol. 21, no. 5, pp. 613-628

Gorard, S. (2001) 'A changing climate for educational research? The role of research capability-building' presentation to the *British Educational Research Association Annual conference*, 13-15th September 2001 University of Leeds

Gorard, S. (1998a) 'Four errors.... and a conspiracy? The effectiveness of schools in Wales' *Oxford Review of Education* vol. 24, no. 4, pp. 459-472

Gorard, S. (1998b) 'Schooled to fail? Revisiting the Welsh school-effect' *Journal of Education Policy* vol. 13, no. 1, pp.115-124

Graham, G. (1999) *'The internet: a philosophical inquiry'* London, Routledge

Green, A. (1997) 'Core skills, general education and unification in post-16 education' in Hodgson, A. and Spours, K. (Eds) *'Dearing and beyond: 14-19 qualifications, frameworks and systems'* London, Kogan Page

Green, B. and Bigum, C. (1993) 'Aliens in the classroom' *Australian Journal of Education*, vol. 37, no. 2, pp.119-141

Green, J. (1997) 'Risk and the construction of social identity: children's talk about accidents' *Sociology of Health & Illness*, vol. 19, pp.14-21

Gregorian, V. (1996) 'Technology, scholarship and the humanities: the implications of electronic information' in Kling, R. (Ed.) *'Computerisation and Controversy: Value Conflicts and Social Choices'* San Diego, Academic Press

Griffiths, M. (1997) 'Internet "addiction": an issue for clinical psychology?' *Clinical Psychology Forum*, vol. 97, pp.32-36

Griffiths, M. (1999) 'Internet addiction: fact or fiction?' *The Psychologist*, vol. 12, no. 5, pp.246-250

Grint, K. and Woolgar, S. (1997) *'The machine at work: technology, work and organisation'* Cambridge, Polity

Haddon, L. (1988) 'The home computer: the making of the consumer electronic' *Science as Culture*, vol. 2, pp.7-51

Halsall, R. (1996) 'Core skills - the continuing debate' in Halsall, R. and Cockett, M. (Eds.) *'Education and training 14-19: chaos or coherence?'* London, David Fulton

Hamilton, R. (1995) 'Despite best intentions: the evolution of the british minicomputer industry' *Business History*, vol. 38, no. 2, pp.81-104

Hammersley, M. (1984) 'Staffroom news' in Hargreaves, A. and Woods, P. (Eds) *'Classrooms and staffrooms: the sociology of teachers and teaching'* Milton Keynes, Open University Press

Hammersley, M. and Atkinson, P. (1995) *'Ethnography: principles in practice'* (Second Edition) London, Routledge

Hargreaves, A. (1982) 'Cultures of teaching' in Hargreaves, A. and Fullan, M. (Eds) *'Understanding teacher development'* London, Cassell

Hargreaves, A. (1994) *'Changing teachers, changing times: teachers' work and culture in the post-modern age'* London, Cassell

Harvey, L (Ed.) (1993) *'Employer views of higher education: proceedings of the second QHE 24-hour seminar'* Birmingham, Quality in Higher Education

Hawkridge, D. (1983) '*New information technologies in education*' London, Croom Helm
Heinz, J. Laumann, E. Nelson, R. and Salisbury, R. (1993) '*The hollow core: private interests in national policy making*' Cambridge, Harvard University Press
Heller, F. (1987) 'The technological imperative and the quality of employment' *New Technology, Work and Employment.* vol. 2, no. 1, pp. 19-26
Hendry, J. (1989) '*Innovating for failure: government policy and the early british computer industry*' Cambridge MA, MIT Press
Hesketh, A. (1998) '*The GET report: graduate employment and training towards the next millennium*' Cambridge, Hobsons
Hickling-Hudson, A. (1992) 'Rich schools, poor schools, boys and girls: computer education in Australian schools' *Journal of Education Policy*, vol. 7, no.1, pp. 1-21
Hicks, B. (1998) 'Blair's paper tiger: an interview with Dennis Stevenson' *Times Educational Supplement* On-line Supplement, 9th January 1998, pp.54
Hockey, J. and Wellington, J. (1994) 'Information technology in the workplace: messages for employment and training' *British Journal of Education and Work*, vol. 6, no. 1, pp.57-74
Hodkinson, P. and Sparkes, A. (1993) 'To tell or not to tell? reflecting on ethical dilemmas in stakeholder research' *Evaluation and Research in Education*, vol. 7, no. 3, pp.117-132
Howe, C. (1998) 'Psychology teaching in the twenty-first century' *The Psychologist*, vol. 11, no. 8, pp.371-374
Hubbard, G. (1981) 'Education and the new technologies' *Proceedings of the Royal Society of Arts*, vol. CXXIX, no.5297, April 1981
Igbaria, M., Schiffman, S., and Wieckowski, T. (1994) 'The respective roles of perceived usefulness and perceived fun in the acceptance of microcomputer technology' *Behaviour and Information Technology*, vol. 13, no. 6, pp. 349-361
Irwin, M. (1987) 'Telecommunications and government: the US Experience' in Wilks, S. and Wright, M. (Eds) '*Comparative government-industry relations: western europe, the United States and Japan*' Oxford, Clarendon Press
Jackson, P. (1993) 'Qualitative research and its public' *Qualitative Studies in Education*, 6, 3, pp.227-231
Jacobs, D. (1988) 'Corporate economic power and the state: a longitudinal assessment of two explanations' *American Journal of Sociology*, vol. 93, pp.852-881
Jeffrey, R. and Woods, P. (1997) 'The relevance of creative teaching: pupil's views' in Pollard, A., Thiessen, D. and Filer, A. (Eds) '*Children and their curriculum: the perspectives of primary and elementary school children*' London, Falmer
Johnston, C. (1999) 'Schools told to invest in hi-tech future' *Times Educational Supplement*, 22nd January 1999, p.2
Jones, S. (1995) '*Cybersociety: computer mediated communication and community*' Thousand Oaks, CA, Sage
Jones, S. (1997) '*Virtual culture: identity and communication in cybersociety*' London, Sage
Jordan, T. (1999) '*Cyberpower: the culture and politics of cyberspace and the internet*' London, Routledge
Jurich, S. (1999) 'Virtual education: trends and potential uses' *TechKnowLogia*, vol. 1, no. 2, pp.35-38
Kainan, A. (1994) 'Staffroom grumblings as expressed teachers' vocation' *Teaching and Teacher Education*, vol. 10, no. 3, pp.281-290
Kavanagh, P. (1998) 'School contracts send RM to top of the class' *Sunday Times*, Section 6, 1st November, p. 12

Kearsley, G. (1998) 'Educational technology: a critique' *Educational Technology*, vol. 38, no. 2, pp.47-51

Keddie, N. (1971) 'Classroom knowledge' in Young, M.F.D (Ed.) *'Knowledge and control'* Macmillan, London

Kenny, J. (1998) 'A fair share of the web: return of the frontier spirit' *Times Educational Supplement* On-line Supplement, 9th January 1998, pp.8-9

Kenway, J. (1995). 'Reality bytes: education, markets and the information superhighway' *Australian Educational Researcher*, vol. 22, no. 1, 35-65

Kenway, J. (1996) 'The information superhighway and post-modernity: the social promise and the social price' *Comparative Education*, vol. 32, no. 2, 217-231

Kenway, J., Bigum, C., Fitzclarence, L, Collier, J. and Tregenza, K. (1994). 'New education in new times' *Journal of Education Policy*, vol. 9, no. 4, 317-333

Kerr, D. (1992) 'The academic curriculum - reform revisited' in Whiteside, T., Sutton, A. and Everton, T. (Eds) *'16-19 changes in education and training'* London, David Fulton

Kerr, S. (1996) 'Toward a sociology of educational technology' in Jonassen, D. (Ed.) *'Handbook of research on educational communications and technology'* New York, Macmillan

Kingston, P., Morgan, J. and Wagstaff, A. (1992) 'The impact of new learning technologies in education' *Education and Training*, vol. 34, no. 5, pp. 7-11

Kitchen, R. (1998) *'Cyberspace: the world in the wires'* Chichester, Wiley

Kitzinger, J. (1994) 'Focus groups: method or madness?' in Boulton, M. (Ed.) *'Methodological advances in social research in HIV/ AIDs'* London, Taylor and Francis

Kling, R. (1996) 'The seductive equation of technological progress with social progress' in Kling, R. (Ed.) *'Computerisation and controversy: value conflicts and social choices'* [Second Edition] San Diego, Academic Press

Knight, P (1995) 'Introduction' in Knight, P. (Ed.) *'Assessment for learning in higher education'* London, Kogan Page

Kreuger, R. (1988) *'Focus groups: a practical guide for applied research'* London, Sage

Labour Party (1997) *'White paper on Education'* London, Stationary Office

Ladner,S. and Tillman, H. (1992) 'How special librarians really use the internet' *Canadian Library Journal*, vol. 49, no. 3, pp.211-216.

Latzer, M. (1995) 'Japanese information infrastructure initiatives: a politico-economic approach' *Telecommunications Policy*, vol. 19, no. 7, pp.515-529

Lave, J. and Wenger, E. (1991) *'Situated learning: legitimate peripheral participation'* Cambridge, Cambridge University Press

Lawton, T. (1992) 'Core skills 16-19' in Whiteside, T., Sutton, A. and Everton, T. (Eds) *'16-19 changes in education and training'* London, David Fulton

Leask, M. and Younie, S. (1999) 'Characteristics of effective on-line communities for teachers: issues emerging from research' paper presented to *European Distance Education Network – 3rd International Open Classroom Conference*, Budapest Technical University, Hungary

Leggett, M. and Robertson, S. (1996) 'Curriculum fragmentation impedes students' understanding of technology and the environment' *Journal of Educational Policy*, vol. 11, no. 6, pp. 681-691.

Lemke, J. (1995) *'Textual politics: discourse and social dynamics'* London, Taylor & Francis

Lepper, M. and Malone, T. (1987) 'Intrinsic motivation and instructional effectiveness in computer-based education' in Snow, R. and Farr, M. (Eds) *'Aptitude, learning and instruction: vol 3,Conative and affective process analysis'* Hillsdale, NJ: Lawrence Erlbaum

Lepper, M. and Chabay, R. (1985) 'Intrinsic motivation and instruction: conflicting views on the role of motivational processes in computer-based education' *Educational Psychology*, vol. 20, no. 4, pp.217-230

Levi-Faur, D. (1999) 'The governance of competition: the interplay of technology, economics and politics in european union electricity and telecom regimes' *Journal of Public Policy*, vol. 19, no. 2, 175-207

Levinson, P. (1997) *'The soft edge: a natural history and future of the information revolution'* London, Routledge

Lindblom, C. (1977) *'Politics and markets: the world's political-economic systems'* New York, Basic Books

Linder, S. (1999) 'Coming to terms with the public-private relationship: a grammar of multiple meanings' *American Behavioural Scientist*, vol. 43, no. 1, pp.35-51

Linn, R., Baker, E. and Dunbar, S. (1991) 'Complex, performance-based assessment: expectations and validation criteria' *Educational Researcher*, vol. 20, no. 8, pp.15-21

Little, J. (1990) 'The persistence of privacy: autonomy and initiative in teachers' professional relations' *Teachers College Record*, vol. 91, pp.509-536

Livingstone, S. (1999) *'Young people new media'* London, London School of Economics

Loader, B. (1998) *'Cyberspace divide: equality, agency and policy in the information society'* London, Routledge

Loveless, T. (1996) 'Why aren't computers used more in schools?' *Education Policy* 10, 4, pp 448-467

Luehrmann, A. (1971) *'Proceedings of the second annual conference on computers in the undergraduate curricula'* Hanover, University Press of New England

Lyon, D. (1988) *'The information society: issues and illusions'* Cambridge, Polity

MacFarlene, A. (1998) 'Information, knowledge and learning' *Higher Education Quarterly*, vol. 52, no. 1, pp.77-92

Mackay, H. and Powell, T. (1998) 'Connecting wales: the internet and national identity' in Loader, B.D. (Ed.) *'Cyberspace divide: equality, agency and policy in the information society'* London, Routledge

Maddux, C.D. (1989) 'The harmful effects of excessive optimism in educational computing' *Educational Technology*, vol. 29, no. 4, pp.23-29

Marriott, N., Selwyn, N. and Marriott, P. (1999) 'Accounting students' use of information and communications technology at two UK universities' in Fletcher, K. and Nicholson, A. (Eds), *'Selected proceedings of the 10th annual CTI-AFM conference'* Norwich, University of East Anglia

Marshall, J. (2000) 'Electronic writing and the wrapping of language' *Journal of Philosophy of Education*, vol. 34, no. 1, pp.135-149

Martin, C. (1993) 'The myth of the awesome thinking machine' *Communications of the ACM* vol. 36, no. 4, pp.120-133

Martin, C. (1995) 'Nature or nurture? sources of firm preference for national health reform' *American Political Science Review*, vol. 89, no. 4, pp.898-913

Marvin, C. (1986) *'When old technologies were new: thinking about electronic communication in the late nineteenth century'* Oxford, Oxford University Press

Marx, L. (1987) 'Does improved technology mean progress?' *Technological Review*, vol. 90, no. 1, pp.33-41

Mayes, T. (2000) 'Pedagogy, lifelong learning and ICT' in Scottish Forum on Lifelong Learning *'Role of ICT in supporting lifelong learning'* Centre for Research in Lifelong Learning, University of Stirling

McNeil, L. (1986) *'Contradictions of control: school structure and school knowledge'* London, Routledge.

McNeil, M. (1991) 'The old and new worlds of information technology in britain' in Corner, J. and Harvey, S. (Eds) *Enterprise and heritage: cross currents of national culture* London, Routledge

Microsoft (1998) *Microsoft in education website* (1998) [http://www.microsoft.com/uk]

Millard, W.B. (1997) 'I flamed freud: a case study in teletextual incendiarism' in Porter, D. (Ed.) *Internet culture* London, Routledge

Miller, A.H., Imrie, B.W. and Cox, K. (1998) *Student assessment in higher education* London, Kogan Page

Miller, H. (1995) 'The presentation of self in electronic life' paper presented to *Embodied Knowledge & Virtual Space* Conference, London, June 1995

Mizokawa, D.T. (1994) *Everyday computing in academe* New Jersey, Educational Technology Publications

Monbiot, G. (2002) 'Schooling up for sale' *The Guardian*, 8th January 2002, p.15

Morgan, D. (1988) *Focus groups as qualitative research* London, Sage.

Morgan, D. and Spanish, M. (1984) 'Focus groups: a new tool for qualitative research' *Qualitative Sociology*, vol. 7, no. 3, pp.253-270

MORI [Market Opinion Research International] (1997) *The British and technology: the Motorola report 1997* Basingstoke, Motorola

Morris, E. (1998) 'Modernising and incentives for excellence' *Teaching Today*, Autumn 1998, p.7

National Council for Educational Technology (1995) *Electronic communications to support special needs co-ordinators* Coventry, NCET

National Council for Educational Technology (1996) *The SENCo electronic communications project* Coventry, NCET

National Council for Educational Technology (1997) 'NCET – response to National Grid for Learning' *Press Release 7th October 1997* Coventry, NCET

National Curriculum Council (1989) *National curriculum: from policy to practice* London, Department of Education and Science

National Curriculum Council (1990) *Core skills 16-19* York, NCC.

Negroponte, N. (1995) *Being digital* London, Coronet

Neill, M. (1995) 'Computers, thinking and schools in "the new world order"' in Brook, J. and Boal, I.A. (Eds) *Resisting the virtual life: the culture and politics of information* San Francisco, City Lights.

Nias, J. (1989) *Primary teachers talking: a study of teaching as work* London, Routledge

Nias, J. Southworth, G. and Yeomans, R. (1989) *Staff relationships in the primary school* London, Cassell

Noble, D. (1991) *The classroom arsenal: military research, information technology, and public education* London, Falmer

Noble, D. (1997) 'A bill of goods: the early marketing of computer-based education and its implications for the present moment' in Biddle, B.J. (Ed.) *International handbook of teachers and teaching* Netherlands, Kluwer

OECD (1998) *Education at a glance: OECD indicators* Paris, Organisation for Economic Co-operation and Development

Ogden, J. (1994) 'Politics in a parallel universe: is there a future for cyberdemocracy?' *Futures*, vol. 26, pp.713-729

Okerson, A. (1996) 'The electronic journal: what, whence and when?' in Kling, R. (Ed.) *Computerisation and controversy: value conflicts and social choices* San Diego, Academic Press

Osmond, R. (1994) 'What do employers want from school leavers: is there an easy answer?' *Teaching Mathematics and its Applications*, vol. 13, no. 1, pp.5-10

Paechter, C. (1995) 'Subcultural retreat: negotiating the design and technology curriculum' *British Educational Research Journal*, vol. 21, no. 1, pp. 75-87

Palast, G. (2000) 'Profit and education don't mix' *The Observer* [Business section], 26th March, p7

Papert, S. (1980) *'Mindstorms: children, computers and powerful ideas'* New York, Harvester Press

Papert, S. (1995) *'Technology in schools: local fix or global transformation'* Remarks to House of Representatives Panel on Technology and Education - 12th October 1995 [http://kids.www.media.mit.edu/project/kids/sp-talk.html]

Parker, B. and Bowell, B. (1998) 'Exploiting computer-mediated communication to support in-service professional development: the SENCO experience' *Journal of Information Technology for Teacher Education*, vol. 7, no. 2, pp.229-246

Parker-Smith, N. (1993) 'Jockeying for position on the data highway' *Upside*, 1st May 1993 [www.upside.com]

Parlette, M. and Hamilton, D. (1972) *'Evaluation as illumination: a new approach to the study of innovative programs'* Occasional Paper 9, Centre for Research in the Educational Sciences, University of Edinburgh

Pateman, T. (1998) 'Aesthetic engagement' *Aspects of Education*, vol. 55, pp.18-24

Pelgrum, W. and Plomp, T. (1991) *'The use of computers in education world-wide: results from the IEA 'computers in education' survey in 19 education systems'* Oxford, Pergamon

Pelgrum, W. and Plomp, T. (1993) *'The IEA study of computers in education: implementation of an innovation in 21 education systems'* Oxford, Pergamon

Penfold, B. (1987) 'Election boosts school micro generosity' *Educational Computing*, June 1987, p.5

Peterson, W.A. (1964) 'Age, teacher's role and the institutional setting' in Biddle, B. and Ellena, W. (Eds) *'Contemporary Research on Teacher Effectiveness'* New York, Holtz, Rinehart & Winston

Phtiaka, H. (1994) 'What's in it for us?' *Qualitative Studies in Education*, vol. 7, no. 2, pp.155-164

Pollard, A. (1987) 'Primary teachers and their colleagues' in Delamont, S. (Ed.) *'The primary school teacher'* Lewes, Falmer

Pollard, A., Thiessen, D. and Filer, A. (1997) 'New challenges in taking children's curricular perspectives seriously' in Pollard, A., Thiessen, D. and Filer, A. (Eds) *'Children and their curriculum: the perspectives of primary and elementary school children'* London, Falmer

Poster, M. (1995) *'The second media age'* London, Blackwell

Poster, M. (1997) 'Cyberdemocracy: internet and the public sphere' in Porter, D. (Ed.) *'Internet Culture'* London, Routledge

Postman, N. (1992) *'Technopoly: the surrender of culture to technology'* New York, Vintage Books

Preston, N. (1992) 'Computing and teaching: a socially critical review' *Journal of Computer Assisted Learning*, vol. 8, pp. 49-56.

Puttnam, D. (1999) 'The challenge to be creative' *ALT Report*, January/February 1999, p.4

Qvortrup, L. (1984) *'The social significance of telematics: an essay on the information society'* [Philip Edmonds, trans.] Philadelphia, John Benjamins

Rachel, J. and Woolgar, S. (1995) 'The discursive structure of the social-technical divide: the example of information systems development' *Sociological Review*, vol. 46, pp.251-273

Reay, D. and William, D. (1999) "I'll be a nothing': structure, agency and the construction of identity through assessment' *British Educational Research Journal*, vol. 25, no. 3, pp.343-354

Reed, L. (2000) 'Domesticating the personal computer: the mainstreaming of a new technology and the cultural management of a widespread technophobia' *Critical Studies in Media Communication*, vol. 17, no. 2, pp.159-185

Reguly, E. (1997) 'British Telecom school net plan put back by OFTEL action' *The Times*, 6th June 1997, p.27

Reich, R. (1991) *'The work of nations'* New York, Random House

Reynolds, D. (2002) 'Misuse of computers' *Times Educational Supplement*, 11th January 2002, p.19

Rheingold, H. (1993) *'The virtual community: homesteading on the electronic frontier'* Reading, Addison Wesley

Richardson, W. (1993) 'The 16-19 education and training debate: 'deciding factors' in the british public policy process' in Richardson, W., Woolhouse, J and Finegold, D. (Eds) *'The reform of post-16 education and training in England and Wales'* Harlow, Longman

Riddell, S. (1989) 'Exploiting the exploited? the ethics of feminist research' in Burgess, R.G. (Ed.) *'The Ethics of Educational Research'* Lewes, Falmer

Roberts, L., Smith, L. and Pollock, C. (1997) 'u r a lot bolder on the net: the social use of text-based virtual environments by shy individuals' paper presented to *International Conference on Shyness & Self-Consciousness*, Cardiff, July 1997

Robertson, D. (1998) 'The University for Industry: a flagship for demand-led training or another doomed supply-side intervention?' *Journal of Education and Work*, vol. 11, no. 1, pp.5-22

Robins, K. (1999) 'Foreclosing on the city? the bad idea of virtual urbanism' in Downey, J. and McGuigan, J. (Eds) *'Technocities'* London, Sage

Robins, K. and Webster, F. (1989) *'The technical fix: education, computers and industry'* London, Macmillan

Robins, K. and Webster, F. (1999) *'Times of the technoculture: from the information society to the virtual life'* London, Routledge

Rolfe, H. (1990) 'In the name of progress? skill and attitude toward technological change' *New Technology, Work and Employment*, vol. 5, no. 2, pp. 107-121

Rorty, R. (2000) *'Philosophy and social hope'* Harmondsworth, Penguin

Roszak, T. (1986) *'The cult of information: a neo-luddite treatise on high-tech, artificial intelligence and the true art of thinking'* Berkeley, University of California Press

Rothschild, M. (1993) 'Techno-policy or techno-pork' *Upside*, 1st March 1993, [www.upside.com]

Sachs, J. and Smith, R. (1988) 'Constructing teacher culture' *British Journal of Sociology of Education*, vol. 9, no. 4, pp.423-436

Sanger, J. with Willson, J., Davies, B. and Whittaker, R. (1997) *'Young children, videos and computer games: issues for teachers and parents'* London, Falmer

Saunders, L. (1992) 'Education, work and the curriculum' *Policy Studies*. vol. 12, no. 2, p 13-26

Savicki, V., Kelley, M. and Lingenfelter, D. (1996) 'Gender and small task group activity using computer mediated communication' *Computers in Human Behaviour*, 12, pp.209-224

Savicki, V., Lingenfelter, D. and Kelley, M. (1997) 'Gender language style and group composition in internet discussion groups' *Journal of Computer-Mediated-Communication*, vol. 2, no. 3, [http://jcmc.huji.ac.il/vol2/issue3/savicki.html]

Sawhney, H. (1996) 'Information superhighway: metaphors as midwives' *Media, Culture and Society*, vol. 18, pp. 291-314

Schiller, H. (1981) '*Who knows? information in the age of the Fortune 500*' Norwood, NJ., Ablex

Schiller, H. (1993) 'The information economy: public way or private road?' *The Nation*, July 12th, pp.64-66

Schiller, H. (1995) 'The global information highway: project for an ungovernable world' in Brook, J. and Boal, I.A. (Eds) '*Resisting the virtual life: the culture and politics of information*' San Francisco, City Lights.

Schoch, N. and White, M. (1997) 'A study of the communication patterns of participants in consumer health electronic discussion groups' *Proceedings of the 60th Annual Meeting of the American Society for Information Science*, vol. 34, pp.280-292

Schofield, J. (1995) '*Computers and classroom culture*' Cambridge, Cambridge University Press

Schwartz, H. (1996) '*The culture of the copy: striking likenesses, unreasonable facsimiles*' New York, Zone

Scott, A. (1998) 'The everyday aesthetics of computer education' in Bromley, H. and Apple, M.W. (Eds) '*Education/technology/power: educational computing as a social practice*' New York, SUNY Press

Seels, B. (1997) 'Taxonomic issues and the development of theory in instructional technology' *Educational Technology*, vol. 37, no. 1, pp.12-21

Sellinger, M. (1998) 'Forming a critical community through telematics' *Computers and Education*, vol. 30, nos. 1/2, pp.23-30

Sellinger, M. and Yapp, C. (2001) '*ICTeachers*' London, Institute for Public Policy Research

Selwyn, L. (1995) 'Efficient public investment in telecommunications infrastructure' *Land Economics*, vol. 71, no. 3, pp.331-342

Selwyn, N. (1997) 'Assessing students' ability to use computers: theoretical considerations for practical research' *British Educational Research Journal*, vol. 23, pp.47-59.

Selwyn, N. (1998) 'A grid for learning or a grid for earning? the significance of the learning grid initiative in uk education' *Journal of Educational Policy*, vol. 13, no. 3, pp.423-431

Selwyn, N. and Bullon, K. (2000) 'Primary school children's use of ICT' *British Journal of Educational Technology*, vol. 31, no. 4, pp.321-332

Selwyn, N. and Gorard, S. (2002) '*The information age: technology, learning and exclusion in Wales*' Cardiff, University of Wales Press

Selwyn, N., Marriott, N. and Marriott, P. (1999) 'Home and overseas students' use of ICT in UK higher education' *Research in Education*, vol. 62, pp.69-71

Selwyn, N., Williams, S. and Gorard, S. (2001) 'E-stablishing a learning society: the use of the internet to attract adults to lifelong learning in Wales' *Innovations in Education & Training International*, vol. 38, no. 3, pp.205-219

Shashaani, L (1993) 'Gender-based differences in attitudes toward computers' *Computers and Education*, vol. 20, no. 2, pp. 169-181

Shilling, C. (1989) '*Schooling for work in capitalist Britain*' London, Falmer

Shipps, D. (1997) 'The invisible hand: big business and chicago school reform' *Teachers College Record*, vol. 99, no. 1, pp.73-116

Simons, H. (1987) '*Getting to know schools in a democracy: the politics and process of evaluation*' Lewes, Falmer

Simons, H. (1989) 'Ethics of case study in education research and evaluation' in Burgess, R.G. (Ed.) '*The Ethics of Educational Research*' Lewes, Falmer

Simons, H. (1995) 'The politics and ethics of educational research in England: contemporary issues' *British Educational Research Journal*, vol. 21, no. 4, pp.435-449 *Education*, 14, 1, pp.39-58

Singh, P. (1997) 'From software design to classroom practice: an Australian case study of the gendered production, distribution and acquisition of computing knowledge' in Marshall, C. (Ed.) *'Feminist critical policy analysis: a perspective from primary and secondary schooling'* London, Falmer

Singh, P. (1993) 'Institutional discourse and practice. a case study of the social construction of technological competence in the primary classroom' *British Journal of Sociology of Education* vol. 14, no. 1, pp.39-58

Siskin, L. (1991) 'Departments as different worlds: subject subcultures in secondary schools' *Educational Administration Quarterly*, vol. 27, no. 2, pp. 134-160.

Slack, J. D. (1984) 'The information revolution as ideology' *Media, Culture and Society*, vol. 6, pp. 247-256

Smith, D. and Keep, R. (1986) 'Children's opinions of educational software' *Educational Research*, vol. 28, no. 1, pp.83-88

Smith, P. (2002) 'Comment' *ATL Report*, February 2002, p.8

Smith, M. and Kollock, P. (1999) *'Communities in cyberspace'* London, Routledge

Smithers, A. (1994) 'The paradox of A-levels' *The Curriculum Journal*, vol. 5, no. 3, pp. 355-363

Snyder, B. (1971) *'The hidden curriculum'* Cambridge, MA, MIT Press

Somekh, B. (1999) 'A level revealed – a bastion of outdated "school knowledge"' *Research Papers in Education*, vol. 14, no. 2, pp.139-142

Spours, K. and Young, M. (1996) 'Dearing and beyond: steps and stages to a unified 14-19 qualifications system' *British Journal of Education and Work*, vol. 9, no. 3, pp. 5-18.

Sproull, L. & Kiesler, S (1996) 'Increasing personal connections' in Kling, R. (Ed.) *'Computerisation and controversy: value conflicts and social choices'* New York, Academic Press

Stevenson Committe (1997) *'Independent commission into information and communications technology in secondary schools 1996/1997'* [http://rubble.ultralab.anglia.ac.uk]

Stewart, D. and Shamdasani, P. (1992) *'Focus groups: theory and practice'* London, Sage

Stivale, C.J. (1997) 'Spam: heteroglossia and harassment in cyberspace' in Porter, D. (Ed.) *'Internet culture'* London, Routledge

Stonier, T. and Conlin, C. (1985) *'The three c's: children, computers and communication'* London, Wiley

Strauss, A.L. (1987) *'Qualitative analysis for social scientists'* Cambridge, Cambridge University Press

Streibel, M. (1988) 'Re-contextualising computers in education: a response to Heinich and Damarin' *Educational Communication and Technology Journal*, vol. 36, no. 3, pp. 153-160

Suppes, P. (1966) 'The uses of computers in education' *Scientific American*, vol. 215, pp. 207-220

Sussman, G. (1997) *'Communication, technology and politics in the information age'* Thousand Oaks CA., Sage

Sutton, R. (1991) 'Equity and computers in the schools: a decade of research' *Review of Educational Research*, vol. 61, no. 4, pp. 475-503

Tasker, M. and Packham, D. (1993) 'Industry and higher education: a question of values' *Studies in Higher Education.* vol. 18, no. 2, p 127-136

Taylor, A. (1998) 'Employability skills: from corporate 'wish list' to government policy' *Journal of Curriculum Studies.* vol. 30, no. 2, p 143-164.

Tehranian, M. (1990) *'Technologies of power: information machines and democratic prospects'* Norwood, NJ, Ablex

Tepper, M. (1997) 'Usenet communities and the cultural politics of information' in Porter, D. (Ed.) *'Internet culture'* London, Routledge

Thiessen, D. (1997) in Pollard, A., Thiessen, D. and Filer, A. (Eds) *'Children and their curriculum: the perspectives of primary and elementary school children'* London, Falmer

Tiffin, J and Rajasingham, L. (1995) *'In search of the virtual class: education in an information society'* London, Routledge

Tight, M. (1998) 'Education, education, education! the vision of lifelong learning in the Kennedy, Dearing and Fryer reports' *Oxford Review of Education*, vol. 24, no. 4, 473-486

Toennies, F. (1957) *'Community and society'* New York, Michigan University Press

Torkzadeh, G., and Angulo, I. (1992) 'The concept and correlates of computer anxiety' *Behaviour and Information Technology*, vol. 11, no. 2, pp. 99-108

Toulouse, C. (1997) 'Introduction' in Toulouse, C. and Luke, T. (Eds) *'The politics of cyberspace'* London, Routledge

Touraine, A. (1969) *'L'societe post-industrielle'* Paris, Fayard

Tribe, J. (1996) 'Core skills: a critical examination' *Educational Review*, vol. 48, no. 1, pp.13-27

Troman, G. (1996) 'No entry signs: educational change and some problems encountered in negotiating entry to educational settings' *British Educational Research Journal*, vol. 22, no. 1, pp.71-88

Truman, D. (1981) *'The government press'* New York, Knopf

Turkle, S. (1984) *'The second self'* New York, Simon & Schuster

Turkle, S. (1995) *'Life on the screen'* New York, Simon & Schuster

UK Net Year (1998a) 'UK netyear will help revolutionise teaching and learning in schools' *Press Release January 1998* Windsor, UK NetYear

UK Net Year (1998b) 'Excite gives every school child in Britain a free email address for life' *Press Release 12th January 1998* Windsor, UK NetYear

UK Net Year (1998c) 'Fujitsu Supports UK NetYear initiative' *Press Release 12th January 1998* Windsor, UK NetYear

Underwood, J. (1997) 'Integrated learning systems: where does the management take place?' *Education and Information Technologies*, vol. 2, no. 4, pp. 275-286

Underwood, J., Cavendish, S. and Lawson, T. (1999) 'Are integrated learning systems good for teachers too?' *Journal of Information Technology for Teacher Education*, vol. 5, no. 3, pp. 207-218

US Presidential Committee on Educational Technology (1997) *'Report to the President on the use of technology to strengthen k-12 education in the United States'* Washington DC, PCAST

Vidal, J. (1999) 'Global trends: muddling along as pests and pollution pile up' *The Guardian*, 29th May 1999, p.16

Vogel, D. (1978) 'Why businessmen distrust their state: the political consciousness of American corporate executives' *British Journal of Political Studies*, vol. 8, pp.45-78

Walker, D. (1998) *'Education in the digital age'* London, Bowerdean

Walkerdine, V. (1998) 'Children in cyberspace: a new frontier' in Lesnik-Oberstein, K. (Ed.) *'Children in culture: approaches to childhood'* London, Macmillan

Watson, D. (Ed.) (1993) *'The ImpacT report: an evaluation of the impact of information technology on children's achievements in primary and secondary schools'* London, King's College, Centre for Educational Studies

Webster, F. (1995) *'Theories of the information society'* London, Routledge

Webster, F. (2000) 'Information, capitalism and uncertainty' *Information, Communication & Society*, vol. 3, no. 1, pp.69-90

Webster, F. and Robins, K. (1986) *'Information technology: a luddite analysis'* Norwood NJ., Ablex

Webster, F. and Smith, A. (1997) *'The post-modern university? contested visions of higher education in society'* London, Routledge

Wedell, K., Stevens, C., Waller, T. and Matheson, L. (1997) 'SENCos sharing questions and solutions: how to make a more convenient phone call' *British Journal of Special Education*, vol. 24, no. 4, pp.167-170

Weil, S. (1986) 'Non-traditional learners within traditional higher education institutions: discovery and disappointment' *Studies in Higher Education*, vol. 11, no. 3, pp. 219-235

Weinholtz, D., Kacer, B. and Rocklin, T. (1995) 'Salvaging quantitative research with qualitative data' *Qualiatative Health Research*, vol. 5, no. 3, pp. 388-397

Wellington, J. (1994) 'How far should the post-16 curriculum be determined by the needs of employers?' *The Curriculum Journal*, vol. 5, no. 3, pp.307-321

Wellman, B. (2001) 'Computer networks as social networks' *Science*, vol. 293 (14th September 2001), pp.2031-2034

Wellman, B. and Gulia, M. (1999) 'Virtual community as communities: net surfers don't ride alone' in Smith, M.A. and Kollock, P. (Eds) *'Communities in cyberspace'* London, Routledge

Wenger, E. (1990) *'Toward a theory of cultural transparency: elements of a social discourse of the visible and invisible'* Palo Alto, CA., Institute for Research on Learning.

White, P. (2002) 'Sins of omission? reciprocity with interviewees in educational research' in Welland, T. and Pugsley, L. (Eds.) *'Ethical issues in qualitative research'* Aldershot, Ashgate

Whitston, K. (1998) 'Key skills and curriculum reform' *Studies in Higher Education*, vol. 23, no. 3, pp.307-319

Wild, M. (1996). 'Technology refusal: rationalising the failure of student and beginning teachers to use computers' *British Journal of Educational Technology*, vol. 27, no. 2, 134-143

Wilks, S. and Wright, M. (Eds) (1987) *'Comparative government-industry relations: western europe, the United States and Japan'* Oxford, Clarendon Press

Williams, R. and Edge, D. (1996) 'The social shaping of technology' in Dutton, W. (Ed.) *'Information and communication technologies: visions and realities'* Oxford, Oxford University Press

Williamson, J., Karp, D. and Dalphin, J. (1977) *'The research craft: an introduction to social science methods'* Toronto, Little Brown

Wills, M. (1999) 'Aiming to be world class' *BETT Trade Show Newsletter*, December 1999, p.3

Wilson, B. (1997) 'Thoughts on theory in educational technology' *Educational Technology*, vol. 37, no. 1, pp.12-21

Wilson, V. (1997) 'Focus groups: a useful qualitative method for educational research?' *British Educational Research Journal*, vol. 23, no. 2, pp. 209-224

Winner, L. (1986) *'The whale and the reactor: a search for limits in an age of high technology'* Chicago, University of Chicago Press

Winner, L. (1993) 'Citizen virtues in a technological order' *Inquiry*, vol. 35, pp.341-361

Winner, L. (1994) 'Three paradoxes of the information age' in Bender, G. and Druckrey, T. (Eds) *'Culture on the brink: ideologies of technology'* Seattle, Bay Press

Wise, J. (1997) *'Exploring technology and social space'* Thousand Oaks CA., Sage.

Wolf, A. (Ed.) (1997) *'GNVQs 1993-97: a national survey report'* Coventry, Further Education Development Agency.

Wood, D. (1998) *'How children think and learn'* Second Edition London, Blackwell
Woods, P. (1984) 'The meaning of staffroom humour' in Hargreaves, A. and Woods, P. (Eds.) *'Classrooms and staffrooms: the sociology of teachers and teaching'* Milton Keynes, Open University Press
Woods, P. (1990) *'The happiest days? how pupils cope with school'* London, Falmer
Wooley, B. (1992) *'Virtual worlds'* London, Penguin
Woolgar, S. (1990) 'Time and documents in researcher interaction: some ways of making out what is happening in experimental science' in Woolgar, S. and Lynch, M. (Eds) *'Representation in scientific practice'* Mass, MIT Press
Woolgar, S. (1991) 'Configuring the user: the case of usability trials' in Law, J. (Ed.) *'A Sociology of monsters: essays on power, technology and domination'* London, Routledge
Woolgar, S. (1991) 'The turn to technology in social studies of science' *Science, Technology and Human Values*, vol. 16, pp.20-50
Woolgar, S. (1996) 'Technologies as cultural artefacts' in Dutton, W.H. (Ed.) *'Information and communication technologies'* Oxford, Oxford University Press
Yeomans, D., Williams, R. and Martin, A. (1995) 'From verbal to horizontal? a longitudinal study of information technology in ten schools' *Journal of Information Technology for Teacher Education*. vol. 4, no. 3, pp. 329-350
Young, M. (1984) 'Information technology and the sociology of education: some preliminary thoughts' *British Journal of Sociology of Education*, vol. 5, no. 2, pp. 205-210
Ziegler, J. (1995) 'Institutions, elites and technological change in france and germany' *World Politics*, vol. 47, pp.341-372
Zuboff, S. (1997) 'In the age of the smart machine' in Teich, A.H. (Ed.) *'Technology and the future'* (Seventh Edition) New York, St. Martin's Press

Index

Access 160-163
Aesthetics 82, 85, 95
A-level 89-102
Art 77-82, 85, 95-6
Assessment 93-4, 105-108, 113-114

Baker, Kenneth 25-6, 28,
BBC (see British Broadcasting Corporation)
Blunkett, David 39-40
British Broadcasting Corporation 32-3
British Journal of Educational Technology 3-4
Bulletin Board 134-155

Castells, Manuel 40
Community 150-155
Computer Literacy 88
Computer Literacy Project 33
Computer Mediated Communication 135-6
Connecting the Learning Society 38
Conservative Party 25-6, 35-6

Data Analysis 18-19
Dearing Report 90
Department for Education 58, 61-3
Discourse Analysis 17-18
Dissemination 164-8

Excellence in Schools 52

Focus Groups 15-16, 75-6
Fun 84

Gates, Bill 60
Gender 86
General National Vocational Qualifications 100

Golding, Peter 175

Higher Education 103-115

Interactivity 176
Interviews 16-17
IT Firms 29-32, 45-7, 52-69

Kenway, Jane 51, 54
Key Skills 90-91, 96-102, 115

Learning trajectories 121-3
Lifelong Learning 119-133
Lobbying 62-3

Microelectronics in Education Programme 27-8, 57
Micros in Schools 26-8
Microsoft 40
Myth 36-7

National Curriculum 29
National Grid for Learning 38-51, 54, 57-69, 74, 134
National Strategy for Information Technology 26
New Labour Government 52-4, 67, 69, 179
New Technology for Better Schools 28
NGfL (see National Grid for Learning)

Open for Learning, Open for Business 63

Papert, Seymour 7, 74
Pedagogy 176-177
Primary School 73-88

Reflexivity 168
Rheingold, Howard 136, 140

Scaffolding 81
Singh, Parlo 74
Stevenson Committee 42

Technical and Vocational Education
  Initiative 27
Technical Fix 50, 172-173
Technological Determinism 47-8
Technology as Text 104-105
Thatcher, Margaret 24-5, 35

Third Way 52-3
Triangulation 10

UK Net Year 39, 41
Undergraduate 103-115
Understanding 87-8, 101
University for Industry 119-120

Value 87
Virtual Community 135-6

Walkerdine, Valerie 86
Winner, Langdon 41